An Apostle for Atheists

Also Available from Bloomsbury

Paul, The Apostle of Obedience, Jason A. Myers
Theology of Paul the Apostle, James D. G. Dunn
The Ritual World of Paul the Apostle, Michael Lakey

An Apostle for Atheists
Paul and the Quest for Radical Philosophy

Ole Jakob Løland

BLOOMSBURY ACADEMIC
LONDON • NEW YORK • OXFORD • NEW DELHI • SYDNEY

BLOOMSBURY ACADEMIC
Bloomsbury Publishing Plc, 50 Bedford Square, London, WC1B 3DP, UK
Bloomsbury Publishing Inc, 1385 Broadway, New York, NY 10018, USA
Bloomsbury Publishing Ireland, 29 Earlsfort Terrace, Dublin 2, D02 AY28, Ireland

BLOOMSBURY, BLOOMSBURY ACADEMIC and the Diana logo
are trademarks of Bloomsbury Publishing Plc

First published in Great Britain 2024
This paperback edition published in 2025

Copyright © Ole Jakob Løland, 2024

Ole Jakob Løland has asserted his right under the Copyright, Designs
and Patents Act, 1988, to be identified as Author of this work.

Cover image © Cathedral St. Sava in Belgrade, reflected in the glass wall of a
modern building. (© florin1961 / iStock)

All rights reserved. No part of this publication may be: i) reproduced or
transmitted in any form, electronic or mechanical, including photocopying,
recording or by means of any information storage or retrieval system without
prior permission in writing from the publishers; or ii) used or reproduced in
any way for the training, development or operation of artificial intelligence (AI)
technologies, including generative AI technologies. The rights holders expressly
reserve this publication from the text and data mining exception as per
Article 4(3) of the Digital Single Market Directive (EU) 2019/790.

Bloomsbury Publishing Inc does not have any control over, or responsibility for,
any third-party websites referred to or in this book. All internet addresses given
in this book were correct at the time of going to press. The author and publisher
regret any inconvenience caused if addresses have changed or sites have
ceased to exist, but can accept no responsibility for any such changes.

A catalogue record for this book is available from the British Library.

A catalog record for this book is available from the Library of Congress.

ISBN: HB: 978-1-3504-2007-6
PB: 978-1-3504-2010-6
ePDF: 978-1-3504-2008-3
eBook: 978-1-3504-2009-0

Typeset by Deanta Global Publishing Services, Chennai, India

For product safety related questions contact productsafety@bloomsbury.com.

To find out more about our authors and books visit www.bloomsbury.com
and sign up for our newsletters.

Contents

Translator's note   vi

Introduction: Paul between faith and reason   1
1 Who is Paul the author: A bluffer or one in search of the truth?   29
2 First Letter to the Corinthians: Criticism of wordly power   51
3 The Letter to the Romans: Introspection and the quest for justice   111
4 Conclusion: Paul: A philosopher for atheists   181

Bibliography   187
Name Index   196
Subject Index   198

Translator's note

Translated from Norwegian by Brian McNeil

I wish to emphasize that the use of masculine terms in speaking of God ("his", "him", etc.) and of terms such as "the kingdom of God" is dictated *exclusively* by stylistic reasons.

The book is published with support from the research group "Biblical Texts, Cultures and Receptions" at the Faculty of Theology, University of Oslo, and the Norwegian Research Council through HUMEVAL (Evaluation of Norwegian research in the Humanities).

Biblical texts are quoted from the New Revised Standard Version (NRSV).

Introduction

Paul between faith and reason

My seat was in the middle of the biggest auditorium in the House of Literature in Oslo. Every single seat around me was occupied, and a long queue of people stood outside in the Norwegian winter cold. They had not been able to get a place in the auditorium because it was so full, and so they had to follow everything via public viewing. A rock star – or more precisely, a philosopher – made his entrance into the auditorium. The Slovenian Slavoj Žižek was to hold his lecture "In Defence of Universalism", an hour-long monologue about the importance of resisting liberalism and mobilizing around a global universalism inspired both by Vladimir Lenin and the Bible.[1] Žižek claimed that the Bible contained a precious idea about a direct access to the universal for all human beings. The Slovenian philosopher maintained that even an atheist ought to acknowledge this. This led me to think of Žižek's enthusiasm for the apostle Paul as the first true universalist, since it was through Paul that Žižek had arrived at the idea that he had presented again and again to full houses everywhere in the world over the past fifteen years: namely, that Christianity's universalist inheritance is too precious to be left in the hands of crazy fundamentalists.[2]

What is a modern philosopher to make of Paul? What do non-Christian philosophers in Europe gain from reading ancient letters from Christianity's first great ideologue – and letters addressed to groups of persons about whom we no longer know anything? What is the point in reading the post that other people sent two thousand years ago? This question must be asked, given

---

[1] The lecture is available on YouTube under the title: "Slavoj Zizek: A Defence of Universalism". It was held on 12 December 2014.
[2] As the philosopher had written: "The authentic Christian legacy is much too precious to be left to the fundamentalist freaks." Slavoj Žižek, *The Fragile Absolute, or, Why is the Christian Legacy Worth Fighting For?*, 2008 ed. (London and New York: Verso, 2000), 2.

that the religion that can be traced back to Paul and to the first believers in Christ is in decline in Europe today, and that religious faith is regarded by many as a stage that our modern societies have left behind them. Indeed, the philosophers' clash with religion is often seen as an important fundament for the emergence of modern society.

After the fall of the Berlin Wall in 1989, parts of the political left underwent a crisis. Radical left-wing philosophers like Žižek felt the urgent need to formulate a new alternative to global capitalism. And after the terrorist attacks on 11 September 2001, these philosophers found themselves in a global public arena where religion had returned. Immigration and the presence of new religious minorities in Europe confronted philosophers with questions such as multiculturalism and religious fundamentalism. The entire world had seen – quite literally – that religion had an explosive political force.

Žižek claimed that the key to the logic behind the growth of fundamentalism lay in Paul's Letter to the Romans. In ch. 7 of this Letter, Paul writes about the relationship between law and sin in a way that, according to the Slovenian philosopher, is completely identical with what today is the dynamic between liberalism and fundamentalism. Just as the law in Romans 7 in reality results in the opposite of what it prescribes, that is to say, human sin, so too liberalism generates its own antithesis, namely, fundamentalism. Žižek sees liberalism as the dominant ideology and law (in the Pauline sense) of our time. Fundamentalism is a reaction to liberalism, but the two are entwined in a poisonous spiral, because neither liberalism nor its counter-reaction, fundamentalism, is capable of solving the problems caused by liberalism.[3] For Paul, the rescue is a divine righteousness with a universal scope and equality for all. For Žižek, the only way to unravel the knot is a renewed political left wing where the idea of equality is built up again by means of a new form of universalism.

The fact that a group of European philosophers in recent decades have highlighted the thinking of the apostle Paul as especially relevant to the great questions of our time has not gone unnoticed. There has long been a widespread view that Paul twisted Jesus' simple message about love of neighbour into

---

[3] *Living in the End Times* (London: Verso, 2010), 154. The same passage is pasted into "The Jew Is within You, but You, You Are in the Jew", in *What does a Jew Want? On Binationalism and Other Specters*, ed. Udi Aloni (New York: Columbia University Press, 2011), 172.

complicated theological formulae and oppressive religious commandments. Where Jesus invited women into his fellowship, Paul told them to keep silence in the assembly (1 Cor. 14.34). And while Jesus said nothing specific about homosexuals, Pauline formulations (Rom. 1.26-27 and 1 Cor. 6.9) have been used for centuries to condemn homosexuality.[4] As if this were not enough, it is claimed that Paul's universalism led to a colonialist mission. Can anything good come from Paul's Letters?

It is not least thanks to the polemic against Paul by the philosopher Friedrich Nietzsche (1844-1900) that Paul has acquired such a bad reputation in the modern age. Nietzsche, Karl Marx (1818-83) and Sigmund Freud (1856-1939) are regarded as the most important thinkers in the modern critique of religion. Nietzsche thunders against Christianity with rhetorical salvos that are targeted particularly at Paul. However, his philosophy is not simply a dismissal of Paul, but an attempt to overcome the inheritance from the apostle by means of a committed reading of his texts. Nietzsche's verbal onslaught on Paul makes the apostle's Letters a central fulcrum for modern philosophy. In other words, the fact that Nietzsche interprets Paul's Letters means that they get an even longer afterlife many centuries after their author's death. When texts are used and interpreted, they live on among new groups of readers in new historical contexts.

Paul in the dock

With his grave accusations against Paul, Nietzsche sets much of the agenda for the question about the value of Paul's thinking today – and not without reason. The French philosopher Jacques Derrida (1930-2004) once wrote that what he most admired in Nietzsche was the German philosopher's "lucidity about Paul".[5] Perhaps it was the Jewish philosopher Jacob Taubes (1923-87) who had whispered this into Derrida's ear on one of the occasions when Taubes

---

[4] The fact that these verses have been used to condemn homosexuality does not mean that we can take it for granted that they are about homosexuality in the modern sense of the term. Neil Elliott, *Liberating Paul: The Justice of God and the Politics of the Apostle*, 2006 ed. (Minneapolis: Fortress Press, 1994), 191-3. See also Dale B. Martin, "Heterosexism and the Interpretation of Romans 1:18-32", *Biblical Interpretation* 3, no. 3 (1995): 332-55.

[5] Jacques Derrida, "A Silkworm of One's Own", in *Acts of Religion*, ed. Gil Anidjar (London and New York: Routledge, 2002), 325.

visited Paris to speak about God with Derrida, another philosopher with a Jewish background.[6] Towards the close of his life, Taubes held some lectures about Paul in the German town of Heidelberg, which were to become highly influential in their later written form. And it was here that Taubes declared that the teacher who had given him the best help to understand the apostle Paul was none other than Nietzsche.[7]

We shall give Nietzsche's interesting criticism a central position here and then evaluate it in the light of later philosophers' readings of the apostle. This means that the question of the appropriateness of Nietzsche's criticism is to some extent delegated to philosophers from our own time who stand in the same tradition of the criticism of religion that Nietzsche helped to found. Something of the potential of meaning in the Pauline texts will be investigated by looking at these philosophers' interpretations of them. Possible and interesting interpretations of the texts will be located in a critical perspective, without postulating that anyone is in possession of the "correct" interpretation. But even given that no one has the definitive answer, we must nevertheless ask whether Paul has acquired a bad reputation that he does not deserve.

This reputation can be evaluated from many different perspectives. It is true that no academic branch has read Paul so often and examined him so closely as theology, but this does not necessarily mean that the theologians' readings are better than the philosophers', nor that believers' interpretations are more appropriate than atheists'. Believers who read Paul through modern philosophers who do not believe in God can discover a content of meaning in the apostle's Letters that they have overlooked. In this way, the philosophers can undergird and enrich the Christians' life of faith. For the growing proportion of the population of Europe who take their distance vis-à-vis Christian faith, the philosophers can point to dimensions of meaning in a cultural heritage that a European atheist has abandoned. The atheist can ask: Did something get lost en route while bidding farewell to the fellowship of the church's faith or the biblical cultural heritage?

One of the most prominent atheists in Europe does not take the trouble to put this question. Thanks to his engaging writings, the evolutionary biologist Richard Dawkins has become one of the most read atheists of our time, who

---

[6] Babette Babich, "Ad Jacob Taubes", *New Nietzsche Studies* 7, no. 3 (2007): 9.
[7] Jacob Taubes, *The Political Theology of Paul* (Stanford: Stanford University Press, 2004), 79.

promises individuals and society a better life if they get rid of belief in God. Dawkins is a modern iconoclast who wants to tear down the image of the Bible as "the Good Book".[8] In doing so, he relies on surprisingly naïve interpretations of the biblical books that are both ahistorical and de-contextualized.[9] Importantly, for Dawkins one prime example of the irrational and destructive aspects of the New Testament is Paul. In Dawkins' eyes, Paul is the origin of an abhorrent doctrine that God became a human being in order that Jesus could be tortured to death as expiation of the sin that was inherited from Adam. According to Dawkins, this Pauline idea is nothing less than sadomasochistic: God demanded the torture and execution of Jesus as payment for the forgiveness of sins.[10] This idea prompts unenlightened believers to humble themselves. At the same time, it makes the Christian faith foster suffering, instead of fighting against it. This is why it is evil; and if Christianity is extirpated, there will thus be less evil. This makes it especially important to help people in our days to liberate themselves from the disgusting ideas of Paul. Dawkins has even inserted at the end of the book a list of the addresses of organizations where people can find help – help to cleanse the mind of Pauline ideas and other intellectual dross, one assumes.

The philosopher Michel Onfray has had a similar public role in France to Dawkins and comparable neo-atheists who have witnessed the return of religion to societal debate and have clearly felt the need to fight for the acceptance of atheism among modern people. After Onfray's manifesto for atheism was published in 2005, it was on the bestseller list in France for months. The neo-atheists see a connection between the diffusion of the Pauline ideas and the impact made by atheism. The more Paul, the less atheism – and vice versa. Onfray devotes much more space than Dawkins to attacking Paul. But Onfray also sees more clearly the danger that threatens European atheism from within, since there are atheist philosophers who embrace Paul. The most prominent of these in Europe are Slavoj Žižek, Giorgio Agamben, and not least the Frenchman Alain Badiou. In his 1997 book *Saint Paul. La fondation de l'Universalisme,* the atheist Badiou uses precisely the apostle Paul as a model for his own philosophy about the truth event and the revival of the

---

[8] Richard Dawkins, *The God Delusion*, 2016 ed. (London: Black Swan, 2006), 268-316.
[9] Arthur Bradley and Andrew Tate, *The New Atheist Novel: Fiction, Philosophy and Polemic after 9/11* (London: Continuum, 2010), 5.
[10] *The God Delusion*, 286-7.

idea of communism. Onfray is disappointed to see a French philosopher on the far left presenting Paul as the model for a radical renewal of the political left wing.[11] Onfray takes the opposite stance: a philosopher ought to warn people against the poisonous thinking of the apostle. In the chapter "The Pauline Infection", Michael Onfray describes Paul with the aid of categories from psychiatry. In a recognizably Nietzschean manner, Onfray jeers at the irrational and sick Paul:

> Paul created the world in his own image. A deplorable image, fanatical, moving with a hysteric's irresolution from enemy to enemy – first Christian, then Gentiles, sick, misogynistic, masochistic. . . . How could we fail to see in our own world a reflection of this portrait of a man so clearly controlled by the death instinct? For the Christian world eagerly experiments with such ways of being and doing – ideological brutality, intellectual intolerance, the cult of poor health, hatred of the vital body, contempt for women, pleasure in inflicting pain, disdain for the here and now in the name of a gimcrack beyond.[12]

Continental philosophy

Although such tirades from the neo-atheists have sold well among ordinary readers, searches in academic databases will show that it is the philosophers who are enthusiastic about Paul that have kindled the interest of scholars. Scholars in the humanities have paid relatively little attention to the thinking of Richard Dawkins and Michel Onfray, but Agamben, Badiou and Žižek have prompted a flood of publications that discuss the philosophical turn to religion in general, and specifically to Paul in recent philosophy.[13] Even researchers into Paul who initially had little interest in modern philosophical readings of these

---

[11] This is evident in the original French edition, where Onfray laments that Badiou takes this position in relation to Paul.
[12] *The Atheist Manifesto: The Case against Christianity, Judaism and Islam,* trans. Jeremy Leggatt (New York: Arcade Publishing, 2007), 132.
[13] This is not the place for a complete bibliography, but a good place to begin studying the turn to religion is Hent de Vries, *Philosophy and the Turn to Religion* (Baltimore: Johns Hopkins University Press, 1998). For a good overview of scholarly contributions and the problems in connection with Paul and philosophy (both ancient and modern), see Ward Blanton and Hent de Vries, *Paul and the Philosophers* (New York: Fordham University Press, 2013).

ancient texts have taken note of this phenomenon or "paradigm".[14] For when self-declared atheists such as Alain Badiou and Slavoj Žižek praise Paul as a radical thinker with great value for our own time, scholars can surely begin to wonder: Why are they ignoring the strong warnings of the neo-atheists and embracing Paul?

As if the embraces were not enough, enthusiasm for Paul has almost bubbled over in philosophers who belong to a philosophical tradition that builds on the religion-critical insights from Marx, Freud and Nietzsche. It is utterly extraordinary to see the Italian Agamben claiming that it is only now, two thousand years later, that it has become possible for us to grasp Paul's Letters in their proper meaning. According to Agamben, they have attained a higher level of readability.[15] Two thousand years of an ecclesiastical monopoly on interpretation have crushed the Jewish messianism in Paul's Letters.[16] But now, at last, the time of these texts has come. They are no longer held hostage to what Agamben claims are the narrow interpretative frameworks of the church: if we are to believe the Italian philosopher, their messianic power, as resistance to the existing order of things, has been unleashed anew.

Accordingly, when these philosophers invoke Paul, they are not appealing for a return to traditional belief and institutionalized religion. On the other hand, they are not particularly convinced by neo-atheists who regard religion as a meaningless superstition generated by the simple failure of believers to recognize reality as natural science has shown it to be. Slavoj Žižek calls Dawkins and like-minded thinkers "vulgar atheists"[17] or "vulgar humanists",[18]

---

[14] Troels Engberg-Pedersen is one of many Pauline scholars who have continued to work as in the past, that is to say, pretty well untouched by the modern philosophers' turn to the apostle. Over the years, however, he has acknowledged the work of these philosophers as a relevant paradigm for research. In 2019, he described the philosophers' readings as one of the four paradigms for Pauline research: in his view, these are the traditional image of Paul, the new image of Paul ("the New Perspective"), the radical image of Paul ("the Radical New Perspective"), and the pictures drawn by modern philosophers. Troels Engberg-Pedersen, "Innledning", in *Paulus og jødedommen*, ed. Troels Engberg-Pedersen (Copenhagen: Akademisk Forlag, 2019), 36. That said, Engberg-Pedersen appears to reduce this fourth paradigm to a reflection of "the more traditional, systematic understanding of Paul in dialectical theology" in a manner that simplifies the complex heterogeneity in this turn to Paul in European philosophy. Troels Engberg-Pedersen, "Paul the Philosopher", in *The Oxford Handbook of Pauline Studies*, ed. Matthew V. Novenson and R. Barry Matlock (New York: Oxford University Press, 2022), 200.

[15] Giorgio Agamben, *The Time That Remains: A Commentary on the Letter to the Romans* (Stanford: Stanford University Press, 2005), 143.

[16] Ibid., 1.

[17] Slavoj Žižek, *Less Than Nothing: Hegel and the Shadow of Dialectical Materialism* (London and New York: Verso, 2012), 14.

[18] *The Puppet and the Dwarf: The Perverse Core of Christianity* (Cambridge, MA: MIT Press, 2003), 171.

because he sees them as defenders of a naïve form of materialism who think that the fiction about God can be torn down from outside the experience of faith and the meaning of the religious texts.[19] According to Žižek, one must pass through the Christian experience in order to become a true materialist and atheist.[20] Žižek understands "God" as what the psychoanalyst Jacques Lacan called *le grand Autre* ("the big Other") who, by means both of the early socialization of the law and of language's function of supplying meaning, gives us expectations that there will be a moral and metaphysical guarantor – an authority that can take many different forms in modern human life.

> So why did Christ have to die? The paradox is that, in order for the virtual Substance (the big Other) to die, the price had to be paid in the real flesh of flesh and blood. In other words, God is a fiction, but for the fiction (which structures reality) to die, a piece of the real had to be destroyed. Since the big Other as a virtual order, a symbolic fiction, is effective in its very inexistence – it does not exist, but it nevertheless works – it is thus not enough to destroy the fiction from the outside, to reduce it to reality, to demonstrate how it emerged from reality (*pace* "vulgar" atheists like Richard Dawkins).[21]

For Žižek, no one becomes an atheist by abjuring God's existence while at the same time living as if there were authorities in the world and in our social order that guarantee what is moral or meaningful. According to the Slovenian philosopher, in order to become true atheists, we must suffer through groundbreaking experiences of an utter lack of meaning, in which our eyes are opened to how groundless both our experiences and the ideologies of our society truly are. If we do not confront this trauma in human existence – to which Christianity already points in the negativity of the cross – we will merely continue to live in a *de facto* trust in an underlying structure that supplies meaning and that tells us what we are to do and not to do. It is easy to believe that we are atheists. It is difficult to live as authentic atheists, according to Žižek, although it can help to take the path via Christianity.

---

[19] The eagerness to aestheticize biological hypotheses from the natural sciences indicate the incoherency of the neo-atheists' approach to religion expressed in aesthetic terms. Bradley and Tate, *The New Atheist Novel: Fiction, Philosophy and Polemic after 9/11*, 9.

[20] "To become a true dialectical materialist, one should go through the Christian experience." *The Puppet and the Dwarf*, 6.

[21] *Less Than Nothing: Hegel and the Shadow of Dialectical Materialism*, 104.

Martin Heidegger (1889-1976) took his own path via Christianity and Paul, en route to an atheism or a moving out beyond Christian faith. Heidegger wanted philosophy to direct its attention to human experience in general. He also gave the inspiration for a renewal of hermeneutics, which found expression through the ideas of Hans-Georg Gadamer (1900-2002) about interpretation and the understanding of texts.

Heidegger was perhaps the foremost thinker in what has been called "continental philosophy" in contrast to "analytical philosophy". While the latter academic current has had its primary centre of gravity among Anglo-Saxon thinkers, continental philosophy has had a strong position on the "Continent", especially in France and Germany. Somewhat schematically, one can say that where analytical philosophers look for answers to what can de facto be true, continental philosophers concentrate their investigations on what gives an existential meaning to life.[22] This makes the continental philosophers more curious about the potential meaning of texts – both literary and religious texts.

Modern philosophy's Paul between faith and knowledge

Etymologically, "philosophy" means "love of wisdom". In ancient Greece, the philosophers defined wisdom on the basis of what led to the good life. There were close links between the philosophical activity that led to certain knowledge and the philosophical activity that led to a good and virtuous life. Simplifying, we may say that it was assumed that if one understood how the world was constituted, one would lead one's life in a prudent and good way. In the early Middle Ages, this classical Greek philosophy was united to Christian theology in a cosmology in which all things in creation had each their God-given goal in a created totality where the unity between knowledge and wisdom, between philosophy and theology, itself was grounded in the harmony of the universe. All of nature was like a divine book. The more one discovered, the more insight one acquired into the divine.

The revolution in the natural sciences in the seventeenth century shattered this world view. The lack of a meaning, of a deeper intention, in all the

---

[22] Simon Critchley, *Continental Philosophy: A Very Short Introduction* (Oxford: Oxford University Press, 2001), 9.

connections that are uncovered in the world became defining for the modern epoch. This is powerfully expressed when the French mathematician and naturalist Blaise Pascal (1623-62) writes, in the light of the natural sciences' discovery of the endless universe that lacks any apparent meaning: "[T]he eternal science of these infinite spaces terrifies me."[23] The truths of science no longer lead automatically to the good life; on the contrary, they cause a feeling of emptiness and foreignness in the world. Like many other scientists at that time, Pascal is a believer. And when he finds the deeper meaning in religion, it is not on the basis of, but despite, the truths of science and philosophy. An abyss arises, or is discovered, between the faith that gives life meaning and the philosophy that gives knowledge of the word. As Pascal wrote on a piece of paper he sewed into the lining of his coat: "God of Abraham, God of Isaac, God of Jacob, not of the philosophers and the learned."[24] Faith and knowledge were to be kept apart – out of consideration both for the religious life and for objective knowledge. For Pascal, faith spoke to the heart, while science strengthened thought.

One of Pascal's contemporaries likewise argued in detail for the distinction between faith and knowledge – not primarily out of consideration for faith, but in order to preserve peace in society. Baruch Benedictus de Spinoza (1632-77) grew up while the wars of religion were devastating Europe, and in his *Tractatus theologico-politicus* (1670), he championed reason and freedom of expression. From the perspective of his hometown, Amsterdam, Spinoza saw religion as a danger to peace in society, because it was such an effective instrument for societal control and the manipulation of the popular masses. This was why biblical interpretation and theology ought not to set boundaries for the reason – especially because the biblical texts were not written on the basis of rational principles. His conclusion, accordingly, was a sharper distinction between faith and knowledge:[25]

> It remains only to show that there is no interaction and no affinity between faith or theology, on the one side, and philosophy, on the other . . . For

---

[23] Blaise Pascal, *Pascal's Pensées* (New York: E.P. Dutton, 1958), 61.
[24] See Michael Moriarty, *Pascal: Reasoning and Belief* (Oxford: Oxford University Press, 2020), 280.
[25] It should be noted that although the distinction was sharpened, revelation was by no means eradicated from Spinoza's thinking. The fascinating necessity of revelation within Spinoza's thinking is admirably explained in Catherine Malabou, "Before and Above: Spinoza and Symbolic Necessity", *Critical inquiry* 43, no. 1 (2016): 84-109.

the aim of philosophy is nothing but truth, but the aim of faith, as we have abundantly demonstrated, is simply obedience and piety ... we have demonstrated that the Bible does not teach philosophical matters but only piety, and everything in Scripture is adapted to the understanding and preconceptions of common people.[26]

In political terms, this was such a powerful attack on the Bible's authority in the Protestant Netherlands, where the Calvinist churches were built on the principle of *sola scriptura,* that Spinoza published his work anonymously in Hamburg. It circulated among intellectuals and was the object of debate, but it was very quickly forbidden in the Netherlands (1674), above all because of Spinoza's rejection of the truth contained in miracles and other supernatural phenomena that are related in the Bible. Besides this, Spinoza's claims about the human influence on the Bible were unheard-of:

Thus, we conclude without reservation that all things that are truly reported to have happened in Scripture necessarily happened according to the laws of nature, as all things do. If anything is found which can be demonstrated conclusively to contradict the laws of nature or which could not possibly follow from them, we must accept in every case that it was interpolated into the Bible by blasphemous persons. For whatever is contrary to nature, is contrary to reason, and what is contrary to reason, is absurd, and accordingly to be rejected.[27]

Spinoza maintained that the Bible did not describe what happened in accordance with the laws of nature. Its aim was rather to inculcate piety and obedience in the broad sectors of the populace. According to the philosopher, the Bible was not written to speak to human beings' reason, but to "influence and captivate their fancy and imagination".[28] The idea that the biblical authors' intention to transmit faith gave rise to accounts that were not historically correct was radically new. Spinoza also argued that the historical lives and personal motives of the biblical authors ought to be analysed;[29] this presupposed knowledge of the original languages in which texts were written. Spinoza was far ahead of

---

[26] Benedictus de Spinoza, *Theological-Political Treatise,* trans. Jonathan I. Israel and Michael Silverthorne (Cambridge: Cambridge University Press, 2007), 184–6.
[27] Ibid., 91.
[28] Ibid.
[29] Spinoza advocated a new type of historical writing about the Bible that is still valid for scriptural scholarship today, when he wrote that this activity ought to "explain the circumstances of all the books of the prophets whose memory has come down to us; the life, character and particular

his own time here. He anticipated the modern biblical scholarship that spread through the Northern European universities in the course of the nineteenth century. Spinoza's levels for biblical interpretation – the distinction between the philological, the exegetical and the historical – have been fundamental for biblical scholarship. He was expelled from the Jewish synagogue because of his harsh criticism of the Hebrew Bible (the Old Testament).[30] He then contrasted the Moses of the Jews with the Paul of the Christians. One striking aspect of Spinoza's radical text is how highly he esteems Paul in comparison to other biblical figures and authors.[31]

> Likewise, it is on this account that Moses, the supreme prophet, put forward no orderly arguments. By contrast, the long deductions and arguments of Paul, such as are found in the Epistle to the Romans, were by no means written on the basis of supernatural revelation. Rather, the Apostles' modes of discourse and discussion in their Epistles reveal plainly that they did not write them on the basis of divine command and revelation.[32]

While Moses completely lacked rational arguments, Paul's Letter to the Romans was full of them. In Spinoza's view, the apostles had written their Letters on the basis of their natural reason, not of any divine revelation. And for Spinoza, Paul in turn had a special position among the apostles. He noted that none of the apostles had philosophized more than Paul,[33] perhaps precisely because he found, or rediscovered, in Paul himself the distinction between natural knowledge and divine revelation.[34] This meant that Paul was also a biblical remedy for what Spinoza regarded as the morbid superstition among people in his own days.[35] One may ask whether this elevation of Paul as a philosopher and as a rational exception to the Bible's irrational authors and

---

interests of the author of each individual book, who exactly he was, on what occasion he wrote, for whom and in what language." Ibid., 101.

[30] Spinoza foresaw the kind of accusations of blasphemy and a lack of respect that his book would prompt: "Those who consider the Bible in its present state a letter from God, sent from heaven to men, will undoubtedly protest that I have sinned 'against the Holy Ghost' by claiming the word of God is erroneous, mutilated, corrupt and inconsistent, that we have only fragments of it, and that the original text of the covenant which God made with the Jews has perished." Ibid., 163.

[31] Taubes, *The Political Theology of Paul*, 77.

[32] Spinoza, *Theological-Political Treatise*, 157.

[33] Ibid., 162.

[34] "Paul mentions that there are two different forms of discourse, one based upon revelation and the other upon knowledge." Ibid., 154.

[35] "That is why none of the Apostles engaged with philosophy more than Paul who was summoned to preach to the Gentiles . . . How happy our age would surely be, were we to see it also free from all superstition." Ibid., 162.

characters was a consequence of Spinoza's original admiration of the apostle Paul or a conscious strategy – since it was precisely by highlighting Paul as a credible biblical witness that Spinoza could present legitimacy from within Christianity's sacred canon as a defence against what he regarded as later misunderstandings and dogmas that had corrupted a more original religion.[36] This higher appreciation of Paul is not unique to Spinoza; we find it again in other modern philosophers who occupy themselves with Paul.

The philosopher Jacob Taubes (1923–87) claimed that modernity had occupied itself with Paul's writings in two situations that were completely decisive for its ideological development.[37] The first was Spinoza, and the second was Nietzsche.[38] But there is another prominent philosopher closer in time to our own days for whom Paul played an interesting and possibly underestimated role, long before Taubes and other philosophers turned to Paul in recent decades.

Sein und Zeit (1927, Eng.: *Being and Time*) by Martin Heidegger remains one of the major philosophical works of the twentieth century. It belongs to a long philosophical tradition that seeks to identify the fundamental aspects of that which exists, the so-called metaphysics or ontology. Heidegger held that philosophy had got stuck in abstractions that were remote from life and had overlooked the philosophical task of uncovering the concrete phenomena that characterize the human being's existence. The intention was to lift the eyes of philosophy beyond that which is the ground or cause of being, and to set philosophy on the traces of the meaning of being: "The question of the meaning of Being must be formulated."[39] With this proclamation, Heidegger introduces the conceptual pair "authentic" and "inauthentic" as possibilities of existence. Confronted with the reality that one must die, the human person

---

[36] Jonathan Israel, "Introduction", in *Theological-Political Treatise* (Cambridge: Cambridge University Press, 2007), xvii.

[37] Paul played a subordinate and equally significant role in Immanuel Kant's philosophy, especially his anthropology. Interestingly, Ch. 7 of Romans 7 resonates with and inspires to Kant's idea of radical evil in human nature. Immanuel Kant, *Religion Within the Limits of Reason Alone*, trans. Theodore M. Greene and Hoyt H. Hudson (New York: Harper Torchbooks, 1960), 25. Leslie Stevenson, "Kant versus Christianity", in *Kant and the Question of Theology*, ed. Chris L. Firestone and James H. Joiner (Cambridge: Cambridge University Press, 2017), 135. For more on Pauline reasoning in Kant's philosophy see Ward Blanton, "Paul and Contemporary Philosophy", in *The Oxford Handbook of Pauline Studies*, ed. Matthew V. Novenson and R. Barry Matlock, *Oxford Handbooks Online* (New York: Oxford University Press, 2022).

[38] Taubes, *The Political Theology of Paul*, 76-7.

[39] Martin Heidegger, *Being and Time*, trans. John Macquarrie and Edward Robinson (Oxford: Basil Blackwell, 1962), 24.

(as "Dasein") is put into an authentic mode where his or her own life is filled with seriousness: "With death, Dasein stands before itself in its own most potentiality-for-Being."[40] The human being recognizes existential possibilities within a special and authentic form of experience of time, in which he or she is summoned to a special decisiveness in the moment: "That *Present* which is held in authentic temporality and which thus is *authentic* itself, we call the 'moment of vision.'"[41] One may object that this sounds rather abstract, and one may ask what is concrete in Heidegger's general reflections. What has given this analysis of existence a concrete shape? What has put flesh on its bones?

Several scholars have noted that central aspects of Heidegger's analysis of human existence in *Being and Time* recall the same philosopher's reading of Paul. In the winter semester of 1920-1, Heidegger lectured on Paul's First and Second Letters to the Thessalonians. He gave the lectures the title: "The Phenomenology of Religious Life".[42] Through detailed and idiosyncratic readings of Paul, Heidegger here distills a vision of an "original" human experience that is to shape his analytic of *Dasein,* which was still not fully developed.[43] As a former student of theology, he draws on historical-critical biblical scholarship when he emphasizes that the First Letter to the Thessalonians is the oldest writing in the New Testament.[44] At the same time, he distances himself from what he regards as an objectifying historical science: this must be replaced by a "phenomenological understanding" of the Letter, where one must expound the de facto way of being in the world that the text expresses.[45] In short, Heidegger finds in Paul an existential praxis that should be understood as a situated life in uncertain expectation. Accordingly, what interests Heidegger is not what Paul and the Thessalonians were expecting, namely the return of Christ (*parousia* in Greek), but what the German philosopher sees as an original way of being in relation to human life, which is lived out in early Christianity.[46] The philosopher Anne Granberg argues that

---

[40] Ibid., 294.
[41] Ibid., 387.
[42] *Phänomenologie des religiösen Lebens,* Vol. 60, Gesamtausgabe (Frankfurt am Main: Klostermann, 1995); English: *The Phenomenology of Religious Life,* trans. Matthias Fritsch and Jennifer Anna Gosetti-Ferencei (Bloomington: Indiana University Press, 2010).
[43] Hans Ruin, "Faith, Grace, and the Destruction of Tradition: A Hermeneutic-Genealogical Reading of the Pauline Letters", *Journal for Cultural and Religious Theory* 11, no. 1 (2010): 19.
[44] Heidegger, *The Phenomenology of Religious Life,* 61.
[45] Ibid., 47.
[46] "The central point that Heidegger is trying to make throughout his WS 1920-21 phenomenological analyses of Pauline Christianity is that the 'immanent sense' of Christian life is best characterized

when Heidegger has his true breakthrough as a celebrated intellectual with *Being and Time,* five or six years later, his presentation of the moment is still marked strongly by his encounter with Paul. Granberg affirms that Heidegger's elaboration of what he regards as an authentic understanding of death is, in fact, purely identical from a structural perspective with the authentic relation to the *parousia.* Like the return of Christ, therefore, death becomes a possibility at every moment that can come "like a thief in the night". She writes that the difference between an authentic and an inauthentic understanding of death reflects the difference between a secular and a Christian understanding of the *parousia.*[47]

In *Being and Time,* Aristotle and Augustine are quoted as if they belonged inside the philosophical canon – but not Paul.[48] Specifically Pauline terms are not found, but the analysis of the de facto experience of life that Heidegger constructed through a detailed reading of Paul is so similar that we are justified in asking whether Paul laid the foundation of its description in *Being and Time.* Was Paul a shortcut or a detour for the philosophical analysis? If Heidegger would have reached this point in any case, Paul can be regarded as a detour. Interpreters of Heidegger such as Jacques Derrida claim, on the contrary, that *Being and Time* has adopted Christian motifs in a substantial manner, and then secularized them:

> Heideggerian thought was not simply a constant attempt to separate itself from Christianity... The same Heideggerian thinking often consists, notably in *Sein und Zeit,* in repeating on an ontological level Christian themes and texts that have been "de-Christianized".[49]

Heidegger could have chosen other figures or other texts on which to build such central parts of his existential philosophy, but he chose Paul, without admitting how great his debt to the apostle was.[50] Nor is this all: Heidegger subordinated

---

in terms of what he later comes to call 'being-in-the-world'." Benjamin D. Crowe, *Heidegger's Phenomenology of Religion: Realism and Cultural Criticism* (Bloomington: Indiana University Press, 2008), 90.
[47] Anne Granberg, "Verken Athen eller Jerusalem – Heideggers Augenblick som 'Kairologisk Tid'," *Norsk filosofisk tidsskrift* 40, no. 4 (2005): 226-7.
[48] With the exception of note vi to Part 2, ch. 1. Heidegger, *Being and Time,* 494.
[49] Jacques Derrida, *The Gift of Death* (Chicago: University of Chicago Press, 1995), 22-3.
[50] When comparing Heidegger's early *Phenomenology of Religion* and his later *Being and Time,* Ward Blanton notes the following: "The basic difference in the content of these two writings may cause some to doubt, or even abandon part of this philosophical canon, as if the real Heidegger has moved on from an early period of interest in early Christianity to a later period of development in which

theology to his own phenomenology, which he regarded as more fundamental than the intellectual theological tradition which he had initially allowed phenomenology to be informed by.[51] At the same time, he translated Pauline faith into a form that could be acknowledged as philosophical knowledge. That the religious element in Paul can be translated to a secular content is also a presupposition of contemporary philosophers' readings of the apostle's texts. When the German philosopher Peter Sloterdijk (1947–) declares his intention of translating the religious element in Paul to something concretely secular, he sees this work of translation as a continuation of the modern Enlightenment project.[52] The Frenchman Alain Badiou sees this secular transcription of Paul as one link in a vast political mobilization against the existing order.

Original texts and later interpretations

The New Testament scholar John Barclay has described the inheritance from Paul as a slow-burning cord on a firework.[53] Over the course of two thousand years, this inheritance began by playing an explosive role and then settled down until it broke out at regular intervals in readings that have shaken up various groups of readers. The Reformation is a clear example. As a professor at the University of Wittenberg, Martin Luther (at that period an Augustinian friar) held lectures on biblical texts. In 1515-17, it was the turn of Paul's Letters to

---

he no longer allows himself to speak in the spirit of Paul or to guarantee the phenomenological approach through a revelation of the early Christian experience of *parousia*." Ward Blanton, *Displacing Christian Origins: Philosophy, Secularity, and the New Testament* (Chicago: University of Chicago Press, 2007), 124.

[51] "Thus the term 'phenomenology' is quite different in its meaning from expressions such as 'theology' and the like." With his starting point in Heidegger's interpretations of Paul, the Dutch philosopher Hent de Vries (1958–) concludes that "Heidegger . . . continues to secondarize religious revelation in favor of a dimension of revealability that makes the former possible in the first place." Vries, *Philosophy and the Turn to Religion*, 242.

[52] Peter Sloterdijk, *You Must Change Your Life: On Anthropotechnics*, trans. Wieland Hoban (Cambridge: Polity Press, 2013), 6. Alain Badiou employs a Pauline concept of grace on the presupposition that it is possible ". . . to extract a formal, wholly secularized conception of grace from the mythological core". Alain Badiou, *Saint Paul: The Foundation of Universalism* (Stanford: Stanford University Press, 2003), 66.

[53] "Paul's legacy is like a slow-burning firework. Explosive at the start, with huge flashes of illumination, it seems to die down for a while, in a steady state of lesser activity, before exploding again, unpredictably, in a huge rush of power and light, then quietly fizzing again before another moment of raw energy and danger." John M. G. Barclay, "Paul and the Philosophers: Alain Badiou and the Event", *New Blackfriars* 91, no. 1032 (2010): 171.

the Romans and the Galatians.⁵⁴ Here, Luther discovered what was to become the core in the Protestant rebellion against the church of the pope: justification by faith alone. According to Luther, it was above all the affirmation in the Letter to the Romans that "in the gospel God's righteousness is revealed from faith to faith" (Rom. 1.16-17) that gave him a religious rebirth.⁵⁵ His readings of Pauline texts kindled Luther's radical protest against the sale of indulgences, and gradually led to the breach with the entire church, so that Luther now became the leader of a reform movement that rapidly spread over the whole of Northern Europe and divided the continent into two – a Protestant and a Catholic part. This religious revolution was, of course, dependent on the political authorities' shifting sides and making common cause with the Protestants. Luther's local prince gave him a wholly decisive support and ensured the Reformer's safety when he was excommunicated. Luther was not burnt at the stake, like any other heretic who posed a danger to the Roman Church; he was given political support to disseminate his message. In all this period, it was ideas that emerged above all in the encounter with Pauline texts that kindled the Reformation fire and thereby set Europe ablaze. Paul played a role in these events because it was primarily formulations from his Letters that became building stones for the theology of the Reformation. Luther maintained, not only that scripture alone (*sola scriptura*) was the fundament of faith, but also that some biblical writings expressed the Word of God more clearly than others. In his ranking of the books of the Bible, Paul occupied the highest position:

> From all this you can now judge all the books and decide among them which are the best. John's Gospel and St. Paul's epistles, especially that to the Romans, and St. Peter's first epistle are the true kernel and marrow of all the books. They ought properly to be the foremost books, and it would be advisable for every Christian to read them first and most.⁵⁶

Luther also lamented that Paul's Letters had been misunderstood by readers before him. The most serious thing was that the real message in Paul's Letter

---

⁵⁴ John Kenneth Riches, *Galatians through the Centuries*, ed. John Sawyer, Christopher Rowland, Judith Kovac, and David M. Gunn, Blackwell Bible Commentaries (Malden: Wiley-Blackwell, 2008), 28.
⁵⁵ James D. G. Dunn, "The Justice of God: A Renewed Perspective on Justification", *Journal of Theological Studies* 43, no. 1 (1992): 1.
⁵⁶ Martin Luther, "Preface to the New Testament", in *Martin Luther's Basic Theological Writings*, ed. Timothy F. Lull (Minneapolis: Fortress Press, 1989), 116-17.

to the Romans had been held back. In his eyes, this Letter was "really the chief part of the New Testament, and is truly the purest gospel".[57] However, the clear meaning of the texts had for a long time been suppressed by traditional readings with their "glosses", that is to say, commentaries alongside Paul's words in the mediaeval editions of the Bible: "Previously, it has been badly obscured by glosses and all kinds of talk, though in itself it is a bright light, almost sufficient to illuminate the entire Holy Scriptures."[58]

One can discuss how clear this meaning in the Letter to the Romans and other Letters of Paul actually is, especially in the light of subsequent contradictory interpretations; and already in the New Testament, some voices maintain that Paul was hard to understand, so that the meaning was distorted (2 Pet. 3.15). What constitutes a distortion of a text is a highly disputable matter, but in any case, this New Testament statement shows that early on, there were conflicting interpretations. This interpretative plurality has proved unavoidable, despite Luther's experience of having finally attained the clear meaning of scripture.

When modern biblical criticism really got going in the course of the nineteenth century, a good many biblical scholars had something of the same expectation as Martin Luther: at long last, it would be possible for the genuine meaning of the biblical texts to be unveiled. While Luther held that the Roman Church had covered up this meaning, nineteenth-century biblical scholars held that it was the church's dogmas that lay like blinkers over the historically correct understanding of the biblical texts. The scholars would employ the historical-critical method to tell, at long last, the true history behind the biblical texts, thereby unveiling their original meaning, which lay hidden behind dogmatic prejudices. Once again, the biblical books and characters were subject to a ranking. This time, it was the apostles, and not least Paul, who obscured the real and historically correct picture of Jesus. Ernest Renan (1823-92) was France's most prominent representative of the modern biblical criticism in the nineteenth century. Like other historical-critical Jesus researchers, Renan wanted to peel away the religious superstition of the gospels in order to get into the original historical core, who Jesus "really was". But Renan regarded Paul's presentations of Jesus as even worse than those in the gospels. In his

---

[57] "Preface to the Epistle of St. Paul to the Romans (1522, Revised 1546)", in *Martin Luther's Basic Theological Writings*, ed. Timothy F. Lull and William R. Russell (Minneapolis: Fortress Press, 2012).
[58] Ibid.

book *Vie de Jésus* (1863, English: *Life of Jesus*), the modern historian of religion described the apostle's texts as distortions of the historical Jesus:

> The evangelists themselves, who have bequeathed us the image of Jesus, are so much beneath him of whom they speak, that they constantly disfigure him, from their inability to reach to his height. Their writings are full of errors and misconceptions . . . On the whole, the character of Jesus, far from having been embellished by his biographers, has been lowered by them. Criticism, in order to find what he was, needs to discard a series of misconceptions, arising from the inferiority of the disciples. These painted him as they understood him, and often in thinking to raise him, they have in reality lowered him.[59]

Behind the apostles' misunderstandings, the historian finds an exceptional human being. In Renan's historiography, Jesus is "the transcendent revolutionary, who essays to renovate the world from its very basis" with higher moral values.[60] Jesus had become the hero, and Paul one of the villains.

It is said that Friedrich Nietzsche gradually lost the faith in which he had been brought up from childhood, after he read *Das Leben Jesu, kritisch bearbeitet*, the historical-critical book about Jesus published in 1835 by David Friedrich Strauss (1808-74).[61] For Strauss, Jesus was a wise man whose superstitious contemporaries had presented him as a magician. Nietzsche also read Renan and seems to have adopted the picture in the contemporary historiography of the rebellious and wise Jesus who brought an originally good message that later apostles, especially Paul, distorted.[62] And it was precisely by being able to show that the original meaning in Jesus' message was completely different from what Paul and Christianity had turned it into that both the historian and the philosopher in the nineteenth century were able to unmask the alleged falsity of Christianity. Today, this antithesis between the text's original meaning and its later interpretations has lost much of its solidity.

---

[59] Ernest Renan, *Life of Jesus* (New York: Random House, 1927), https://www.gutenberg.org/cache/epub/16581/pg16581.html.
[60] Ibid.
[61] Blanton, *Displacing Christian Origins: Philosophy, Secularity, and the New Testament*, 190.
[62] Nietzsche mentions both Strauss and Renan in *The Anti-Christ*. He reacts against Renan's belief in progress and against Strauss' ambition to uncover what is historically genuine, but Nietzsche largely seems to have adopted the picture of the relationship between Jesus and Paul. Friedrich Nietzsche, *The Anti-Christ, Ecce Homo, Twilight of the Idols, and Other Writings*, trans. Judith Norman (New York: Cambridge University Press, 2005), 15, 26, 28-9.

First of all, belief in the objectivity of history and in the possibility of access to the most authentic historical reality behind the texts is much weaker. Already the German theologian Albert Schweitzer (1875-1965) criticized the nineteenth-century historians for being too subjective and for bearing the imprint of the contemporary ideological project of liberating the masses from religious dogmas. He argued that Jesus was turned into an instrument in this Enlightenment project:

> The historical investigation of the life of Jesus did not take its rise from a purely historical interest; it turned to the Jesus of history as an ally in the struggle against the tyranny of dogma . . . each individual created Him in accordance with his own character. . . . For hate as well as love can write a Life of Jesus, and the greatest of them are written with hate: that of Reimarus (. . .) and that of David Friedrich Strauss. It was not so much hate of the Person of Jesus as of the supernatural nimbus with which it was so easy to surround Him, and with which He had been surrounded.[63]

Aversions in the form of commitment against something can supply energy to readings, but it can also make them unfocused and imprecise vis-à-vis the texts that are the historical sources. We must also ask how we can best understand these sources. Biblical texts have a limited value as windows onto a past reality. We often lack sources for a reasonably certain and complete reconstruction of the historical context to which the texts point and in which they came into being. Historical-critical research has achieved great results, but every generation of historians is confronted by Schweitzer's challenge: Have they created the historical figures and events of the biblical texts in their own image?

In the reading of texts over the course of history, different readers have understood the same texts differently, and sometimes extremely differently. This, however, need not mean that how readers perceive texts is completely arbitrary, nor that the act of reading is merely a subjectivist projection.[64] And yet, readers are always influenced by their own historical period, personal interests, cultural preferences and prior understandings. Human

---

[63] Albert Schweitzer, *The Quest of the Historical Jesus: A Critical Study of Its Progress from Reimarus to Wrede* (Baltimore: Johns Hopkins University Press, 1998), 4.

[64] As Hans-Georg Gadamer writes, "*Understanding is to be thought of less as a subjective act than as participating in an event of tradition*, a process of transmission in which past and present are constantly mediated." Hans-Georg Gadamer, *Truth and Method* (London: Continuum 2004), 291.

interpretation always includes subjective dimensions that make completely objective readings impossible. But the prior understandings and prejudices with which we encounter texts are formed in the culture to which we belong and are therefore to a large extent collective. This gives the experience of reading a strongly intersubjective dimension, which is strengthened when the readings "wrestle" with other and deviant readings in free discussions. Our interpretations are formed as a part of the large cultural fellowship today, and they are also influenced by the history of reception of the texts since they came into being.[65] Texts can also be interpreted and explained on the basis of their linguistic and literary structure. This gives the interpretation a less subjective and more technical character. Texts have not only strong messages that call for interpretation but also a linguistic structure that can be decoded.[66]

The Enlightenment philosopher Spinoza demanded that science should delineate the historical circumstances under which the biblical texts came into being. In particular, the intention of every biblical author behind the text must be reconstructed. He thus gave birth to two ideas that were fundamental for historical-critical biblical scholarship. At the same time, Spinoza maintained the necessity for the new biblical scholarship to identify various types of reception. He wrote that biblical scholars ought to describe "how it was received and whose hands it came into" and also "how many variant readings there have been of its text".[67]

The history of reception studies how texts are received, interpreted and employed by readers in specific historical contexts. In recent years, reception studies have occupied a more prominent role in biblical scholarship. On the basis of Spinoza's two mandates for this type of scholarship, one can ask: What supplies the deepest understanding of the texts – historical-critical knowledge about the genesis of the texts or knowledge about the reception of the texts? The biblical scholar John Riches concludes that there is at least as much to learn about the biblical texts by studying the various ways in which they are read,

---

[65] Hans-Georg Gadamer emphasizes the subordination of the reader – which is both unconscious and involuntary – to the history of reception: "If we are trying to understand a historical phenomenon from the historical distance that is characteristic of our hermeneutical situation, we are always already affected by history. It determines in advance both what seems us worth inquiring about and what will appear as an object of investigation." Ibid., 300.
[66] Paul Ricoeur, "What Is a Text? Explanation and Understanding", in *Hermeneutics and the Human Sciences: Essays on Language, Action, and Interpretation*, ed. John B. Thompson (Cambridge: Cambridge University Press, 1981).
[67] Spinoza, *Theological-Political Treatise*, 101.

how they have been used and have formed the readers' lives, as from attempts to reconstruct the authors' original intention when they wrote them.[68] Another biblical scholar, Brennan W. Breed, goes further than this. He asks how precise such a reconstruction can be, given that the authors and redactors of the Bible, just like other creators of texts, presumably had half-hearted and unconscious intentions when they wrote things down.[69] It has proved difficult to enter into the interior dimension of the author and recreate the same process that gave birth to the work or text.[70] This has led several text theorists to conclude that the author is dead, while the text lives. As the literary theorist Roland Barthes puts it:

> As soon as a fact is *narrated* no longer with a view to acting directly on reality but intransitively, that is to say, finally outside of any function other than that of the very practice of the symbol itself, this disconnection occurs, the voice loses its origin, the author enters into his own death, writing begins.[71]

This means that the writing that is to be interpreted is read independently of what the author may have intended, and the historical origin of the narrator's voice in the text is largely effaced. It is, therefore, difficult to fulfill this aspect of the task Spinoza set for biblical scholarship, namely, to describe the author's intention. What about Spinoza's demand that the historical circumstances of the biblical author should be described?

In 2005, a meeting took place at the University of Syracuse in the United States between the philosophers Alain Badiou and Slavoj Žižek and historians whose special field of interest was Paul, including Dale Martin, E. P. Sanders, Daniel Boyarin and Paula Fredriksen. Fredriksen held that there was an essential difference between the ways in which Paul's Letters were read by the philosophers and the historians: while the philosophers cultivated an interpretative freedom in the encounter with the texts, the historians were obliged to let the texts speak out of their historical context. Scholars like Fredriksen herself had to preserve what she called "historical integrity". Unlike

---

[68] "I have long suspected that there is at least as much to be learnt about texts from examining the ways in which they have been read and have shaped the lives of their readers, indeed of whole communities of readers, as from our attempts to reconstruct their author's original intention." Riches, *Galatians through the Centuries*, xi.

[69] Brennan W. Breed, *Nomadic Text: A Theory of Biblical Reception History* (Bloomington: Indiana University Press, 2004), 107.

[70] Ricoeur, "What Is a Text? Explanation and Understanding", 149.

[71] Roland Barthes, *Image, Music, Text*, trans. Stephen Heath (New York: Hill and Wang, 1977), 142.

the philosophers, the historians could not impose their own interests on the texts.⁷² As I have mentioned, it is doubtful whether it is possible to read texts from a lost past without projecting onto them something of the prejudices and presuppositions of one's own time. This means that the contrast Fredriksen constructed may be exaggerated. We cannot simply affirm that whereas philosophers read their meaning into the texts, the historians bring out the meaning that already lies in them; the difference between philosophizing and exegesis is not so great. And on the other hand, it is not the case that historians are able to reconstruct the context of ancient texts (in keeping with Spinoza's second demand) without something of the interpretative freedom that, in Fredriksen's eyes, is the philosophers' privilege. For this freedom is also the historians' privilege, or rather, their demanding task: when they reconstruct and demarcate a historical context, this too is a creative activity involving the active selection of some elements that have their place alongside many other elements. We then interpret them in such a way that we give the preference to some interpretations rather than to others, and ourselves bear the responsibility for these choices.⁷³ It is difficult to establish a clear boundary between the historical context of the genesis of the texts and their reception by subsequent readers, especially in the case of biblical texts about which so much is uncertain (e.g. their dating).

The historian who attempts to reconstruct the original historical meaning of the texts for those who heard them at that time is herself or himself a part of the history of the impact and the reception of these same texts. This is another reason why the distinction between original texts and later interpretations is not so watertight or so clear as some would suggest. Accordingly, one can approach the question of the meaning of the texts on the basis of Spinoza's third mandate to biblical scholarship: namely, the history of reception. By uncovering various readings of one and the same text in the course of time, the historian of reception seeks to demonstrate recurrent and constant tendencies in the way in which persons in differing contexts read one and the same text. Texts can indeed mean many strange things, but there are nevertheless

---

⁷² "[W]e have to work hard to reconstruct their world, not project upon them concerns from ours." Paula Fredriksen, "Historical Integrity, Interpretative Freedom: The Philosopher's Paul and the Problem of Anachronism", in *St. Paul among the Philosophers*, ed. John D. Caputo and Linda Martín Alcoff (Bloomington: Indiana University Press, 2009), 72.
⁷³ Breed, *Nomadic Text: A Theory of Biblical Reception History*, 99.

some tendencies over time. Studies of reception increase our knowledge of what kinds of meaning – within the great variety of interpretations – texts can generate, that is to say, what texts can accomplish for their readers.[74] This means that the idea that Paul played a role in the Reformation is not sheer speculation. Texts influence readers. They can have power over them. And the Reformer Martin Luther let himself be influenced by the Letters of Paul. There was an explosion; something unexpected happened. The Pauline texts acquired a decisive influence that they had not always possessed.

In a similar way, there were not so many who foresaw the intense interest in Paul among European philosophers around the turn of the millennium. There was considerable surprise when philosophers who were so critical of religion became enthusiastic about the author who, perhaps more than any other, had stood as the symbol of Christian conservatism and dogmatism. While the Swedish theologian Jayne Svenungsson has called this a "hype",[75] John Barclay, whom we have mentioned earlier, has described it as dramatic.[76]

As texts, the Letters of Paul contain in general terms the potential to signify and mean something for human beings. In this book, we shall look at something of the potential for meaning that has been actualized and demonstrated through the philosophers' readings of the apostle. There is no reason to tacitly accept the philosophers' readings, just as there is no reason to dismiss them as irrelevant or mistaken on the grounds that they are not reading Paul in a historically correct manner. The philosophers' readings can be embraced, opposed or deconstructed by pointing to other potential aspects of the texts' meaning that have been, or that can be, actualized through concrete interpretations. This is how the meaning of the Pauline texts is investigated, and this is how we get a broader and deeper understanding of what these ancient Letters can mean – for individuals and for society, for good and for ill.

No one has "the" answer. Nonetheless, we can ask: Has Paul acquired an undeservedly bad reputation? And is he so attractive to atheistic philosophers today because he can solve philosophical problems for us? In that case, what are these problems?

---

[74] Ibid., 140.
[75] Jayne Svenungsson, "Nykter Motbild Till Filosofernas Paulus-Hajp", *Svenska Dagbladet*, https://www.svd.se/nykter/motbild-till-filosofernas-paulus-hajp. The Swedish "hajp" is derived from the English word "hype".
[76] Barclay, "Paul and the Philosophers: Alain Badiou and the Event", 171.

Structure of the book

The overall structure of the book is based on the assumption that there are primarily two letters from the Pauline corpus that modern philosophers have been compelled to read and engage with. An introductory chapter and a general presentation of Paul in light of the philosophical images of him are therefore followed by one chapter on the reception of First Corinthians in modern philosophy and thereafter one on the reception of Romans in the same line of thought. Led by an interest in which parts and aspects of these letters that interest these philosophers, these two chapters move chronologically through the letters while discussing the philosophers' readings of them. In that way, the chapters can also serve as introductions to Paul's arguably most important writings through the philosophers' lens on them. Given that Friedrich Nietzsche's extensive engagement with Paul's letters has been of such importance for the reception of Paul in modern philosophy, a fragment of Nietzsche's criticism is placed at the beginning of each chapter and serves as a continuous point of reference for the discussions in the book.

This first chapter has introduced the reader to the two contradictory approaches to Paul taken by atheist thinkers of today. While the so-called neo-Atheists dismiss the apostle as an irrational fanatic in ways reminiscent of Nietzche's intense criticism of him, atheist thinkers in the continental philosophical tradition have come to appreciate Paul's thought as valuable for their secular philosophies. Paul played a key role in the genealogy of the modern separation between faith and reason in the early modern philosophy of Spinoza, comparable to the one in Heidegger's philosophy in the twentieth century. Like any readings of biblical texts, these philosophical readings exemplify some of the potential meaning of these texts – a potential that forever disturbs a stable delineation between original historical meanings and later philosophical ones.

Chapter 2 parts from Nietzsche's claim that Paul was a bluffer entirely guided by a lust for power to tyrannize the masses. This image of Paul is constructed through an exaggeration of the level of institutionalization and social influence of the Pauline communities during Paul's lifetime. Similar to Nietzsche, Sigmund Freud also imagines the apostle to suffer from a guilt complex from breaking the law – a psychologization of the apostle that can be said to have more in common with later Protestant reception than what we read in the Pauline Letters. The effect of the turn to Paul in recent continental philosophy has been to displace this Protestant and religious perception of Paul by interpreting the apostle as primarily a political and philosophical figure. In that way, the philosophers' interest in Paul inscribes him into the canon of the history of philosophy.

Chapter 3 demonstrates how Paul's First Letter to the Corinthians functions as Nietzsche's target for his critique of religion, because the German philosopher assumes that the apostle is the great hindrance preventing the human being from taking on his or her new form as *Übermensch*. It is especially the exaltation of the weak, in the form of the crucified Jesus, expressed through Paul's doctrine of the cross in the first chapter of the letter that is under attack from Nietzsche. Alain Badiou rejects Nietzsche's aristocratic *Übermensch* and regards instead Paul as the inspiration of a radically new politics. But although Paul is meant to be the inspiration for a radical change of material circumstances, the outcome is nevertheless a strikingly idealistic philosophy of the subject. Against these idealistic interpretations of the First Letter to the Corinthians, the chapter suggests that there is a potential of a materialism for collectives in the letter.

Chapter 4 shows how Nietzsche describes Paul as a psychologically unstable type that through the struggle for a new freedom attempts to abolish the law. In a rare instance of a recognition of an authentic insight not based on lies, Nietzsche seems to valorize Paul's insight into the subject divided between its conscious will and its more unconscious impulses. While Freud considers Paul's message of salvation a fantasy, the founder of modern psychoanalysis recognizes some truth in the apostle's notion of original sin. Inspired by Freudian psychoanalysis, philosophers like Jacques Lacan, Julia Kristeva and Slavoj Žižek find deep insights about the human psyche in Paul's Letter to the Romans. In particular, Paul's tragic description of the intertwinement of law and sin in ch. 7 calls for interpretations by the philosophers. Departing from these interpretations, the chapter explores a wider philosophical meaning of the Letter for the Romans in light of the philosophical ethics of Jacques Derrida and Emmanuel Levinas.

The book concludes that it is precisely the tragic dimensions of human life in Paul that inspire the atheist philosophers to read him. In this way the philosophers construct an image of Paul as a precursor of modern psychoanalysis and not as an irrational religious fanatic antithetical to its secularized forms of confession. Furthermore, Paul's epistles are interpreted as models for a human ability and possibility of a radical break with the political status quo. Without counting on divine interventions in a secular world where God does not exist, Paul's gesture can be repeated in new circumstances. From Spinoza's praise of Paul as the most rational writer in the Bible, up until Alain Badiou's recent claim that there is an entirely secularized form of grace to be appreciated from the apostle's letters, there is a modern trajectory of reading Paul as an apostle for atheists.

1

Who is Paul the author

A bluffer or one in search of the truth?

The life, example, teachings, death, meaning, and rights of the whole evangel – nothing was left after this hatred-inspired conspirator realized what he and he alone could use.[1]

Friedrich Nietzsche in *The Anti-Christ*

"Paul an apostle – sent neither by human commission nor from human authorities, but through Jesus Christ and God the Father, who raised him from the dead." This is how Paul presents himself in the opening words of the Letter to the Galatians (1.1). A critic of religion like Friedrich Nietzsche could ridicule Paul for believing in God, just as Nietzsche did in the scene he created of a mentally ill man who walks round the market square with a candle lit in the middle of the day and cries out. "I'm looking for God!"[2] The apostle Paul is depicted by Nietzsche as a madman, but also as a clever man with a colossal power – for, according to Nietzsche, Paul is the author of a number of strokes of genius that have kept Europe tied down in chains and opened the path to the oppression of the human being by the church and religion. Nietzsche understood Paul as a fatal continuation of Plato's high esteem for the ideal and the mental at the expense of the physical and material, of real human life. This is why Nietzsche saw the struggle for the human being's freedom as a struggle against the popular Platonism with which Christianity poisoned the masses:

---

[1] Nietzsche, *The Anti-Christ, Ecce Homo, Twilight of the Idols, and Other Writings*, 38.
[2] *The Gay Science: With a Prelude in German Rhymes and an Appendix of Songs*, trans. Josefine Nauckhoff (Cambridge: Cambridge University Press, 2001), 119.

> But the struggle against Plato, or – to speak plainer, and for the "people" – the struggle against the ecclesiastical oppression of millenniums of Christianity *(for Christianity is the Platonism for the "people")*, produced in Europe a magnificent tension of soul, such as had not existed anywhere previously; with such a tensely strained bow one can now aim at the farthest goals.[3]

By liberating oneself from the pressure exerted by Christianity, the human person now has undreamt-of possibilities to aim far in the free unfolding of one's life. The human being who has abandoned Christianity's slave morality – a morality born of the thirst for revenge and hatred vis-à-vis superior power and strength – is no longer bitter and full of hate about life as it is. Behind Christianity's talk about compassion and love of neighbour lies, in reality, a concealed hatred of life, a moral hypocrisy and, not least, a will to seize power. It was this that Paul sought when he *invented* Christianity. Nietzsche declared: "What *he* needed was *power*."[4] Alongside Plato, Paul is Nietzsche's most prominent target. In the fight against the Christian religion, Platonism for the people, it is not enough to label its originator mad. Paul is not merely "superstitious". He is just as much "ambitious" and "importunate",[5] a claim that Nietzsche substantiates not only by means of a purely philosophical argument but also historically. His strategy is to unmask Paul as one who invents Christianity by twisting the historical starting point: the Jesus of the gospels.

> On the heels of the "glad tidings" came *the very worst ones of all*: Paul's. Paul epitomizes a type that is the antithesis of the "bringer of glad tidings," the genius in hatred, in the vision of the hatred, in the merciless logic of hatred. . . . The life, example, teachings, death, meaning, and rights of the whole evangel – nothing was left after this hatred-inspired counterfeiter realized what he and he alone could use. *Not* reality, *not* the historical truth! And once again, the Jew's priestly instinct perpetrated the same enormous crime against history, – he simply crossed out Christianity's yesterday, its day before yesterday, *he invented for himself a history of the first Christianity*.[6]

---

[3] Friedrich Wilhelm Nietzsche, *The Essential Nietzsche: Beyond Good and Evil: The Genealogy of Morals* (New York: Chartwell Books, 2018). 10.
[4] Nietzsche, *The Anti-Christ, Ecce Homo, Twilight of the Idols, and Other Writings*, 39.
[5] *Daybreak: Thoughts on the Prejudices of Morality*, trans. R. J. Hollingdale (Cambridge: Cambridge University Press, 1997), 39.
[6] *The Anti-Christ, Ecce Homo, Twilight of the Idols, and Other Writings*, 38.

Nietzsche's picture of Paul as a falsifier of history has stuck to the apostle's reputation in modern times. In Nietzsche's version of the story, Paul came after Jesus and distorted his "glad tidings". The life of this historical person, his example that was to be imitated, and his concrete life are quite simply set aside and eradicated in Paul's version of the whole story. Nietzsche has a certain sympathy with Jesus, whom he regards as an apolitical idiot who, like many at that time, ends up on a cross. And he spares the evangelists from the tirades he pours out upon Paul. It is as though, despite everything, he is confident that something in the contents of the gospels represents a historical kernel. Unlike the author of the Second Letter of Peter (3.16), he does not admit that Paul's texts or other books can be difficult to understand, but he does struggle with the gospels: "I have to admit, there are not many books I have found so difficult as the Gospels."[7]

Independently of the kind of motivation that one attributes to Paul (and Nietzsche succeeds in tracing not a few intentions in the mind of the deceased apostle), the basis of the argument is that Nietzsche himself has access to something about Jesus that is more original than what Paul wrote. The philosopher proclaims that he is in search of historical truths, liberated from the apostle's fiction. Much of Nietzsche's persuasive power here draws its strength from the common view among historians such as Strauss and Renan in the nineteenth century, namely, that the gospels were written earlier than Paul's Letters. This, however, is not the case. And since historical science has made new discoveries and the historians have adhered to new hypotheses about the genesis of the New Testament, time has run away from a central part of Nietzsche's criticism of Paul.

Nevertheless, the picture of Paul as the dogmatic falsifier, and of Jesus as the wise man in search of love, has retained its place in the inheritance from the nineteenth century. Jacob Taubes underlines in his lectures on Paul that when a Jewish dialogue philosopher like Martin Buber (1878-1965) approaches Christianity, one can detect goodwill in relation to Jesus – but a corresponding reluctance to read Paul as a Jewish figure becomes clear. Taubes claims that while Liberal Judaism may have some pride in counting Jesus as "one of its own", the situation with regard to Paul is not so good.[8] Slavoj Žižek maintains

---

[7] Ibid., 26.
[8] Taubes, *The Political Theology of Paul*, 5-7.

that today, it is precisely the more liberal persons who criticize Paul for an intolerant and missionary universalism that fails to show enough tolerance for other faiths and ways of thinking. The recurrent liberal refrain about the apostle says that it is Paul who corrupts Jesus' original message of love and distorts it into dogmas of faith for an oppressive institution.[9] As I have mentioned, Richard Dawkins and Michel Onfray follow in the same track. But what the critics of Paul see as reasons to hold him at arm's length motivates Žižek to embrace the apostle. He affirms that the action of organizing collective realities on the basis of orthodox doctrinal propositions does not show how oppressive Christianity is – quite the contrary is true. Far too many well-meaning radicals yield precisely to a liberal and individualistic unwillingness to mobilize collectively and to hold fast to ideology. When the political left buys the big narrative of degeneracy – namely, that Marx had a liberating message that was subsequently misused by Lenin – this has a demobilizing and paralyzing effect on what Žižek regards as necessary radical action. Žižek holds both that the problems began already in Marx's utopianism and that the left must in one way or another go back to Lenin, the man of mobilization and action while being fully aware that no political project will be perfect. For the Slovenian philosopher, the liberal hegemony that legitimates global class differences is much worse. And it is precisely in Paul's institutionalization of Jesus' message that Žižek sees the close relationship between Marxism and Christianity:

> The authentic Christian legacy is much too precious to be left to the fundamentalist freaks. Even those who acknowledge this direct lineage from Christianity to Marxism, however, usually fetishize the early "authentic" followers of Christ against the Church's "institutionalization" epitomized by the name of Saint Paul: yes to Christ's "original authentic message"; no to its transformation into the body of teaching that legitimizes the church as a social institution. What these followers of the maxim "yes to Christ, no to Saint Paul" (who, as Nietzsche claimed, in effect invented Christianity) do is strictly parallel to the stance of those "humanist Marxists" from the mid-twentieth century whose maxim was "yes to the early authentic Marx, no to this Leninist ossification." And in both cases, one should insist that such a "defence of the authentic" is the most perfidious mode of its betrayal: *there is*

---

[9] Slavoj Žižek, *On Belief* (London: Routledge, 2001), 142-4.

not Christ outside Saint Paul; in exactly the same way, there is no "authentic Marx" that can be approached directly, bypassing Lenin.¹⁰

The existence of the founders depends on later interpretations. The search for the authentic is a blind alley, because every attempt necessarily entails a retrospective and secondary interpretation. The "rock star" philosopher Žižek thereby turns Nietzsche's point on its head by saying: Yes, Paul transformed Jesus' message into dogmatic propositions and consolidated these in a societal institution. And this is precisely why the Christian inheritance is much too precious for left-wing radicals to abandon it and hand it over to crazy fundamentalists. This is part of the background to what the left-wing radical atheist did in 2011 when he stood alongside Occupy Wall Street demonstrators in New York and condemned the financial elite as "pagans worshipping blasphemous idols". He praised the egalitarian demonstrators as the realization of nothing less than the Holy Spirit.¹¹

Who was Paul?

Paul was a Greek-speaking diaspora Jew who probably received a training in rhetoric in the city of Tarsus in today's Turkey. After becoming a believer in Christ, he travelled around in the eastern part of the Roman Empire to spread his message. It is highly likely that he worked in Rome before the fire in 64 CE and before the Jewish War, which ended with the destruction of the Temple in Jerusalem by the Romans in 70 – a traumatic experience for Jews who venerated the Temple as a centre for their worship of God.

It seems in a way logical that we first have the more down-to-earth accounts of Jesus' life in the form of the four gospels, which are then followed by the apostles' Letters with their more far-reaching speculations about Jesus'

---

[10] Žižek, *The Fragile Absolute*, xxix–xxx.
[11] "Communism failed absolutely, but the problems of the commons are here. They are telling you we are not American here. But the conservative fundamentalists who claim they really are American have to be reminded of something: What is Christianity? It's the holy spirit. What is the holy spirit? It's an egalitarian community of believers who are linked by love for each other, and who only have their own freedom and responsibility to do it. In this sense, the holy spirit is here now. And down there on Wall Street, there are pagans who are worshipping blasphemous idols." "Slavoj Žižek Speaks at Occupy Wall Street: Transcript", *Impose Magazine*, https://imposemagazine.com/bytes/slavoj-zizek-at-occupy-wall-street-transcript.

divinity. First the original history and then religious faith. This would also accord well with Nietzsche, but it accords badly with the conclusions drawn by the overwhelming majority of scholars who work historical-critically on the New Testament texts. The picture of Paul as a historical "counterfeiter" has no doubt drawn nourishment from the experience that Nietzsche and others who read Paul's Letters can have: the man who wrote these Letters is not interested in Jesus!

There is a striking absence in Paul's Letters of references to, or accounts of, Jesus' earthly life, his miracles and his teaching. As I have mentioned, Paul the itinerant charismatic claims to have received the message directly from God (Gal. 1.1), and on the rare occasions when he does quote Jesus, he does not state that these words are written down anywhere. The First Letter to the Corinthians contains one of the strikingly rare examples in Paul's Letters of words attributed to Jesus. The apostle begins the quotation by writing: "For I received from the Lord what I also handed on to you" (1 Cor. 11.23). He does not refer to a written text, and the usual historical explanation of this quotation is that oral traditions of the words of Jesus began to circulate at an early date. It is not by chance that it is Jesus' words of institution of the eucharist that Paul reports here, because precisely these words took on a ritual function in the worship services of the earliest believers in Christ, words that also were recited, remembered and handed on to an author like Paul. In the same Letter, we find the example of logia from Jesus about marriage (7.10, "the wife should not separate from her husband") and that "those who proclaim the gospel should get their living by the gospel" (9.14). This is why preachers like Paul should not take material goods with them on their travels for the sake of the gospel.

There are several reasons why descriptions of Jesus' life and reiterations of logia from Jesus are not central in Paul. First, there is his interest in exploring the cosmological significance of Jesus' death and resurrection. Second, he is attempting to interpret the Christ event in relation to the Temple and the Law, which were central phenomena in the Judaism within which Paul works. And third, Paul is writing in order to influence practical situations in the groups of persons whom he addresses.

Paul is convinced that the crucified Jesus is the centre of a cosmic drama which he can also express in a form that exhibits traces of a different linguistic form than we find elsewhere in the Pauline Letters. This applies, for example, to Phil. 2.6-11, which the so-called form criticism has isolated as a separate text because it has the appearance of a hymn and introduces a stylistic breach into the epistolary text.[12] Accordingly, while the Italian philosopher Gianni Vattimo (1936–2023) traces the idea of the emptying-out of the deity, or *kenosis*, back to Paul,[13] biblical scholars trace it even further back. Here, we probably have a hymn that was used in the community in Philippi to which Paul wrote and possibly in other communities too. It was probably composed and elaborated by a collective of believers, rather than by Paul as an individual author.[14] Such texts therefore belong to the oldest material we encounter in the New Testament. Although Paul's First Letter to the Thessalonians is regarded as the oldest Letter, the hymn in Philippians may be even older.

Paul's transmission of words of this kind can be seen as a strategy for institutionalizing belief in Christ. He anchors his own message in something older, something that is already shared by a large number of persons and that therefore possesses a certain authority. There is, however, a constant risk of exaggerating the importance of Paul's work for an institutionalization that was in its infancy in the apostle's own time and that took on a genuinely powerful form only under Emperor Constantine nearly more than three hundred years after Paul's death. The fact that Paul speaks about stoning and scourging (2 Cor. 11.25) and imprisonment indicates that he encountered a brutal superior power – not that he was a powerful figure in his own time.[15] It is also worth recalling that the dogma of the Trinity in the Nicene Creed was elaborated under the same Emperor (and at the Council of Constantinople in 381). When Nietzsche writes about Paul that "the intractable lust for power reveals itself as an anticipatory reveling in divine glories",[16] his criticism has roots in the

---

[12] Wayne A. Meeks, *The First Urban Christians: The Social World of the Apostle Paul* (New Haven: Yale University Press, 1983), 144-5.

[13] "Divinity announces itself by subtractions, withdrawal, kenosis, free negation, as when Christ speaks of gaining one's soul by losing it. Or when Paul speaks in the letter to the Philippians of the truth of Christianity as kenosis, divine self-emptying, the privileging of the nothings and nobodies, the 'least of these.' Here we have a God who ceases to reign as Imperial father, renouncing sovereign power in order to become our brother as Christ, not a master but a friend and servant." Richard Kearney and Jens Zimmermann, *Reimagining the Sacred. Richard Kearney Debates God with James Wood, Catherine Keller, Charles Taylor, Julia Kristeva, Gianni Vattimo, Simon Critchley, Jean-Luc Marion, John Caputo, David Tracey, Jens Zimmermann, and Merold Westphal*, Insurrections: Critical Studies in Religion, Politics, and Culture (New York: Columbia University Press, 2015), 48.

[14] "Acts and the Pauline letters provide only tantalizing glimpses of the rituals practiced by the Pauline groups, but those glimpses are enough for us to see that they had adopted or created a rich variety of ceremonial forms." Meeks, *The First Urban Christians: The Social World of the Apostle Paul*, 163.

[15] Paula Fredriksen, *Paul: The Pagans' Apostle* (New Haven: Yale University Press, 2017), 168.

[16] Nietzsche, *Daybreak: Thoughts on the Prejudices of Morality*, 41-2.

apostle's cosmological speculations and theology. But if Paul was genuinely aiming at power and was driven by a lust for domination, it was surely rather silly, around the year 50 CE, to cultivate the belief that a crucified criminal was the Messiah. If the aim was to "tyrannize the masses" in the first century, as Nietzsche puts it,[17] it was counterproductive (to put it mildly) to join a suspect Christ-cult. This new variant of Judaism was not yet a mass movement, and Paul was a pretty unimportant figure in his own time, as we see from the lack of references to him in other sources. This means that if we want to know something about Paul's life, our primary source is his own Letters. And Friedrich Nietzsche had read them. He writes about Paul's persecution of lawbreakers in the name of God:

> Paul had become at once the fanatical defender and chaperone of this God and his law, and was constantly combating and on the watch for transgressors and doubters, harsh and malicious towards them and with the extremest inclination for punishment. And then he discovered in himself that he himself – fiery, sensual, melancholy, malevolent in hatred as he was – *could* not fulfill the law, he discovered indeed what seemed to him the strangest thing of all: that his extravagant lust for power was constantly combating and on the watch for transgressors and doubters.[18]

It is in the chapters of the Letter to the Galatians that we find probably the richest historical source for the life of Paul. He writes here that he "was violently persecuting the church of God and was trying to destroy it" (Gal. 1.13). He thus presents himself as nothing less than a persecutor of the believers in Christ. The apostle emphasizes: "I advanced in Judaism beyond many of my people of the same age, for I was far more zealous for the traditions of my ancestors" (1.14). But we do not find evidence in the apostle's autobiographical passages for Nietzsche's claim that Paul experienced at this time that he was persecuting others for breaking a law that he himself was unable to keep.

Nietzsche goes even further and claims that Paul had a guilty conscience. The German philosopher also maintains that Paul himself indicated that he was responsible for a terrible immorality.

---

[17] *The Anti-Christ, Ecce Homo, Twilight of the Idols, and Other Writings*, 39.
[18] *Daybreak: Thoughts on the Prejudices of Morality*, 40.

Many things lay on his conscience – he hints at enmity, murder, sorcery, idolatry, uncleanliness, drunkenness and pleasure in debauch – and however much he tried to relieve his conscience, and even more his lust for domination, through the extremest fanaticism in revering and defending the law, there were moments when he said to himself: "It is all in vain! The torture of the unfulfilled law cannot be overcome."[19]

In other passages where Paul describes something of his life before he became a Jewish believer in Christ, there is nothing to suggest that he had special problems about following the Jewish law, or that he took pleasure in "riotous parties". On the contrary, Paul insists that he was "a Pharisee" who was "as to righteousness under the law, blameless" (Phil. 3.5-6).[20]

In his 1939 book *Moses and Monotheism*, Sigmund Freud (1856-1939) writes that the Jewish people was overwhelmed by a continuously increasing consciousness of guilt around the beginning of the Common Era, a consciousness of guilt that Paul called "original sin".[21] The father of modern psychoanalysis saw Paul as a religious innovator who had special individual presuppositions that allowed him to elaborate the specific form of "salvation fantasy" that became the Christian faith.

He was a man with a gift for religion, in the truest sense of the phrase. Dark traces of the past lay in his soul, ready to break through into the regions of consciousness.[22]

The historian of religion Stanley K. Stowers has said that, as a historian, he cannot imagine a Freud without an Augustine first.[23] He has also shown how dependent Augustine was on Paul, especially in the elaboration of his anthropology. There is, in other words, a trajectory from Paul to Freud, and Jacob Taubes substantiates this link when he maintains that no one after Paul and Augustine had developed a more radical doctrine of original sin than Sigmund Freud.[24] But are these links built on a psychologization of Paul

---

[19] Ibid.
[20] Krister Stendahl, *Paul among Jews and Gentiles and Other Essays* (Philadelphia: Fortress Press, 1976), 80.
[21] Sigmund Freud, *Moses and Monotheism* (Buckinghamshire: Chrysoma, 2007), 42.
[22] Ibid.
[23] Stanley K. Sowers, *A Rereading of Romans: Justice, Jews, and Gentiles* (New Haven: Yale University Press, 1994), 2.
[24] Jacob Taubes, *From Cult to Culture: Fragments Towards a Critique of Historical Reason* (Stanford: Stanford University Press, 2010), 337.

that has no roots in the apostle's own life? If there is nothing in Paul's Letters about dark traces from the past, or about immorality such as murder and wild parties, where do Nietzsche and Freud get this from?

The theologian and bishop Krister Stendahl (1921-2008) lamented that Protestant Christianity has had a tendency to interpret Paul's consciousness of sin on the basis of Martin Luther's accounts of his individual struggle with his conscience. He argues that this is to misinterpret Paul.[25] It is symptomatic that Nietzsche sometimes writes about Paul in the same breath as Luther, as if the psychology of these two persons were almost identical.[26] Nietzsche's readings bear recognizable traces of Protestant Pietism,[27] while Freud's readings may be the expression of a Jewish desire for assimilation and acceptance in a Protestant German culture.[28] This means that their understanding of Paul may be formed on the basis of typical Protestant readings.[29] This applies not least to the view taken about who the "I" in Romans 7 is. Who has come into the wretched situation described in v. 15 of this chapter: "For I do not do what I want, but I do the very thing I hate"? If the "I" is Paul and describes the apostle's personal experience, the entire chapter becomes at once a rich source for Paul's inner life. But the text can also be read as an example of a conventional rhetorical strategy in antiquity, the so-called *prosopopeia,*[30] where an "I" speaks as the personification of an absent person. This absent person may be typical non-Jew (7.9, "I was once alive apart from the law"), but it can also represent the human person in general – either before or after this person accepted faith in Christ. There are several possible interpretations, and most scholars reject the idea that the "I" expresses Paul's individual experience.

---

[25] Stendahl, *Paul among Jews and Gentiles and Other Essays*, 79.
[26] "[. . .] and similarly to Luther, who one day began to hate the spiritual ideal and the Pope and the saints and the whole clergy with a hatred the more deadly the less he dared to admit it to himself, a similar thing happened to Paul." Nietzsche, *Daybreak: Thoughts on the Prejudices of Morality,* Aphorism 68. Translation: http://nietzsche.holtof.com/reader/friedrich-nietzsche/daybrake/aphorisms.
[27] Ward Blanton, *A Materialism for the Masses: Saint Paul and the Philosophy of Undying Life* (New York: Columbia University Press, 2014), 15.
[28] Eric L. Santner, "Freud's Moses", in *Sexuation,* ed. Renata Saleci (Durham: Duke University Press, 2000), 59.
[29] "The negative influence from Luther's conversion and his rediscovery of justification by faith can be characterized in four ways, all of which are a result of projecting Luther's experience – or, for that matter, to some extent Augustine's conversion more than eleven hundred years ago – back onto Paul." James D. G. Dunn, "The Justice of God: A Renewed Perspective on Justification", 2-3.
[30] Fredriksen, *Paul: The Pagans' Apostle*, 123.

This passage is doubtless grist to the mill of Nietzsche's psychologizations of Paul and the alleged similarities to a Reformer who lived one and a half thousand years later. And thinkers after Luther continue to see similarities between Paul and subsequent Christian thinkers whom they regard as so relevant to philosophy that they do not abandon totally the intellectual concepts of Christianity. When Simon Critchley, a self-declared atheist, was asked why he could not simply abandon religion, as other modern philosophers do, he replied:

> Because what interests me about the call – in the visceral register of subjective and intersubjective life – is to be found in religious thinkers like Paul, Augustine, Pascal, and Kierkegaard. These people, it seems to me, are asking exactly the right questions in the right way – even if I cannot accept their theological conclusions, their answers.[31]

What did Paul write?

The New Testament scholar Jorunn Økland has called Paul an urban globetrotter, unlike the Galilean fishers and craftsmen who were the core of the fellowship of disciples around Jesus,[32] because he set out for urban centres in the Eastern Roman Empire, where he founded small groups of believers in Christ and kept in touch with them.[33] The reactions from the local authorities, who were likely responsible for what he calls "my imprisonment" (Phil. 1.7), indicate that the apostle also visited public squares and spaces to spread the message.[34] The Acts of the Apostles relate that Paul travelled to Athens and ended up discussing with Epicurean and Stoic philosophers on the public square (Acts 17.18) before he addressed the city's influential judges in his Areopagus speech (17.22):

---

[31] Kearney and Zimmermann, *Reimagining the Sacred. Richard Kearney Debates God with James Wood, Catherine Keller, Charles Taylor, Julia Kristeva, Gianni Vattimo, Simon Critchley, Jean-Luc Marion, John Caputo, David Tracey, Jens Zimmermann, and Merold Westphal*, 152.
[32] Jorunn Økland, "Innledende Essay", in *Paulus' Brev*, Verdens Hellig Skrifter (Oslo: Bokkluben, 2010), xxxi.
[33] Fredriksen, *Paul: The Pagans' Apostle*, 12. Meeks, *The First Urban Christians: The Social World of the Apostle Paul*, 9.
[34] John Dominic Crossan and Jonathan L. Reed, *In Search of Paul: How Jesus's Apostle Opposed Rome's Empire with God's Kingdom* (New York: HarperSanFrancisco, 2004), 71.

> Athenians, I see how extremely religious you are in every way. For as I went through the city and looked carefully at the objects of your worship, I found among them an altar with the inscription, "To an unknown god." What therefore you worship as unknown, this I proclaim to you. (Acts 17.22-23)

The New Testament scholar Hans Conzelmann (1915-89) has called this speech the most monumental Christian document from the beginning of a very special confrontation between Christianity and philosophy, which was to continue throughout the whole of Western history.[35] Paul concludes his speech by proclaiming that the unknown god whom the Athenians worship without knowing him has raised up a chosen human being from the dead: "When they heard of the resurrection of the dead, some scoffed; but others said, 'We will hear you again about this'" (17.32). When Slavoj Žižek compares today's philosophers, who so easily brush aside radical political ideas, with the Greek philosophers who laughed ironically when they heard Paul's proclamation of the resurrection of Jesus, he is building on this story – without apparently sowing doubt about the historical content in the many stories about Paul in the Acts of the Apostles.[36] Among scholars who read the New Testament historical-critically, on the other hand, there are few who are confident that this episode about Paul is based on a historical event. Conzelmann affirms that the speech on the Areopagus Hill is assuredly not a genuine sermon by Paul but is rather a literary construction by the author.[37] Biblical scholarship has long operated with the hypothesis that the same author wrote both the gospel of Luke and the Acts of the Apostles; this also entails that some of the most substantial narratives about Paul in the New Testament may have been written down almost half a century after Paul's oldest Letters.[38] Accordingly, when scripture scholars compare the Acts of the Apostles with the Letters of

---

[35] Hans Conzelmann, "The Address of Paul on the Areopagus", in *Studies in Luke-Acts: Essays Presented in Honor of Paul Schubert*, ed. Paul Schubert, J. Louis Martyn, and Leander E. Keck (Nashville: Abingdon Press, 1966), 217.

[36] Žižek, *The Puppet and the Dwarf*, 99. In another text too, Žižek seems to accept the historicity of the episode in the Acts of the Apostles – in other words, that Paul actually held this address. See *Less Than Nothing: Hegel and the Shadow of Dialectical Materialism*, 650-1.

[37] Conzelmann, "The Address of Paul on the Areopagus", 218. "We must also ask whether the more public settings in Acts may not often reflect some of the of the author's subtle literary allusions, such as the several hints of Socrates in the encounters in the agora and Aeropagus in Athens, or sometimes simply the pattern of the author's day rather than of Paul's." Meeks, *The First Urban Christians: The Social World of the Apostle Paul*, 26.

[38] Todd Penner, "Madness in the Method? The Acts of the Apostles in Current Study", *Currents in Biblical Research* 2, no. 2 (2004): 42.

Paul, they trust his words more than the Lukan two-volume historical work (the gospel of Luke and the Acts of the Apostles). Conzelmann also underlines that literary constructions of this kind were not restricted to early Christian historians. He points out that ancient historians like Thucydides (460-395 BCE) used great freedom in composing when they wanted to fill in gaps in their narrative.[39] The Greek historian explains in the introduction to his account of the Peloponnesian War how he went about this:

> As to the speeches that were made by different men, either when they were about to begin the war or when they were already engaged therein, it has been difficult to recall with strict accuracy the words actually spoken, both for me as regards that which I myself heard, and for those who from various sources have brought me reports. . . . And the endeavor to ascertain these facts was a laborious task, because those who were eye-witnesses of the several events did not give the same reports about the same things, but reports varying according to their championship of one side or the other, or according to their recollection.[40]

Thucydides does not exclude the mystical and the divine, but he behaves with considerable freedom when he presents historical events in the way that he thinks the actors would have spoken and acted. If, therefore, the evangelists share the same presuppositions as one type of ancient historians, we can expect a certain amount of freedom in their dealings with history. This does not mean that the evangelists who wrote a couple of decades after Paul were writing pure fiction. But it means that they were working on, and handing on, oral and written traditions informed by the past.[41] Nor does it mean that the New Testament authors were alone in writing with religious presuppositions about earthly matters. There was no purely secular historiography in the modern sense, making a strict distinction between faith and knowledge. Even Polybius (200-120 BCE), a unique source for the history of the Roman Empire in the second century before the Common Era, writes on the basis of an overarching supposition that there is a divine providence:

---

[39] Conzelmann, "The Address of Paul on the Areopagus", 218.
[40] Thucydides, *Peloponnesian War* 1.22. Loeb Classical Library.
[41] "The Synoptic evangelists were, for the most part, not writing creative fiction but rather reconfiguring traditions informed by the past." Dale C. Allison, *Constructing Jesus: Memory, Imagination, and History* (London: SPCK, 2010), 8.

> For what gives my work its peculiar quality, and what is most remarkable in the present age, is this. Fortune has guided almost all the affairs of the world in one direction and has forced them to incline toward one and the same end; a historian should likewise bring before his readers under one synoptical view the operations by which she has accomplished her general purpose.[42]

The fact that the New Testament authors interpreted earthly history on the basis of their conviction that the events had a deeper divine meaning thus does not mean that they are useless as historical sources. It is unclear to what extent the evangelists knew Paul's Letters, but there is a broad consensus that the oldest Letters of Paul are the texts in which we come closest in historical terms to the first successors to the Jesus movement.

Nietzsche writes that the New Testament is "a kind of rococo of taste". He claims that "to have bound this New Testament along with the Old Testament into one book" is perhaps the greatest sin on the conscience of literary Europe.[43] The anthology of texts is organized in such a way that the longest apostolic Letters come first in a Christian process of canonization that was not based on any exact dating of these texts in the modern sense of the word. But not all the apostolic Letters that have Paul as their biblical author were written by Paul himself. At some point, pseudonymous authors began to appeal to Paul's authority in order to win acceptance for their own interests in the growing movement; this was not unusual praxis in antiquity and can, for example, be traced in an essentially different structure of the sentences in Greek, or in the absence of linguistic phrases that are typical of the genuine Pauline Letters. When, accordingly, Slavoj Žižek discovers in Paul in the Letter to the Ephesians (6.12) what he regards as a surprisingly relevant definition of political struggle, or when Giorgio Agamben claims that it is Paul who has employed a particular expression in the Letter to the Colossians, some biblical scholars would frown,[44] since the authenticity of these two Letters (as well as of Paul's Second Letter to the Thessalonians) is regarded as a matter of dispute. It is doubted whether they were written by Paul himself. The doubts loom particularly large in the case of the third group of Pauline Letters: the Letter to

---

[42] Polybius, *The Histories* 1.4. Loeb Classical Library.
[43] Nietzsche, *The Essential Nietzsche: Beyond Good and Evil: The Genealogy of Morals*, 52.
[44] Žižek, *Living in the End Times*, xv. Agamben, *The Time That Remains: A Commentary on the Letter to the Romans*, 13, 68, 90.

Titus and the two Letters to Timothy were written in all probability by other leaders in Christian fractions some decades after Paul's death.[45]

The philosopher Alain Badiou, on the other hand, has informed himself about dominant hypotheses in modern biblical scholarship. With the German scholar Günther Bornkamm, a pupil of Bultmann, as his explicit source,[46] Badiou is fully aware that the Pauline specialists regard only seven of the thirteen New Testament Letters as non-pseudonymous.[47] This means that we have seven authentic Letters of Paul, four of which have been known as the *Hauptbriefe* ("principal Letters") in a branch of research that in the past was dominated by German speakers: Romans, First and Second Corinthians and Galatians. Badiou brushes aside the accounts in Acts of Paul's journeys as "Hollywood versions" of the same journeys the apostle writes about in the epistolary literature.[48] This may appear a particularly apt metaphor, if one accepts the hypothesis that Paul in the Acts of the Apostles is adapted to the grand narrative of this historical work, which is a relatively Empire-friendly story of how the gospel is spread from the geographically limited area of Jerusalem to Rome, the end of the world. The Acts of the Apostles gives Paul a more exalted status, inter alia by making him a Roman citizen, than he has in the reality that seems to be reflected in the authentic Letters.[49] He himself says nothing in the Letters about this; instead, he undergoes treatment at the hands of the authorities that was perhaps unworthy of a Roman citizen. This uncertainty reminds us of the hypothetical element in the historical readings, which are based on probability and interpretations, not on unambiguous evidence.

Political texts

Friedrich Nietzsche claimed that one of characteristics of theologians is that we (including the author of this book) do not have the art of reading well. We

---

[45] Fredriksen, *Paul: The Pagans' Apostle*, 169.
[46] Badiou, *Saint Paul: The Foundation of Universalism*, 3.
[47] Ibid., 32.
[48] Ibid., 27.
[49] Crossan and Reed, *In Search of Paul: How Jesus's Apostle Opposed Rome's Empire with God's Kingdom*, 5.

lack the ability to "read facts *without* falsifying them", because we are notorious liars.⁵⁰ One of the aims of modern biblical scholarship, which is sometimes dominated precisely by theologians, is to read better, through philological and historical expertise. While theologians in the past traditionally read the letters of Paul as eternally valid theological treatises, modern scripture scholars have insisted on the elements in the apostle's texts that are determined by specific situations and historical circumstances – because they are letters.⁵¹ The Letter to the Romans is the longest Letter and contains lengthy passages that resemble treatises, but the New Testament scholar Jacob Jervell (1925–2014) emphasized that it is conditioned to a large degree by Paul's situation.⁵² While the Letters to the Galatians and the Corinthians are strongly marked by the writer's desire to intervene in internal situations among the recipients, the Letter to the Romans is written in order that Paul may obtain help from the Romans. The lengthy arguments in the Letter may be caused by Paul's need to introduce the recipients to fundamental aspects of the new faith, so that he can legitimate his projected visit to them in Rome. In other words, the temperature in the Pauline Letters varies in accordance with the situation. This is why the laborious style of argumentation in Romans is so different from the confrontational tone in Galatians that we see in the introductory words to the Letter: "If anyone proclaims to you a gospel contrary to what you received, let that one be accursed!!" (Gal. 1.9).

Both Nietzsche and Christianity have seen Paul through the lens of a pietistic priestly figure, and we must shake up this understanding. Large parts of the church have also cultivated understandings of Paul as an apolitical figure who is relevant primarily to the religious sphere and the private life of faith. When the historians locate Paul in a material philosophy, and the philosophers read the apostle politically, this can prepare the way for new understandings. It can also create a situation in which a philosopher like Jacob Taubes with a Jewish background reminds Christians of how immune they have been against seeing the dramatic element in Paul's reinterpretation of his own Judaism.⁵³ This is also why some argue in favour of translating the

---

⁵⁰ Nietzsche, *The Anti-Christ, Ecce Homo, Twilight of the Idols, and Other Writings*, 51.
⁵¹ Fredriksen, *Paul: The Pagans' Apostle*, 62.
⁵² Jacob Jervell, *Gud og hans fiender: Forsøk på å tolke Romerbrevet* (Oslo: Universitetsforlaget, 1973).
⁵³ "For Paul, the task at hand is the *establishment and legitimation of a new people of God*. This doesn't seem very dramatic to you, after two thousand years of Christianity. But it is the most dramatic process imaginable in a Jewish soul." Taubes, *The Political Theology of Paul*, 28.

Letters with concepts that alienate readers who think they know what Paul means when they encounter in his Letters religiously charged concepts such as "faith", "grace" and "justification". The theologian Theodore Jennings (1942–2020) suggested eliminating "faith" in favour of "loyalty" and replacing "grace" with "generosity" and "justification" with "justice",[54] since this would also defy an exaggerated individualization and spiritualization of Paul's concepts. This reflects a disinclination to reduce Paul's thought to nothing other than Platonism for the people (to use Nietzsche's dismissive phrase). It likewise expresses an awareness that the use of language continually changes and that certain terms that in the past have been employed to translate New Testament Greek have become rather empty of meaning in everyday speech.

Since Paul is regarded as the first in the line of theological pillars such as Augustine, Thomas Aquinas, Martin Luther and John Calvin, he is almost understood as the *primus motor* of an ecclesiastical institution that was established only several centuries later. This means that Paul's Letters are seen as channels of spiritual ideas for Christian communities or churches. But Paul is a Jew who does not know the word "Christian", and we may perhaps associate the term "community" or "church" with a group of persons who come together once a week in a church building with a pastor. This is very remote from the associations of the Greek word *ekklêsia,* which we translate as "community" or "church". This term was used of free citizens who met in an assembly that had a political character.[55] This is as if Paul were to apply a technical term for an Athenian democracy that excluded women and slaves from politics to a different kind of fellowship for both women and men, both slaves and free citizens (Gal. 3.28). And that is to transform the more religious understanding of Paul's concept, making it a sort of alternative town council.[56] The distinction between religion and politics with which we operate in the modern period did not exist at that time. When the philosopher Alain Badiou prefers to speak of Paul's addressees as "cells" or "enclaves" rather than as "communities", he brings out something of the numerically marginal quality, and the potential for

---

[54] Theodore W. Jennings, *Outlaw Justice: The Messianic Politics of Paul* (Stanford: Stanford University Press, 2013), 3. In classical antiquity, *pistis* and its Latin pendant *fides* tended rather to have connotations of "steadfastness", "conviction" and "loyalty". Fredriksen, *Paul: The Pagans' Apostle,* 120.
[55] Stathis Gourgouris, *The Perils of the One* (New York: Columbia University Press, 2019), 130-1.
[56] Blanton, *A Materialism for the Masses: Saint Paul and the Philosophy of Undying Life,* 178.

criticism of wordly power, of small groups that venerated a crucified criminal as their supreme authority in municipal centres in the Roman Empire.[57]

Paul is accused of watering down the Judaism of his own time, because he insists that those who accept the faith without being Jews are not obliged to follow Torah – since he believes that the last days have come, when all the peoples are to be united in the faith in the Messiah. When Paul is accused, he must defend himself. And because there are fractions and conflicts of interest, Paul's Letters are one-sided contributions to ongoing debates. And because only fragments of these debates have been preserved for posterity, we can soon lose sight of this when we read Paul's Letters in isolation. And this makes Alain Badiou's designation of the Pauline Letters as "interventions" useful.[58] They are not so much coherent theoretical treatises with a watertight system, as attempts to intervene in discussions and to provoke action. One of Paul's most important goals was unity within the cells and self-control in conduct. The leaders were to drop the demand for Jewish legal piety as a sign of loyalty to Christ. The Letters can be said to be a manifesto for this.[59]

This means that they are texts meant to provoke reactions, rather than to impress the readers with their elegant language or their philosophical originality. The philosopher Søren Kierkegaard (1813-55) went even further than Badiou in emphasizing the stylistic inferiority of Paul's texts in comparison with the great masters of philosophy:

> As a genius, Paul cannot stand comparison with either Plato or Shakespeare; as an author of beautiful parables, he comes rather low down on the list; as a stylist, he is a completely obscure name.[60]

For Kierkegaard, the apostle is eternally different from other human beings (including the geniuses), because he is sent. It is the authority with which the apostle speaks that makes Kierkegaard willing to listen to him – not the aesthetic quality or the lack of it.

---

[57] Badiou, *Saint Paul: The Foundation of Universalism*, 95, 100.
[58] Ibid., 20, 31.
[59] Meeks, *The First Urban Christians: The Social World of the Apostle Paul*, 109.
[60] Sören Kierkegaard, *Tvende ethish-religieuse Smaa-afhandlinger*, http://sks.dk/forside/skr.asp (accessed 05 May 2021).

Paul and the philosophical canon

The philosopher Badiou writes that he has never thought of Paul as a religious figure.[61] He has always read him as one of the classics, among whom he lists Plato and Wittgenstein alongside Paul. Badiou, who gives Paul a place in his philosophical canon, claims that there is nothing especially holy about the Letters. A canon is a list of books and authors; but unlike a closed canon (such as the Bible), the canon of philosophy is more open and is the object of continuous negotiation about who is to be voted in and voted out. In the light of feminist critique, it has become clearer that there have also been clear limits to how open the philosophical canon has been.[62] Thus, the contrast between the closed biblical canon and the open philosophical one is not as unambiguous as is often suggested. Nonetheless, the great interest in Paul in continental philosophy in recent decades has moved the apostle's name into philosophical discussions to which he did not belong so strongly in the past. This helps to make Paul part of a widened philosophical canon to which students are often introduced. One of those who have helped to move the apostle closer to the canon of philosophy is Slavoj Žižek, who has declared that he interprets the value of Christianity "following Alain Badiou's path-breaking book on Paul".[63] His simple indifference to most of the historical perspectives on Paul means that the Pauline texts acquire the status of classics in Žižek's philosophy – no anachronism is too extreme in Žižek's treatment of these Letters that are two thousand years old, and no phenomenon is too modern for Paul to be able to shed light on it. Žižek continually moves him into unexpected situations where he is set to work to solve a philosophical problem. The question, however, is whether the apostle in reality is a detour or a shortcut to finding the solution.

One reason why Paul can be mentioned in the same breath as Karl Marx is the endeavours by philosophers like Jacob Taubes and Giorgio Agamben to inscribe the apostle in a kind of sidetrack or supplement to the canon of philosophy, namely, in Jewish messianism. Both philosophers argue that messianic expectations of a transformation of earthly realities and a re-establishing of peace and justice through a messianic saviour-figure have

---

[61] Badiou, *Saint Paul: The Foundation of Universalism*, 1.
[62] See for instance Genevieve Lloyd, *The Man of Reason. "Male" and "Female" in Western Philosophy* (Minnesota: University of Minnesota Press, 1993).
[63] Žižek, *The Fragile Absolute*, xxix.

been kept in check for centuries by conservative forces in churches and synagogues.[64] Taubes depicts Pauline Christianity as a markedly messianic movement in which the eschatological hope in earthly transformation was crushed by the death of the Messiah-figure, and then reinterpreted in a manner that directed the messianic faith into the internal dimension of the human being – because the brutal concrete circumstances made the external transformation of the world impossible, and postponed it.[65] Salvation was put on hold, and at the same time anticipated through love of neighbor, which Paul proclaimed as the fundament of the existence of new non-Jewish fellowships of believers in Christ.

At irregular intervals, however, these messianic impulses broke out within both Christianity and Judaism, and this explosive power has been canalized in modern times into secular forms such as Marxism. Even if religion is weakened, the impulses do not vanish, according to Taubes: they are only canalized in other ways, often in periods and situations marked by great human suffering. This is why Taubes claims that the proletariat takes on the figure of a saviour in Karl Marx's philosophy, where the expectation that the drama in world history will be decided through revolution becomes a secularized eschatological drama.[66]

Accordingly, when Agamben wishes to re-establish the status of Paul's Letters as fundamental texts in the messianic tradition, he takes the path via the Marxist and Jewish philosopher Walter Benjamin (1892-1940), who was clearly inspired by messianism. Agamben refers to Benjamin's allegory of the hunchbacked dwarf in the first thesis in the text about the concept of history that Benjamin wrote while escaping from Nazism in 1940.[67] The dwarf hides under a chessboard and ensures that a puppet would win the game. In the allegory, the puppet is called "historical materialism". Benjamin writes: "It can easily be a match for anyone if it enlists the services of theology." He mentions that the dwarf could not bear the light of day, because he was "wizened and has to keep out of sight".[68] Ever since the text was published by Theodor Adorno in

---

[64] Agamben, *The Time That Remains: A Commentary on the Letter to the Romans*, 1.
[65] Taubes, *From Cult to Culture: Fragments Towards a Critique of Historical Reason*, 5.
[66] *Occidental Eschatology* (Stanford: Stanford University Press, 2009), 184-6.
[67] Benjamin committed suicide on 26 or 27 September 1940, after he was informed that the Spanish authorities would close the border to refugees and send them in the direction of the German occupying power – into France.
[68] Walter Benjamin, *Illuminations. Essays and Reflections* (New York: Pimlico, 2007), 253.

1955, it has fascinated many people and inspired a variety of interpretations. When Giorgio Agamben wrote his commentary on the Letter to the Romans in 2000, he concluded with some thoughts on whom Benjamin has in mind when he writes about the dwarf, which no one up until that time had succeeded in identifying. Agamben quotes from another section of the text about the concept of history:

> In other words, our image of happiness is indissolubly bound up with the image of redemption. The same applies to our view of the past, which is the concern of history. The past carries with it a temporal index by which it is referred to redemption. There is a secret agreement between past generations and the present one. Our coming was expected on earth. Like every generation that preceded us, we have been endowed with a *weak* Messianic power, a power to which the past has a claim.[69]

Benjamin wants to introduce here a concept of history that has space for a mystical fellowship between the present and the past, between the living and the dead, as an alternative to a historical science that one-sidedly objectivizes the past and hence is unable to distinguish the essential from the inessential and to see the truly tragic and the struggle of the oppressed. At the same time, Benjamin wants to link the salvation of the human being to a historical task or a messianic vocation that comes from the past, from those who have preceded us, and above all, from the victims of oppression. But how are we to understand the weak element in the messianic power?

Agamben's key is Paul. According to the philosopher, the apostle is the dwarf behind the chessboard, and the weak messianism in Benjamin has literary roots in Paul's Second Letter to the Corinthians. When Paul writes about what he believes is a divine intention in his own suffering, which he calls "a thorn in the flesh" (2 Cor. 12.7), he summarizes the meaning of this experience as follows: "Power is made perfect in weakness" (12.9), and then declares: "Therefore I am content with weaknesses, insults, hardships, persecutions, and calamities for the sake of Christ; for whenever I am weak, then I am strong" (12.10). Agamben holds that Benjamin most likely had this biblical passage in mind when he wrote.[70] And as if that were not enough, the philosopher claims

---

[69] Ibid., 254.
[70] Agamben, *The Time That Remains: A Commentary on the Letter to the Romans*, 140.

that Benjamin's text about the concept of history is influenced in its entirety by a Pauline vocabulary of this type.[71]

Walter Benjamin is perhaps the twentieth century's leading interpreter of Jewish messianism and its mediator to philosophy. His importance is acclaimed by Theodor Adorno, Hannah Arendt and Jacques Derrida. The parallel between the apostle and Benjamin, and their ideological relatedness, locate Paul in the undercurrent of Jewish messianism that throughout history has swirled around on the outskirts of Christian Europe in both religious and secular forms. This relatedness between the allegedly Christian Paul and the allegedly Jewish Benjamin is one of several ideas in the interest for Paul in philosophy that dislocate the boundaries between Christianity and Judaism, and between religion and philosophy.

The picture of Paul as a precursor of Walter Benjamin is in sharp contrast to Nietzsche's picture of the apostle as the mendacious priestly figure who seeks nothing but power. Paul becomes, not a symbol of power, but – together with Benjamin – a symbol of powerlessness. Both were denigrated and persecuted in their lifetimes. And both ended their days as victims of empires that liquidated political opponents.

---

[71] Ibid., 144. Not everyone is equally convinced about the literary dependence that Agamben postulates between Paul and Benjamin. Roland Boer, *Criticism of Religion: On Marxism and Theology, Ii* (Leiden: Brill, 2009), 187. "Paul of the Gaps. Agamben, Benjamin and the Puppet Player", in *Paul in the Grip of the Philosophers,* ed. Peter Frick (Minneapolis: Fortress Press, 2013). "Agamben exaggerates the case of Benjamin and Paul." Brian Britt, "The Schmittian Messiah in Agamben's The Time That Remains", *Critical Inquiy* 36, no. 2 (2010): 262-287. See also Sigrid Weigel, "In Paul's Mask: Jacob Taubes Reads Walter Benjamin", in *Genealogies of the Secular: The Making of Modern German Thought*, ed. Willem Styfhals and Stéphane Symons (Albany: State University of New York Press, 2019).

2

First Letter to the Corinthians
Criticism of wordly power

This reminds me again of the invaluable words of Paul. "The weak things of the world, the foolish things of the world, the base things of the world, and the things that are despised, hath God chosen": this was the formula; decadence was victorious in hoc signo.[1]

Friedrich Nietzsche in Anti-Christ (1888)

The First Letter to the Corinthians is written or dictated by someone who calls himself Paul and intends to address a group in Corinth, the Roman provincial capital in Greece. If we are to believe ch. 18 of the Acts of the Apostles, Paul founded the community on his second journey in this region. The information we have in the Letters indicates that Paul wrote several Letters to this group.[2] This one is called the First Letter to the Corinthians because it is the first of these Letters that is preserved in the collection of writings that became the canonical New Testament. The best-known passage in it is surely the text about love in ch. 13, not least because it is frequently used in worship and in popular culture. But the dispute in European intellectual history has first and foremost concerned the first chapter in the Letter. It is this part of Paul's message to the Corinthians that has drawn the greatest attention from the philosophers. Etymologically, "philosophy" means "love for wisdom". Accordingly, when Paul

---

[1] Nietzsche, *The Anti-Christ, Ecce Homo, Twilight of the Idols, and Other Writings*, 50-1.
[2] The Second Letter to the Corinthians can be divided into several minor letters, but research has so far not reached a consensus of whether the letter should be divided into two, three or even five letters. Margaret M. Mitchell, "Paul's Letters to Corinth: The Interpretative Intertwining of Literary and Historical Reconstruction", in *Urban Religion in Roman Corinth: Interdisciplinary Approaches*, ed. Daniel N. Schowalter and Steven J. Friesen (Cambridge: Harvard Divinity School, 2005), 318.

draws a contrast between "the wisdom of the world" and "the message about the cross" (1 Cor. 1.18), this touches some of philosophy's basic questions: What is wisdom, and what is not wisdom? Paul constructs this contrast on the basis of his own alleged lack of "eloquent wisdom":

> For Christ did not send me to baptize but to proclaim the gospel, and not with eloquent wisdom, so that the cross of Christ might not be emptied of its power. For the message about the cross is foolishness to those who are perishing, but to us who are being saved it is the power of God. For it is written, "I will destroy the wisdom of the wise, and the discernment of the discerning I will thwart." Where is the one who is wise? Where is the scribe? Where is the debater of this age? Has not God made foolish the wisdom of the world? For since, in the wisdom of God, the world did not know God through wisdom, God decided, through the foolishness of our proclamation, to save those who believe. For Jews demand signs and Greeks desire wisdom, but we proclaim Christ crucified, a stumbling block to Jews and foolishness to Gentiles, but to those who are the called, both Jews and Greeks, Christ the power of God and the wisdom of God. For God's foolishness is wiser than human wisdom, and God's weakness is stronger than human strength. (1 Cor. 1.17-25)

There is thus a reason why Paul does not preach with fine-tuned and impressive rhetoric. The impressive rhetorical forms through which the wisdom of the world is expressed are utterly unsuited to communicate the saving message about the cross. Paul divides the human race into three groups here on the basis of their reaction to the foolishness that is preached. Jews reject the gospel of the Crucified because they prefer other signs, while Greeks seek this world's wisdom, which God has already shown to be foolishness. The third group consists of those who believe and are called, and this group can include both Jews and Greeks. The group of believers in Christ thus admits to membership both Jews and Greeks who see Christ as being nothing less than the wisdom of God. In this way, Paul has constructed an effective contrast between those who mistakenly revere a foolishness with its origin in this world and those who live out of a deeper form of wisdom with its origin in both God and the cross.

Paul uses the rest of the Letter to give further content to these groups and categories. The addressees must make their choice in relation to the groups. Will the Corinthians believe, or not believe? Will they put their trust in "a wisdom for those who are mature?" (2.6), or will they trust in a wisdom that belongs to the rulers of this world, who crucified "the Lord of glory" (2.8) and who will certainly perish after God's judgement when "the end" comes (1.8)? When contrasts of this kind are the existential fundament in the new life in Christ, the urgent question is how the believers ought in fact to live in this world before the end comes. The apostle claims that "the appointed time has grown short" (7.29), and this leads him to give some remarkable pieces of advice in this matter. He recommends that the believers who have a wife should "be as though they had none" (7.29), and that "those who mourn" should live "as if they were not mourning" (7.30).

In recent times, modern philosophers have paid close attention to Paul's exhortation in ch. 7 about the attitude or position to which God has called the believer in the messianic age (7.29-31), and it is these verses that Jacob Tauber called "the nihilistic passage".[3]

Nietzsche's readings of Paul

Nihilism is a concept that Nietzsche applies to the rejection of the supposition that there exist objective foundations for religion, morality and knowledge as a whole. He sees this form of nihilism as the necessary remedy for an ideological epidemic that has spread mental poison over Europe since Paul. But Paul's Christianity is also a form of nihilism, because it spread a murderous form of the denial of life that emptied existence here on earth of meaning and transposed meaning over into that which lies beyond death. According to Nietzsche, this world-denying nihilism was made possible by a large-scale reassessment of values:

> Jesus himself had done away with the very concept of "guilt," he denied that there was any gulf fixed between God and man; he *lived* this unity between God and man, and that was precisely *his* "glad tidings"; . . . And *not* as a mere

---

[3] Taubes, *The Political Theology of Paul*, 53. I wonder whether Gianni Vattimo has taken this over from Taubes, when he too reads a form of nihilism out of these verses: "I come back to Saint Paul and his notion of *hôs mê*, 'as if they do not' [1 Corinthians 7:29-31]. This is a Pauline equivalent of the ontological difference: being is other than what it is. It is nihilism defined as a certain respect for distance and difference. Like Max Scheler says of the phenomenological epoché, it gives us a form of 'moral detachment,' a form of freedom of negation and suspension." Kearney and Zimmermann, *Reimagining the Sacred. Richard Kearney Debates God with James Wood, Catherine Keller, Charles Taylor, Julia Kristeva, Gianni Vattimo, Simon Critchley, Jean-Luc Marion, John Caputo, David Tracey, Jens Zimmermann, and Merold Westphal*, 146-7.

privilege! From this time forward the type of the Savior was corrupted, bit by bit, by the doctrine of judgment and of the second coming, the doctrine of death as a sacrifice, the doctrine of the *resurrection,* by means of which the entire concept of "blessedness," the whole and only reality of the gospels, is juggled away – in favor of a state of existence *after* death! . . . St. Paul, with that rabbinical impudence which shows itself in all his doings, gave a logical quality to that conception, that *indecent* conception, in this way: "*If* Christ did not rise from the dead, then all our faith is in vain" – And at once there sprang from the gospels the most contemptible of all unfulfillable promises, the *shameless* doctrine of personal immortality. . . . Paul even preached it as a *reward*.[4]

Nietzsche sees Christianity's entangling of guild, sin and bad conscience as an instrument that oppressed what the philosopher held to be the instinctive freedom in the human being. It is not Jesus' fault that Christianity carries out a remarkable reappraisal of values that drives people to lead a life based on fear of what comes after death, instead of leading a life that finds pleasure in what is here on earth. It is Paul, at 1 Cor. 15.14, who "at one blow" turns Jesus' good news into a pessimistic message about human guilt feelings vis-à-vis the deity, which must be expiated in order to avoid punishment after this life. Pauline Christianity twists the gospel of Jesus, and the result is "a record amount of guilt consciousness".[5] Christianity introduces a religious system in which the invention and the idea of punishment or reward by the deity after death wreak psychological terror on the human being. It is Paul who is responsible for this, and it is in ch. 15 of the First Letter to the Corinthians that the fatal step is taken, when the apostle invents what Nietzsche calls "the doctrine of personal immortality".

The philosopher Friedrich Nietzsche appoints himself a "genealogist of morals" and sees in his mind's eye a world history in which a caste of knights has opposed a caste of priests. While the warriors have cultivated a healthy relationship to their own bodies and a physical strength through adventurous hunting and armed struggles, the priests have been left behind as the powerless ones. Their noticeable physical inferiority has generated a hatred

---

[4] Friedrich Nietzsche, *The Anti-Christ,* trans. Thomas Common (1889), reprint by Luarna Ediciones (www.luarna.com), 96-7.
[5] Nietzsche, *The Essential Nietzsche: Beyond Good and Evil: The Genealogy of Morals,* 262.

of the noble ones who hold power in the world.⁶ The Jews, as the priestly people, have nurtured more strongly than any others this grudge against the superior aristocratic power, and their prophets initiate the fatal melting down of aristocratic values such as "rich", "godless", "violent" and "sensual" into "the world" that was the great object of the Jews' hatred. They were a people "born for slavery" in the eyes of the ancient world, and this reappraisal of morals was in reality a settling of accounts, where the morality of slaves clashes with the morality of masters.⁷ And the people of slaves held tenaciously to the idea that the poor were the blessed, and the weak the good. Powerlessness was linked to moral exaltation, and the Jewish reappraisal of values culminated in Paul's invention of the crucified Jesus as savior. This degraded doctrine displays the worst attack by the Jewish priestly instinct on the aristocratic Roman values, and Nietzsche quotes 1 Cor. 1.20-21 and 25-29 in *The Anti-Christ* as proof of the worst kind of psychology that is the fruit of the slave morality – of what Nietzsche, with a concept borrowed from the lowest caste in India, berates as "Chandala morality". He calls this Pauline passage "a first-rate testimony to the psychology of every Chandala morality".⁸ This is the germ of a struggle for equal rights for all human beings, because Nietzsche sees "Chandala morality" as the lowest imaginable instinct, which prepares the ground for an uprising against all privileges. This uprising has its fundament in a hatred that destroys everything that truly has value, replacing it with sympathy for what is weak and abused. According to Nietzsche, this is one of the main problems with the New Testament, and with the First Letter to the Corinthians in particular: "You cannot read the New Testament without feeling a certain affection for what it abuses, – not to mention the 'wisdom of this world,' which an insolent windbag tries to confound 'through foolish preaching'".⁹

Nietzsche sees Paul's disparagement of "the wisdom of this world" in the First Letter to the Corinthians and his exaltation of what is weak as a deadly blow against the morality of the masters, and as Christianity's victory over it through its continuation of the Jews' slave morality. He writes that there has never been a greater event than *this* struggle of "Rome against Judea", a

---

⁶ Ibid., 214.
⁷ Ibid., 94. With the phrase "born for slavery", Nietzsche adopts what can be called Roman propaganda about the Jewish people.
⁸ Nietzsche, *The Anti-Christ, Ecce Homo, Twilight of the Idols, and Other Writings*, 44.
⁹ Ibid., 45.

struggle he summarizes in the final words of his *Ecce Homo* in the aphorism: "Have I been understood? – *Dionysos versus the crucified.*"[10] Nietzsche writes that if one is to understand him, one must grasp what "the crucified" means, and what faith in him leads to.

> The great numbers gained control; the democratism of Christian instinct had *won* . . . Christianity was not "national," not the function of race, – it appealed to all the types that had been disinherited by life, it had its allies everywhere. Christianity is based on the rancor of the sick, the instinct *against* the healthy, *against* health. Everything well-constituted, proud, high-spirited, beauty above all, hurt their ears and eyes. This reminds me again of the invaluable words of Paul. "The *weak* things of the world, the *foolish* things of the world, the *base* things of the world, and the things that are *despised,* hath God chosen": *this* was the formula; decadence was victorious *in hoc signo* . . . Christianity won, and with this, a *nobler* sensibility was destroyed, – Christianity has been the worst thing to happen to humanity so far.[11]

Once again, Nietzsche quotes 1 Cor. 1.20, to explain why the lofty aristocratic values are rejected. This was the formula for the "decadence", that is to say, the moral degeneration for which Christianity paved the way through its lack of nationalism and racial consciousness. What won was what Nietzsche calls the democratic instinct, thanks to Christianity's appeal among the poor and "those with no inheritance". And precisely because he believes that the relationship of the entire human race to morality, and the path away from religion that can save all human beings, are at stake in this struggle, he goes back to Paul to uncover the root of the evil. One is prevented from unleashing the *Übermensch* in oneself by the victory of the Pauline preference for the weak over the ruling class' cultivation of strength and health, a victory that has set in stone a life-denying way of thought. One says "no" to a psychologically healthy, life-affirming, and not least, artistically creative existence because one yields to the bad conscience one feels vis-à-vis that which is weak – a consequence of the fantasies and the foolishness of the slave morality. In Nietzsche's eyes, it is in the First Letter to the Corinthians that the Pauline madness becomes most powerfully visible. As Jacob Taubes has noted, it is

---

[10] Ibid., 151.
[11] Ibid., 50-1.

there the Pauline texts that Nietzsche regards as the craziest are to be found.[12] Nietzsche's own philosophical ideas undergird his argumentation against the alleged irrationality in the worship of the Crucified in Christianity. But he also employs historical arguments, since he holds that the Pauline ideas were decisively important for the last two thousand years and that the idea of a crucified God gave people in antiquity a terrible experience. He thus postulated a historical break that was brought about by Paul's theology of the cross:

> Modern men, with their obtuseness as regards all Christian nomenclature, have no longer the sense for the terribly superlative conception which was implied to an antique taste by the paradox of the formula, "God on the Cross." Hitherto there had never and nowhere been such boldness in inversion, nor anything at once so dreadful, questioning, and questionable as this formula: it promised a transvaluation of all ancient values.[13]

Nietzsche thus claims that Pauline Christianity brought about a kind of intellectual revolution that had begun in the Judaism that was its origin. This Pauline transformation had kept people in subjection right down to Nietzsche's own days. And while Paul affirms that this intellectual revolution saves people, Nietzsche affirms that the opposite is true: it condemns the human being to self-hate and to an obsession with an existence beyond death – either heaven or hell – which in any case is merely an illusion.

Jacob Taubes: What did Nietzsche get right about Paul?

The philosopher Jacob Taubes largely follows Nietzsche's reading of Paul. Taubes too was a philosopher who was familiar with what the historians of his day were writing about classical antiquity, especially about early Christianity. And like Nietzsche, Taubes in the twentieth century can also combine historical and philosophical arguments.[14] When Taubes in the 1960s examines afresh Nietzsche's readings of Paul from the 1880s, historical-critical biblical scholarship had reached new conclusions, but without displaying any interest

---

[12] Taubes, *The Political Theology of Paul*, 79.
[13] Nietzsche, *The Essential Nietzsche: Beyond Good and Evil: The Genealogy of Morals*, 50.
[14] Taubes referred frequently to the so-called History of Religions School (*Religionsgeschichtliche Schule*) in his doctoral dissertation. See Taubes, *Occidental Eschatology*.

worth mentioning in the philosopher Nietzsche. Despite this, Taubes maintains that there lies a historical insight in Nietzsche's writings that the historical-critical exegetes have not yet improved upon, since it was precisely Nietzsche's desire to tear down Christianity with its roots that led the philosopher to the historical break that Paul made manifest. Taubes claims that Nietzsche was the first who succeeded with complete legitimacy in localizing this break in 1 Cor. 1.20.

Taubes believes that Paul is making history when he shifts the focus in 1.17 from internal conflicts in the Corinthian fellowship to his doctrine about the cross: "For Christ did not send me to baptize but to proclaim the gospel, and not with eloquent wisdom, so that the cross of Christ might not be emptied of its power" (1 Cor. 1.17). When Paul contrasts the rhetorical skill and wisdom that he rejects with the cross of Christ that he embraces, he has exalted a crucified human being in ways that are completely foreign to the conceptual world of antiquity. Through his worship of the Crucified, Paul gives a slap in the face to what Nietzsche terms the noble ethos in antiquity.[15] Accordingly, what Paul says is something unheard-of for hearers in antiquity. Taubes thus agrees with Nietzsche that Paul's words about the cross constitute a reappraisal of the values of that time, since his preaching kindled associations in hearers in antiquity with something "most wretched and cruel". A reference to a statement by the Roman politician Cicero (106-47 BCE) could have given further support to Nietzsche's view, which is seconded by Taubes. As a representative of the Roman aristocracy, Cicero urged the people not to use the word "cross", since it was unworthy of a Roman citizen even to mention this word.[16] This means that when Paul does just this in the First Letter to the Corinthians, he is breaking with the imperative of the Roman upper class and bringing shame upon both himself and his fellow conspirators. As a free man, and possibly a Roman citizen, he is naming explicitly a punishment that was typically meted out to a slave who disobeyed his master. For Taubes, the first mention of the cross in the New Testament and the formulation about salvation through the Crucified is a historic and original contribution by Paul.[17] In this sense, he

---

[15] *From Cult to Culture: Fragments Towards a Critique of Historical Reason*, 17.
[16] Marcus Tullius Cicero, "Pro Rabirio Perduellionis", in *The Loeb Classical Library. Cicero lx* (Cambridge, MA: Harvard University Press, 1927), 465-7.
[17] Taubes, *From Cult to Culture: Fragments Towards a Critique of Historical Reason*, 85.

agrees with Nietzsche that it was the apostle who invented the theology of the cross that transforms values.

Taubes also confirms Nietzsche's picture of Pauline fellowships consisting of societal rejects such as poor persons and others "with no inheritance" (to use Nietzsche's term). Taubes points out that Paul emphasizes how the weak and those from lower social classes who are not particularly noble have been chosen by God, while the upper classes, with the wise and the powerful, stand under God's judgement:

> Consider your own call, brothers and sisters: not many of you were wise by human standards, not many were powerful, not many were of noble birth. But God chose what is foolish in the world to shame the wise; God chose what is weak in the world to shame the strong; God chose what is low and despised in the world, things that are not, to reduce to nothing things that are, so that no one might boast in the presence of God. (1 Cor. 1.26-29)

According to Taubes, on the basis of the societal criteria in Corinth, the members of the community are not even counted as human beings – and Paul sees them as chosen by God. Taubes holds that this idea of divine election transforms the world's values as a sign of the power in the cross.[18] He shares much of Nietzsche's view of Paul, but the adversary for Taubes is Nietzsche, rather than Paul: for where Nietzsche praised the aristocracy, Taubes took the side of the oppressed who hope for revolutionary change. Taubes remained loyal to what he saw as a Pauline transformation of values, with its origin in a shared and explosive Jewish-Christian messianism that had erupted in Paul's historic formulations about the Crucified. But where Nietzsche held that the revolution had been carried out through the Christian church, Taubes held that it had been neutralized by the church after Constantine: when Emperor Constantine makes the cross one of the icons of the Empire, the memory of Jesus' suffering and death is effaced. And this is why Nietzsche is wrong to claim that the victory belongs to the Pauline transformation and exaltation of that which is weak. In Taubes' view, it is the Roman Empire, with Constantine, that is victorious over Christianity and that prevents the Pauline messianism

---

[18] Ibid., 83.

from erupting in the church and in society.[19] Nevertheless, the Pauline element is an impulse that lies latent throughout history.

Taubes sees Paul as a Jewish messianist who seeks truth through the event of the cross, as an event that turns human history upside down – and especially for the Jewish people. He is not the cynical bluffer of Nietzsche's depiction. On the contrary, he is an apostle who endeavours to convince others that the Crucified is the Messiah and that the identity of the people of God is now fundamentally new, so that the Gentiles can become a part of it. Paul's harsh words about "the world's wisdom" are a consequence of his belief in the election and revelation in that which is of no account: namely, in the Crucified and in all those who are far down in the hierarchy of society.

Taubes thus largely follows Nietzsche in his reading of Paul, although he does not share Nietzsche's sympathy for the aristocracy, his contempt for the new Pauline evaluation of that which is weak, or his enthusiasm for the *Übermensch* who is to come in the place of God. However, he believes that the level of precision in Nietzsche's reading of Paul is weakened when Paul's attack on "the world's wisdom" is interpreted by Nietzsche in *The Anti-Christ* as an expression of the apostle's rejection of science and learning in general:

> A religion like Christianity, which is completely out of touch with reality, which immediately falls apart if any concession is made to reality, would of course be mortally opposed to the "wisdom of the world," which is to say *science*. . . . Paul *understood* that lying – that "belief" was necessary; later, the church understood Paul. – The "God" that Paul invented for himself, a God who "confounds all worldly wisdom" (to be exact, the two great rivals of all superstition, philology and medicine) is in truth just Paul's firm *decision* to do it himself: to call his own will "God," torah, that is Jewish to the core.[20]

Nietzsche depicts Christian faith as remote from reality, and science as close to reality – the former is an illusion produced by a sheer act of will on the apostle's part. In his crass confrontation with Christianity, the critic of religion equates Paul's concept of "the world's wisdom" with modern science, especially those branches of science that Nietzsche himself regards as the most effective against religious superstition. Here, Nietzsche moves the opposite pole to Paul from the ancient aristocracy to sciences such as philology and medicine. The

---

[19] Ibid., 95.
[20] Nietzsche, *The Anti-Christ, Ecce Homo, Twilight of the Idols, and Other Writings*, 46.

perspective of societal class is displayed by a question about human rationality. What Paul's God "shames" (1 Cor. 1.27) now is human knowledge in general. In this way, Nietzsche has constructed a sheer antithesis between faith and knowledge; Taubes sees this as an inaccurate account the position that Paul takes in the Letter.[21] He also sees the kind of general contrast that Martin Heidegger paints in the introduction to a new edition of his inaugural lecture as professor in 1929 as too imprecise.[22] Heidegger quotes Paul's rhetorical question at 1 Cor. 1.20b, "Has not God made foolish the wisdom of the world?", and then goes on to ask: "Will Christian theology one day resolve to take seriously the word of the apostle and thus also the conception of philosophy as foolishness?"[23]

It is as if Heidegger here presupposes that Paul rejected philosophy and laid the foundations for a sharp antithesis between faith and knowledge. This is why he looks for a theology that draws the consequence from the words of the Letter to the Corinthians, and treats philosophy as idiocy when compared to the theological truths. But ought the author of the First Letter to the Corinthians to be understood as a pure opponent of philosophy? Ought the Pauline inheritance to be understood in Nietzsche's sense as an irrational power directed against science?

Badiou: Paul as a theoretician of the truth event

Alain Badiou (born 1937) is a French philosopher who was appointed in 1999 to the prestigious chair in philosophy at the École normale supérieure in Paris. His predecessors in this professorship at the elite French university include Jean-Paul Sartre, Michel Foucault, Jacques Derrida and Badiou's own teacher, Louis Althusser. In addition to a prolific philosophical œuvre, Badiou has published novels and plays, including the play L'Incident d'Antioche ("The Incident at Antioch") in 1982, a piece of political theatre in which the protagonist is given the female name "Paula" and appears as actor under

---

[21] Taubes, *From Cult to Culture: Fragments Towards a Critique of Historical Reason*, 77.
[22] Ibid.
[23] Heidegger's introduction was written for the fifth edition of his inaugural lecture as professor in 1939. Martin Heidegger, "Introduction to 'What is Metaphysics?'", in *Pathmarks*, ed. William Hardy McNeill (Cambridge: Cambridge University Press, 1998), 288.

headings such as "The Road to Damascus" and "The Incident at Antioch". This play is a tragedy that begins with an awakening and ends under the heading "The Council at Nicaea", where a definitive end is put to the new possibilities that this awakening had brought to light.[24] It stages central themes from Badiou's philosophical work, such as universalism and the concept of truth,[25] but it is also influenced by Badiou's autobiography. A few years before this, the philosopher had written about his experience during the 1968 protests in Paris, which he called his own "Road to Damascus".[26]

This identification with Paul is made all the more paradoxical by the fact that Badiou does not identify with the apostle's faith. In his 1997 book *Saint Paul: La fondation de l'universalisme*, he proclaims that he could not care less about the gospel Paul preaches, since (according to Badiou) Paul reduces Christianity to one single affirmation: Jesus is risen. Jesus' birth, his teaching and his death can be counted as historical facts, but Badiou sees the core of Paul's message as a fable. And as a modern atheist, he cannot believe in fables spun about a man who was crucified and rose from the dead.[27] In his book *The Ticklish Subject*, published two years later, Slavoj Žižek reacted with enthusiasm to Badiou's readings of Paul and agreed with his resolute reject of belief in the resurrection. Žižek too holds that the breakthrough of modern science makes it impossible to accept this belief.[28] But although the Pauline hope in resurrection is an obsolete stage that modern philosophy has superseded, the manner in which Paul formulates this hope is nevertheless relevant. The content is dead, but the uncompromising attitude to his content remains wholly up to date:

> What he provides is the first detailed articulation of how fidelity to a Truth-Event operates in its universal dimension: the excessive, *surnuméraire* Real of a Truth-Event ("Résurrection") that emerges by Grace (i.e. cannot be accounted for in the terms of the constituents of the given situation) sets in

---

[24] Kenneth Reinhard, "Introduction", in *The Incident at Antioch/L'Incident d'Antioche: A Tragedy in Three Acts/Tragédie en Trois Actes*, ed. Susan Spitzer and Kenneth Reinhard (New York: Columbia University Press, 2013), xxviii.
[25] Mads Peter Karlsen, "'Episoden i Antiokia': En teologisk scene i Alain Badious filosofiske teater", in *Den store fortælling: Festskrift til Geert Hallbäck*, ed. Søren Holst and Christina Petteson (Copenhagen: Anis, 2012).
[26] Reinhard, "Introduction", xxviii.
[27] Badiou, *Saint Paul: The Foundation of Universalism*, 4-5.
[28] Slavoj Žižek, *The Ticklish Subject: The Absent Centre of Political Ontology*, 2008 ed. (London: Verso, 1999), 164.

motion, in the subjects who recognize themselves in the call, the militant "work of Love," that is, the struggle to disseminate, with persistent fidelity, this Truth in its universal scope, concerning everyone.[29]

In one sense, Badiou and Žižek accept the premise by Nietzsche and other critics of religion that a life after death must be understood as a religious invention, and hence as an illusion. But when Badiou takes hold of the same verse as Nietzsche in the fifteenth chapter of First Corinthians, he does not do so in order to unmask the apostle's invention of an immortality of the person or of the soul. Nor does he do so in order to demonstrate that the apostle's irrationality is in conflict with science. As Badiou reads him, Paul is not attempting here to prove the resurrection of Jesus. Its proclamation does not aim to confirm or refute science. It is not a case of an exception to the laws of nature, as a supernatural miracle would have been.[30] On the contrary, the resurrection belongs to another dimension – the literary dimension.[31] Badiou holds that there are four spheres in which philosophical truth manifests itself to the human being: a political, a scientific, an artistic and an amorous sphere.[32]

"Resurrection" should be regarded as a literary metaphor for the paradoxical event that opens up a possibility that did not exist before.[33] Badiou sees the resurrection as the great truth event for Paul *qua* subject, just as other truth events can be *the* great truth event in our own day. The special point in Paul is that he establishes a new form of subjectivity by putting a new name to the pure truth event that breaks with utter unpredictability into human lives. It does not break in as a supernatural power; rather, it should be understood in a secular sense, as an unexpected immanent irruption in the world and in a specific situation, which may have a political, cognitive or aesthetic character. It can also be experienced as the love that arises between human beings. But

---

[29] Ibid., 165.
[30] Badiou, *Saint Paul: The Foundation of Universalism*, 45.
[31] "Paul is a poet-thinker of the event." This statement is ambiguous in relation to the question whether Paul belongs in one of Badiou's four spheres of truth. Since he rejects the possibility that religion can be a sphere of truth, or that Paul is primarily a religious figure, are we perhaps left with the possibility that Paul may have a place in the artistic sphere, since he exemplifies the truth-event with what Badiou regards as literary means – that is to say, with a fable?
[32] *Ethics: An Essay on the Understanding of Evil* (London: Verso, 2001), 28.
[33] Mads Peter Karlsen points out that Badiou's book on Paul employs central concepts that he had already elaborated in a more comprehensive philosophical work, *L'être et l'événement*. Seen in this way, the Letters of Paul become a literary exemplification of what Badiou elsewhere in his philosophy calls a "truth-process". Mads Peter Karlsen, "Alain Badious Paulus-Læsning", *Dansk teologisk tidsskrift* 73, no. 1 (2010): 64.

the break constitutes an event that was so surprising that it could not have been predicted on the basis of what the human being knew beforehand.

> It is thus an *immanent break*. "Immanent" because a truth proceeds *in* the situation, and nowhere else – there is no heaven of truths. "Break" because what enables the truth-process – the event – meant nothing according to the prevailing language and established knowledge of the situation.[34]

It is thus not a question of an objective truth that competes with science. Here, according to Badiou, Nietzsche has got it wrong. When Paul proclaims: "If there is no resurrection of the dead, then Christ has not been raised" (1 Cor. 15.14), the apostle is not inventing an illusion of an existence beyond death in order to tyrannize people with his priestly instinct, as Nietzsche claims. What the apostle is doing is to go from the singular to the universal, by making the resurrection valid for everyone, not only for one individual. For Badiou, Nietzsche is so deeply provoked precisely by the universalism that entails equality among all human beings. "Nietzsche is Paul's rival far more than his opponent", Badiou writes[35] – his "rival" because the German philosopher wants to replace the Pauline universalism with a particularism that, in reality, is a communitarianism with a racial basis for a few privileged persons. Badiou notes that Nietzsche rails against Pauline Christianity because it was neither national nor determined by race.[36]

First of all, it is Paul who puts a name to the truth event through his specific proclamation that Jesus has won the victory over death and has risen from the dead. Second, Paul is a man who displays pure fidelity to the truth event, and this fidelity finds expression through a genuinely new way of thinking and acting that breaks with the past. Third, Paul forces himself with his truth upon previous truths and "knocks holes" in them.[37] Paul thus illustrates general traits from Badiou's philosophy in a way that few others do.

> To be faithful to an event is to move within the situation that this event has supplemented, by *thinking* (although all thought is a practice, a putting to the test) the situation "according to" the event. And this, of course – since

---

[34] Badiou, *Ethics: An Essay on the Understanding of Evil*, 42-3.
[35] *Saint Paul: The Foundation of Universalism*, 72.
[36] Ibid., 62.
[37] *Ethics: An Essay on the Understanding of Evil*, 70.

the event was excluded by all the regular laws of the situation – compels the subject to *invent* a new way of being and acting in the situation.[38]

Truth in this sense is nothing that can be observed or calculated. Truth is something the subject cultivates and generates in loyalty to the radically new conditions that are the consequence of the truth event. It is only when the human animal demonstrates loyalty to this event that he or she becomes a subject, something more than all the others, becoming "a human animal among others, which nevertheless finds itself *seized* and *displaced* by the evental process of a truth".[39] What Paul introduces is thus not new rules for living, but a new form of existence that is independent of the laws that existed in the situation in which the event took place. This new form of existence unfolds through a completely new language in the First Letter to the Corinthians, according to Badiou. In loyalty to the event, Paul invents a new language in which foolishness, stumbling stone and weakness take the places of reason, good order and power.[40] Badiou finds something in the Pauline text that points in this direction – but what?

The breach with Jew and Greek

Badiou takes up Paul's affirmation that the gospel is to be preached in such a way that "the cross of Christ might not be emptied of its power" (1 Cor. 1.17). According to Badiou, this entails that the character of the event to which the cross points (that is to say, the resurrection) makes it impossible for it to be proclaimed either by the Greek philosophical wisdom that is armed with rhetorical skill, or by the Jewish prophethood that interprets signs from above, from the transcendent realm.[41] When Paul writes that "Jews demand signs and Greeks desire wisdom", as two contrasting figures to the apostle himself and to the believers who "proclaim Christ crucified" (1.22-23), Badiou affirms that Paul is not referring to two different nations or groups with their own way of life, territory or language. Nor is Paul distancing himself from religions,

---

[38] Ibid., 41-2.
[39] Ibid., 91.
[40] *Saint Paul: The Foundation of Universalism*, 47.
[41] Ibid., 28.

since in Badiou's perspective Paul is not founding a new religion. "Jews" and "Greeks" in this text indicate two subjective ways of being, from the intellectual world that Paul knows. Badiou speaks in this context of regimes of discourse, that is to say, ways of structuring human communication.[42] Accordingly, this does not show how most Jews or Greeks actually thought or acted, nor is it an expression of anti-Semitism, if we are to believe Badiou.[43] Instead, these are types or figures who base their knowledge on ways from which Paul distances himself. When "Jews demand signs" (1.22), this indicates a discourse based on the exception: either on the miracle or the divine election that has its origin in a transcendence outside the immanent or the given world. To look for signs is to track down the exception to the order or regularity of the natural world, something that the typical prophet does. The expression "Greeks desire wisdom" refers to a discourse based on the totality of the given world or the order of the universe. It sees wisdom as the knowledge of the interconnections or laws of nature. The figure here is not the prophet, but the wise man. While the Jewish discourse is based on the law that is given in the exceptional instance or in the divine election, the Greek discourse makes itself dependent on the law of nature.[44]

Paul breaks with both of these. The apostle's message cannot be reconciled with any law. His Christian discourse is illegal and acosmic. It proclaims faith, not law. It cannot be integrated into the law of election or the law of nature, into the Jewish or the Greek discourse. This is why it is a "scandal" (literally, a "stumbling stone") for the Jews, since the event cannot be grasped on the basis of the logic of the Jewish discourse: whereas this discourse looks for signs of divine strength, Christ is manifested as weakness. This weakness is "foolishness" for the Greek discourse, because the word about the cross puts a halt to the wise man's speech and rhetoric. The event makes language limp and collapse, because the previous categories that put a name to things before the irruption of the event are incapable of putting a name to the new reality that the event constitutes. The break is complete, and the old language cannot comprehend it. This is why Paul invents a completely new discourse. And he cannot do this by building on the established philosophical wisdom; instead, he must

---

[42] Badiou claims that Paul is positing a schema of various discourses here, in a manner similar to what the psychoanalyst Jacques Lacan did.
[43] Badiou, *Saint Paul: The Foundation of Universalism*, 43.
[44] Ibid., 40-7.

undermine this and complete the break by means of an anti-philosophy.[45] And this, according to Badiou, is why Paul does not establish any new Christian philosophy in the First Letter to the Corinthians.[46] Instead, he intervenes in the established discourses with his starting point in a proclamation of an event that makes sense in a totally new and completely unexpected way. Badiou claims that when Paul writes: "God chose things that are not, to reduce to nothing things that are" (1.29), the apostle makes all previous knowledge and all that exists incomparable to the Christ event. This event brings that which is not, rather than that which is, to bear witness to the apostle's God. That which is not is the impossible thing that, thanks to the irruption of the event into existence, makes possible that which is radically new, and invites all subjects to make this possible by inventively drawing the consequences from what has occurred.

There will be differences. There will be both Jews and Greeks. And many customs and rites will continue to exist. But this is on the particular plane, and they are like shadows compared with the ideals and principles that are a consequence of the universalism of the truth event. The empirical differences that exist between human beings and cultures are in reality nonexistent when the subject, in loyalty to the truth event, rises up to the universal level, where the egalitarian holds sway. This is because loyalty to the universally valid truth event makes all the particular collapse and the egalitarian flower. Paul exemplifies this in Badiou's eyes:

> For though I am free with respect to all, I have made myself a slave to all, so that I might win more of them. To the Jews I became as a Jew, in order to win Jews. To those under the law I became as one under the law (though I myself am not under the law) so that I might win those under the law. To those outside the law I became as one outside the law (though I am not free from God's law but am under Christ's law) so that I might win those outside the law. To the weak I became weak, so that I might win the weak. I have become all things to all people, that I might by all means save some. (1 Cor. 9.19-22)

Badiou sees this, not as an expression of opportunism, but as an expression of a principled indifference to differences. These particular differences no longer play any role in the universalistic project that Paul champions. When

---

[45] Ibid., 28.
[46] Ibid., 47.

Paul lives "as one under the law" or "as one outside the law", his universalism finds expression through his cultural adaptation and adoption of the particular. There is no need to eliminate these special cultures, traditions, or religions. They are to be tolerated. But this tolerance must be accompanied by a fundamental indifference to the particular differences. This indifference makes the adaptation legitimate and possible for the universalist.

Paul in Corinth – the militant figure we need?

What kind of philosophical problem is it that Badiou and Žižek want to solve by using what they regard as an "anti-philosopher"? According to them, the anti-philosopher Paul was the first to articulate a position that expresses the militant and consistent attitude to a truth event, and they believe that there is a precarious scarcity today of precisely this militant attitude, with its fight on behalf of a universalism. They claim that our historical epoch, after the fall of the Berlin Wall, is marked by the reduction of politics to particular interests and to the globalization of capitalism. According to Alain Badiou, the world community is moving in the wrong direction:

> . . . that the – perfectly obvious – reality of the situation is characterized in fact by the unrestrained pursuit of self-interest, the disappearance or extreme fragility of emancipatory politics, the multiplication of "ethnic" conflicts, and the universality of unbridled competition.[47]

Capitalism is, of course, a universal project, but the two philosophers maintain that it is a universalism without substantial contents. It is an abstract universalism that, in accordance with Karl Marx's descriptions, is disseminated as a world-encompassing market. Žižek claims that when injustice comes to light, it is often explained, especially by the political left wing, as due to a lack of tolerance and rights for ethnic groups, women and sexual minorities. This is what Badiou regards as closed identities, since not every person can join them.[48] But since this type of measure does not embrace all persons, nor affect the fundamental antagonism or conflict in society (which Žižek sees

---

[47] *Ethics: An Essay on the Understanding of Evil*, 10.
[48] *Saint Paul: The Foundation of Universalism*.

through Marxist spectacles and identifies as the class struggle), politics is reduced to the interests of particular groups. Here, according to Žižek, lies the apostle's relevance today; unlike a philosopher such as Charles Taylor, he does not believe that one should pay heed to the demands for recognition that are made on behalf of cultural fellowships such as ethnic minorities. Paul breaks resolutely with every form of communitarianism, which the Slovenian understands as a philosophy that states that the values a society must build on what grows out of socially integrated local milieus that cultivate their own culture and lifestyle:

> The key dimension of Paul's gesture is thus his break with any form of communitarianism: his universe is no longer that of the multitude of groups that want to "find their voice," and assert their particular identity, their "way of life," but that of a fighting collective grounded in the reference to an unconditional universalism.[49]

Since particularistic communitarianism and multiculturalism are allowed to dominate, political mobilization today all too often culminates in identity politics, not least because all the universalistic projects are actively opposed. Badiou writes that a recognition of the catastrophic outcomes of the revolutions tips over into a constant rejection of the mere possibility or desirability of revolutionary change:

> Such is the accusation so often repeated over the last fifteen years: every revolutionary project stigmatized as "utopian" turns, we are told, into totalitarian nightmare. Every will to inscribe an idea of justice or equality turns bad. Every collective will to the Good creates Evil. This is sophistry at its most devastating.[50]

In antiquity, the sophist was one who was experienced in rhetoric and was often regarded as the wise man. However, voices such as Plato warned against the sophists' lack of knowledge of the truth and against their dangerous potential as seducers of the people and demagogues. When he speaks of "sophistry", Badiou, inspired by Paul, rejects the warnings against the pervasive universalistic ideas in our time as seductive words: those who deny that the universal manifests itself in concrete situations and constitutes events containing truths for all human

---

[49] Žižek, *The Puppet and the Dwarf*, 130.
[50] Badiou, *Ethics: An Essay on the Understanding of Evil*, 13.

beings are dangerous sophists. And these sophists of our time relativize that which is true, employing the lack of complete knowledge in concrete situations as a pretext for demobilizing. Because fewer people support universalistic movements and ideas that have consequences for all human beings, politics is paralyzed. In this way, societal hierarchies and economic class distinctions are set in stone. Radical egalitarianism is crushed when every attempt to introduce it is rejected as impossible. At the same time, our contemporary ideologies continue to legitimate the capitalist system. According to Žižek's criticism of ideology, the main problem here is not Christianity. The German sociologist Max Weber wrote more than a century ago in *The Protestant Ethic and the Spirit of Capitalism* about how Christian Protestantism had generated an ethical praxis of life that contributed to the emergence of capitalism in the West. The critique of Christianity has become to such an extent a part of the status quo that the Slovenian Marxist finds it neither original nor liberating to repeat it. And if we are to believe Žižek, Pauline Christianity is not particularly trendy – he claims, instead, that imported versions of oriental religions are consumed by Western individuals through today's culture industry, and that these make them apathetic, as if they were opium for the people. "If Max Weber were alive today, he would definitely write a second, supplementary volume to his *Protestant Ethic*, entitled *The Taoist Ethic and the Spirit of Global Capitalism*", as he pointedly puts it.[51] Oriental religion that seeks harmony in a cosmic hierarchy goes hand in glove with a hegemonic capitalism that Asia has embraced: they reinforce each other mutually. Unlike this, Paul's theology undermines hierarchies created by human beings:

> The oriental or Buddhist logic accepts the primordial void or chaos as the ultimate reality and, paradoxically, for this very reason, prefers organic social order with each element in its proper place. At the very core of Christianity, there is a vastly different project: that of a destructive negativity, which does not end in a chaotic void but reverts (and organises itself) into a new order, imposing it on to reality. For this reason, Christianity is antiwisdom; wisdom tells us that our efforts are in vain, that everything ends in chaos, while Christianity madly insists on the impossible. Love, especially a Christian one, is definitely not wise. This is why Paul said: "I will destroy the wisdom of the wise" ("*Sapientiam sapientum perdam*", as his saying is

---

[51] Žižek, *On Belief*, 13.

usually known in Latin). We should take the term "wisdom" literally here: it is wisdom (in the sense of "realistic" acceptance of the way things are) that Paul is challenging, not knowledge as such. With regard to social order, this means that the authentic Christian tradition rejects the wisdom that the hierarchic order is our fate, that all attempts to mess with it and create another egalitarian order have to end up in destructive horror.[52]

Badiou called ideologies in our own times "sophistry". In a similar way, Žižek sees the wisdom that Paul attacks when he quotes Isaiah's words, "I will destroy the wisdom of the wise" (1 Cor. 1.19), as an expression of these ideologies. There is thus in the "authentic" Christian tradition (for Žižek holds that much of what came later crushed the Pauline radicalism in order to make Christianity palatable to those who held power)[53] a madness that champions the impossible. The atheist Žižek sees the value of Pauline Christianity, not in an optimism or a positive thinking, but in the audacity of hoping in the impossible in such a way that this hope never ends in, or falls into, fatalism. The resurrection of Jesus is an impossibility of this kind, and this is why Paul's brief confession of faith and his original name for the truth event illustrate Badiou's philosophy of truth and event so well. Žižek builds further on this philosophy when he reads Paul.

Žižek underlines that what Paul rejects is not knowledge per se, but the wisdom that is led by the dominant "common sense" to express scepticism about radical change. What is needed then is a risky leap of faith that in any case will look like madness, indeed foolishness.[54] What is needed is a passionate loyalty to the truth event that appears incomprehensible to the sceptic who has little faith in the possibility of overcoming the human and political limitations. The sceptic calculates in advance what is possible within the given hierarchical societal order, whereas the militant person is an uncompromising advocate for egalitarianism, no matter what the cost.

This militant figure who emerges from these readings of Paul is not only one who (like the martyr) is willing to sacrifice everything for the cause; this

---

[52] *Living in the End Times*, 116-17.
[53] In Žižek's historical narrative of Christianity, all the great theologians like Augustine and Thomas Aquinas attempt to accommodate Christianity's original anti-hierarchical message to the societal hierarchies that exist in their own days. They want to tame what are seen as "exaggerations" in the more original Pauline message. *Less Than Nothing: Hegel and the Shadow of Dialectical Materialism*, 114.
[54] *In Defense of Lost Causes*, 2nd ed. (London: Verso, 2008), 2.

is also a figure who is no longer willing to wait for the right moment to act, because that would merely postpone the event. If one has to wait for the perfect moment to act, one can wait forever.[55] And since the truth event is produced by the subject who champions it and fights for it, it must be brought about by the subject personally. The subject must put a name to an event in the world and give it the meaning of a genuine truth event that is worth living for, an event with consequences that are worth drawing from it. The fundamental Christian attitude that Žižek finds in Paul is that, now that the Messiah has come, the believers are already redeemed. The time for nervous expectation is over, and we live in the wake of the event. The event has taken place, and this means that we must now bear the almost unlivable burden of living up to the event, that is to say, of drawing the consequences from it through concrete action. This entails an extreme urge to act in order to live out what loyalty to the event means.[56] The loyal subject is an activist of the militant type, the one who does not flinch from fighting for the cause that is at stake – what Žižek calls unconditional universalism. Paul *qua* model is thus a pretext for acting. It is time to act.

It is this militant attitude that attracts Žižek and that he reads out of the Letters of Paul. But how can a modern atheist like Žižek be inspired by a religious faith from Paul without becoming Christian or religious? How can a modern atheist remain loyal to science while at the same time maintaining that faith is necessary? And is Paul an arbitrarily chosen figure from the pantheon of heroes of faith and religious thinkers in the world religions?

The apostle of demythologization

Badiou and Žižek insist on combining the philosophical inspiration from Christianity's earliest author with a consistently modern belief in progress. They are certain that enlightenment and knowledge move the world forwards, and they regard those who take a different view as postmodern relativists. Badiou claims that the true task of philosophy is mathematical in its core: it is mathematics that is the basis for ontology (the philosophical investigation of

---

[55] *The Puppet and the Dwarf*, 133.
[56] Ibid., 136.

that which exists). And while Paul's truth event (namely, the resurrection of Jesus) is a fable, the truth event of science is real. It moves knowledge forwards in ways that new generations must take into account. "After Einstein's texts of 1905, if I am faithful to their radical novelty, I cannot continue to practice physics within its classical framework", says Badiou.[57] Scientific revolutions or paradigm shifts of this kind are genuine truth events. At the same time, religion is not totally illusory. Paul's truth event is "real enough", as the British literary critic Terry Eagleton (born 1943) writes:

> Like divine grace, a truth event represents an invitation which is available to everyone. Before the truth, we are all equal. Such truth events for Badiou are real enough – indeed, more real than the shabby set of illusions which commonly pass for reality. . . . The resurrection for Christians is not just a metaphor. It is real enough, but not in the sense that you could have taken a photograph of it had you been lurking around Jesus's tomb armed with a Kodak. Meanings and values are also real, but you cannot photograph them either. They are real in the sense that a poem is real.[58]

Badiou swears that he does not believe in the Pauline fabulation about Jesus' resurrection; but for Eagleton, it is a metaphor and yet at the same time "more real". More real than what? It is just as real as a poem or as moral values. Eagleton writes that the truth event resembles divine grace, but is not divine grace. How can it resemble it, but not be equivalent to it? Alain Badiou emphasizes that it is possible to extract a completely secularized form of grace from the mythological kernel in the apostle's message.[59]

In the Letters to what Badiou calls the "cell" in Corinth, he finds traces of an author who clearly believed in miracles – a belief that Badiou calls obscurantism, a denial of reality that rejects rational enlightenment. At the same time, however, Paul does not make belief in miracles a necessary fundament for faith in, or proclamation of, the event.[60] In other words, Badiou acknowledges that Paul's world view is different from his own, not least because he believes in a resurrection from the dead that Badiou rejects. The apostle lives in a premodern world in which both supernatural miracles and

---

[57] Badiou, *Ethics: An Essay on the Understanding of Evil*, 42.
[58] Terry Eagleton, *Reason, Faith, and Revolution: Reflections on the God Debate* (New Haven: Yale University Press, 2009), 118-19.
[59] Badiou, *Saint Paul: The Foundation of Universalism*, 66.
[60] Ibid., 50-4.

resurrections are possible, while the French professor lives in a modern world that has drawn the consequences from discoveries in the natural sciences. However, the two phenomena have a different status in Paul's thinking. As Badiou reads him, belief in miracles is not a part of the apostle's discourse about the truth event. This subordinate position is particularly clear when Paul writes: "If I speak in the tongues of mortals and of angels, but do not have love, I am a noisy gong or a clanging cymbal" (1 Cor. 13.1). Badiou calls this an "empty subjectivism" that is worth nothing in comparison with the love that finds expression in loyalty to the truth event. Badiou finds an affirmation in Paul that fits his own philosophy: love "rejoices in the truth" (1 Cor. 13.6).[61] We may put this in Badiou's vocabulary: loyalty to the truth event is the origin of all enjoyment. For love alone is pure loyalty to the watershed event that gives truth.

Badiou's book on Paul abounds in references to the primary texts (Paul's Letters), but is virtually free of references to secondary literature. He does, however, recommend two academic studies of Paul in the foreword. One of these is the book about Paul published in 1969 by the German biblical scholar Günter Bornkamm (1905-90), a pupil of Rudolf Bultmann (1884-1973). Badiou appears to have read Bornkamm's work thoroughly, since the Frenchman's understanding of the apostle's Letters is very close to the German's. Bornkamm's book is a typical historical-critical reading of Paul in the mid-twentieth century, when Bultmann's insistence on the necessity of interpretation, as a mediator between the world view of the biblical texts and our own world view, stood high on the agenda. Bornkamm too underlined the historically conditioned element in the Christian message and the need for new understandings of this message in a new period:

> Nor can we say anything about the concepts and categories of thought in which primitive Christian faith was variously expressed and developed, whether they were adequate or open to criticism. They are time-conditioned and almost incomprehensible to us, however relevant and necessary for their time, and in every case constantly require fresh interpretation and elucidation.[62]

---

[61] Ibid., 91.
[62] Günter Bornkamm, *Paul* (Minneapolis: Fortress Press, 1995).

It is possible that the French atheist was trying to take seriously this kind of attitude to the biblical texts when he sought to translate Paul's premodern thinking into a modern age and to "extract" a secular understanding of grace. Bornkamm's teacher Rudolf Bultmann pointed out how remote and mythical the New Testament world view was for modern persons, depicting as it does a world where supernatural powers intervene in natural processes and human decisions, and where miracles occur. Bultmann claimed that one could not require modern persons to believe in this world view, since faith is not a question of taking one particular stance on how the universe hangs together. World views are something we live with, not something we believe in, and this is why the New Testament texts must be demythologized. The existential understanding of the human being in these texts must be uncovered behind the mythical world view, for it is the truth in this existential understanding that modern persons could believe in or reject.[63] In one sense, Badiou radicalizes Bultmann's demythologization. Badiou's reading of Paul rejects the world view that is reflected in the texts, and we are left with a purely secular understanding of the message.

As I have mentioned, Spinoza held that Paul was the New Testament author who philosophized most. Bultmann claimed that demythologization was introduced in the New Testament, and that it was Paul who took the first decisive step by departing from the cosmic determinism that (according to Bultmann) is dominant elsewhere in the biblical texts, and by interpreting the Christ event in a manner that confronted the human being with a choice. Instead of letting the human being be an object for fate and spiritual powers, Paul radicalized the message in such a way that the reaction to this message became an existential choice.[64] Like Bultmann's theology, Badiou's philosophy is a form of existentialism. For Bultmann, the human being's existence is at stake in the encounter with God's word. For Badiou, the human being can become a genuine subject only by deciding to live in loyalty to the truth event. In both cases, it is an either-or.[65]

---

[63] Rudolf Bultmann, "New Testament and Mythology", in *The Historical Jesus: Vol. 1: The History of the Quest: Classical Studies and Critical Questions*, ed. Craig A. Evans (London: Routledge, 2004), 323-30.
[64] *Jesus Christ and Mythology* (New York: Scribner, 1958), 33.
[65] The other central source of inspiration for Badiou's readings of Paul is Stanislas Breton, a theologian who was likewise inspired by Bultmann's demythologization. Ward Blanton, "Dispossessed Life",

When the philosopher Simon Critchley approaches Paul, his presupposition is that philosophy begins in disappointment, first of all in the religious disappointment that God is dead. However, he rediscovers a secular concept of faith in Paul's Letters, in the form of loyalty to an infinite demand. This is a form of faith that can be shared and experienced by those he calls "faithless".[66] It is, in other words, a faith to which one is called on the basis of a demand that cannot be limited to a religious life, but can affect or be heard by everyone. Once again, the philosopher finds in Paul something universal that can be secularized.

An apostle for the extreme left wing?

Like Badiou, Critchley is concerned with the motivation for political resistance. The English philosopher finds it unproblematic to envisage a politics without religion, but asks whether, in practice, politics can do without the religious dimension.[67] If Paul is counted as a religious figure, the philosophical interest in him in recent decades can suggest a recognition of the limitations of a totally secularized politics. For Critchley, a politics that is completely stripped free of religion lacks, above all, motivation – an insight he draws in particular from the Enlightenment philosopher Jean-Jacques Rousseau (1712-78) and his ideas about "civil religion". But what is the real problem? What kind of politics is it that requires a religious dimension?

Critchley points to Barack Obama as an exemplary combination of the religious and the political,[68] while a philosopher like Žižek claims that the choice between a Democrat and a Republican as the president of the United States is a false alternative.[69] And while Critchley presents the non-violent protests against the American invasion of Iraq in 2003 as the type

---

in *A Radical Philosophy of Saint Paul*, ed. Stanislas Breton (New York: Columbia University Press, 2011), 25.

[66] Simon Critchley, *The Faith of the Faithless: Experiments in Political Theology* (London: Verso, 2012), 18.
[67] Ibid., 10.
[68] Ibid., 24-5.
[69] Slavoj Žižek, *Did Somebody Say Totalitarianism?: Five Interventions in the (Mis)Use of a Notion* (London: Verso, 2001), 240. In 2016, on the other hand, Žižek held that there was a real alternative in the American presidential election, and his hope was that Donald Trump would win, in order to provoke strong contrary reactions.

of political resistance we need, Žižek dismisses them as ineffective. All they achieved was to give a good conscience to the demonstrators who trudged around in the streets.[70] Žižek's political diagnosis is somber. Within the liberal democracy and its political parties and forms of government, there is a space for negotiations between the particular interests of groups and for small-scale reforms but not for any thoroughgoing reforms that would offer an alternative to global capitalism. It may well be easier for Norwegian eyes to gauge how far Žižek is inconsistent in his diagnoses of contemporary politics – for while the Slovenian delights in downgrading social democrats to liberal reformists who lack all traces of a revolutionary spirit, he has also praised the productivity of Norwegian society, although without mentioning how open the Norwegian economy is for global free trade and free market forces:

> This is why, as a counter-position to the ideology of choice, countries like Norway should be held up as models: although all the main agents respect a basic social agreement and ambitious social projects are enacted in a spirit of solidarity, productivity and dynamism remain at extraordinarily high levels, flatly denying the common wisdom that such a society ought to be stagnating.[71]

According to the Slovenian philosopher, "common sense" (or the wisdom of our age) would reject the possibility of achieving what Norway has achieved. He is no doubt influenced by his many years of a hectic touring activity at North American universities; even a slight acquaintance with many debates in North American politics, for example in the Democrats' primary campaigns, will show the existence of a dominant scepticism vis-à-vis the Scandinavian welfare model.[72]

In addition to the sceptic as the figure for the wise man whom Paul attacks in Corinth, we find another figure in Žižek's thinking who is a constant threat to the militant search for truth that is inspired by Paul – namely, the postmodern sophist.[73] As I have mentioned, Badiou identified sophistry as the sceptical

---

[70] Critchley, *The Faith of the Faithless: Experiments in Political Theology*, 227.
[71] Žižek, *Living in the End Times*, 359.
[72] Bernie Sanders was beaten by Joe Biden in the race to be the Democrats' challenger in the American presidential election. Sanders met strong opposition when he spoke in favour of a "socialism" that we practice in Scandinavia.
[73] Here, we also find some of the roots of Žižek's admiration of Badiou, and thus also of Žižek's interest in the Frenchman's readings of Paul, in "Badiou's desperate struggle against postmodernist-

rejection of every revolutionary political project. The postmodern sophist is not the sceptic who is content with a cool calculation that it is impossible to implement radicalism in practice. According to Žižek, the postmodern sophist is one who simultaneously admires the idealism in the revolution (in Marx) and warns that enthusiasm for the revolution will tip over into fatal, unethical mistakes. Respect for one's fellow human being will invariably lead this type of sophist to criticize every enthusiastic identification of the promise of a universal improvement in human living conditions with a de facto political event, movement or ideology. This sophist thinks that such a transformation of society for the better will never be totally realized before the transformation tips over into new forms of oppression. In the eyes of the sophist, therefore, the truth event is postponed indefinitely, as a promise of something that is to come, as a messianism that is never willing to embrace a genuine event as the truth event. In Žižek's philosophy, this sophist is inspired above all by Jacques Derrida and his philosophy of "a democracy to come".[74] Derrida writes that this philosophy is inspired by a type of Marxism that he claims is distinguishable from other types of Marxisms that end up in a one-party state and totalitarianism.[75] This is a Marxist spirit that is willing to engage in constant self-criticism and is open to its own change and reappraisal.[76] Žižek counters that, precisely because this Marxism is so self-critical, it finds it very difficult to commit itself wholeheartedly to any concrete political project.[77] Its aversion to such commitments or "leaps of faith" means that it contributes in reality only to setting the status quo in stone, to a paralysis that makes action impossible, and to conservatism.[78] There are no truth events in the world of the postmodern sophist. Nothing happens in the true sense of the word.[79] Accordingly, even if this sophist sincerely wishes that politics may not harm people, in reality

---

deconstructionist 'sophists'" and "his heroic Platonic insistence on Truth as independent of historical language games". Žižek, *Less Than Nothing: Hegel and the Shadow of Dialectical Materialism*, 76.

[74] *The Ticklish Subject: The Absent Centre of Political Ontology*, 153.

[75] For Derrida, this idea is also closely linked to an idea of a messianic force that is devoid of messianism and has no specific Messiah-figure. Jacques Derrida, *Specters of Marx: The State of the Debt, the Work of Mourning and the New International*, trans. Peggy Kamuf, 2012 ed. (New York: Routledge, 1994), 81.

[76] Ibid.

[77] Žižek complains that this kind of return to Marx has "become an academic fashion". He ascribes this fashion to "postmodern sophists". Žižek, *On Belief*, 2.

[78] The ethics that Badiou identifies in Levinas and Derrida results in what Badiou calls "a disturbing conservatism". Badiou, *Ethics: An Essay on the Understanding of Evil*, 16.

[79] Žižek, *The Ticklish Subject: The Absent Centre of Political Ontology*, 154-5.

all that he or she does is to cause economic injustice to continue, with class distinctions remaining intact. Žižek is willing to go further, in the sense that he wants to breathe new life into concepts from which Derrida distances himself, such as "the dictatorship of the proletariat".[80] This dictatorship did indeed end up in an oppressive Stalinism, but this is not the entire truth for Žižek, who has set out to break liberal taboos.[81] It is an indisputable fact that he succeeds in doing precisely this; but apart from this, we see in any case that Badiou and Žižek cite the Pauline inheritance, not as militating against scientific truth, but as an inspiration in the existential and political struggle against what they see as the sophistry and relativism of our age.

In principle, Badiou's reading of Paul and Žižek's subsequent actualization of it in his philosophy need not be tied to any special political or ideological current. The philosophy of the truth event that is inspired by Paul need not necessarily lead to the right or to the left in a political sense. For example, Terry Eagleton has illustrated the politics of the truth event by fighting against gender discrimination and racism.[82] These are political struggles that Badiou has reduced to a specific identity politics that does not include the universalist element, and this demonstrates the flexibility in Badiou's philosophy of the event. Badiou can claim that some events are pointless reforms, empty of truth (that is to say, not authentic revolutions), but others can claim that these are genuine truth events with far-reaching political consequences. But when Badiou does give examples of political events that count as truth events, it is completely clear that he wishes to legitimate an extreme left wing. And while it can indeed be taken for granted that Einstein's theory of relativity is a truth event in science, in general, and in physics, in particular, it is not so easy to swallow the claim that the same status in politics should be ascribed to the Communist Revolution in Russia in 1917. Many can share the enthusiasm for the French Revolution of 1793, but the view Badiou takes of the Cultural Revolution in China (1965-7) suggests that, in his eyes, the heritage from Paul is best preserved on the left wing.[83] And Žižek's descriptions of Paul as a "proto-Leninist" who organized the movement in the same way as Lenin strengthens the impression that this inspiration from Paul is limited to those

---

[80] *In Defense of Lost Causes*, 7.
[81] *Did Somebody Say Totalitarianism?: Five Interventions in the (Mis)Use of a Notion*, 3.
[82] Eagleton, *Reason, Faith, and Revolution: Reflections on the God Debate*, 119-20.
[83] Badiou, *Ethics: An Essay on the Understanding of Evil*, 41.

in the "community" on the extreme left wing.[84] But is it legitimate to appeal to Paul on behalf of a left-wing radicalism that wants to revolutionize human beings' material living conditions? Are not the apostle's writings exhortations to devote oneself to a spiritual life exalted far above the material dimension?

Max Weber: From First Corinthians to modern capitalism – and back

Friedrich Nietzsche criticized Paul for emptying earthly things of all meaning and directing human beings' attention to what lies beyond death. Žižek held that oriental religion had supplanted Protestantism in offering a work ethic that functioned as a catalyst for capitalism, with reference to Max Weber's classic work from 1904/5. Weber's original hypothesis was that the rationalization of the life of faith that the Reformation introduced, and that culminated in the Puritan sects, prepared the ground for modern capitalism, since this new Protestant ethic combined God's call to sobriety and hard work with capitalism's hunt for profit and its need to save in order to invest.

In Max Weber's grand narrative, the call from God is decisively secularized during the Reformation. Now that monasticism is eradicated and the special monastic vocation is then seen as worthless, the human being is called to carry out the worldly duties of everyday life.[85] The worldly calling of the baker and the craftsman is given the same dignity as that of the priest. Weber bases this secularization of the call during Martin Luther's Reformation on a reading of early Christianity and especially of Paul. According to Weber, Luther attributes great importance to the worldly professions, whereas Paul is utterly indifferent to them. He writes:

> In the apostolic era as expressed in the New Testament, especially in St. Paul, the Christian looked upon worldly activity either with indifference, or at least essentially traditionalistically; for those first generations were filled with eschatological hopes. Since everyone was simply waiting for the coming of the Lord, there was nothing to do but to remain in the station and the worldly occupation in which the call of the Lord had found him,

---

[84] Žižek, *The Ticklish Subject: The Absent Centre of Political Ontology*, 272. *The Puppet and the Dwarf*, 9.
[85] Max Weber, *The Protestant Ethic and the Spirit of Capitalism* (London: Harper Collins, 1991), 81.

and labour as before. Thus he would not burden his brothers as an object of charity, and it would only be for a little while.[86]

What happens with the emergence of Lutheran Protestantism, according to Weber, is that the orientation of the Pauline ethic of the call shifts from that which comes after death to that which happens here on earth. And the core text in Paul where Weber picks up this indifference to the world can be found in the First Letter to the Corinthians:

> In the first years of his activity as a reformer he was, since he thought of the calling as primarily of the flesh, dominated by an attitude closely related, in so far as the form of world activity was concerned, to the Pauline eschatological indifference was expressed in 1 Cor. Vii. One may attain salvation in any walk of life; on the short pilgrimage of life there is no use in laying weight on the form of occupation. The pursuit of material gain beyond personal needs must thus appear as a symptom of lack of grace, and since it can apparently only be attained at the expense of others, directly reprehensible.[87]

The glowing eschatological expectations in Paul and his successors have cooled down in Luther's understanding of the call, although Weber sees a more Pauline attitude in the Reformer's early phase. But gradually, Martin Luther discerns the present-day historical circumstances as a direct result of God's will. The believer is to remain in his or her position and state of life. Unconditional obedience to one's superiors becomes Lutheranism's imperative, according to Weber,[88] before the ascetical sense of duty in Calvinism is rationalized in ways that contribute to the spirit of capitalism, or to the culture on which modern capitalism is based. Along the way, the Pauline calling has become a modern work ethic and an integrated part of the modern division of labour.

Weber's interpretation of some verses in the seventh chapter of First Corinthians forms the basis of his summary of the Pauline calling as indifference to the worldly dimension in an intense expectation of what would come after death. By the time we reach this chapter of the letter, the author has admonished the readers to practice a greater harmony within the group in Corinth. He has warned against the formation of fractions (chs 3 and 4) and reacted to reports about immoral behaviour in legal contexts and in sexual

---

[86] Ibid., 84.
[87] Ibid.
[88] Ibid., 85.

praxis (chs 5 and 6), before giving practical advice about marriage, to help the believers avoid sexual misconduct (ch. 7). Both the individual bodies and the fellowship of the believers as the body of Christ are under constant pressure and risk being polluted or invaded by sexual misconduct (*porneia*) and other forms of immorality that can make them unclean before the time of the Lord's coming (4.5). *Porneia* here is almost a cosmic concept for the totality of the sinful world that can overwhelm the believers' bodies.[89] In addition to matters concerning marriage, the author advises the Corinthians about what they ought to do, now that they have undergone a moral purification with the help of baptism (1.13-16) and the working of the Spirit (2.10-15). Paul has emphasized the contrast between the word of the cross and the wisdom of the world, and he has pointed to all the dangers that lurk in the form of immorality in the believers' environment. We might therefore expect that the Corinthians would be told to isolate themselves from the allegedly clever thinkers of this world (1.20) whom God puts to shame (1.27) and from persons who want to lead them into a catastrophic immorality. But the apostle does not prescribe social isolation, for ". . . you would then need to go out of the world" (5.10). Although the Corinthians now lead the new life in Christ, they are to live as they have done previously: "However that may be, let each of you lead the life that the Lord has assigned, to which God called you" (7.17). They are thus to live in the realization that everything has in fact changed after the Christ event – and at the same time, they are to live as they have always done. This applies, no matter whether one is a slave or free:

> Let each of you remain in the condition in which you were called. Were you a slave when called? Do not be concerned about it. Even if you can gain your freedom, make use of your present condition now more than ever. For whoever was called in the Lord as a slave is a freed person belonging to the Lord, just as whoever was free when called is a slave of Christ. You were bought with a price; do not become slaves of human masters. In whatever condition you were called, brothers and sisters, there remain with God. (1 Cor. 7.20-24)

In his commentary on the Letter to the Romans, the Italian philosopher Giorgio Agamben studies this passage in depth, in order to identify what Paul

---

[89] Halvor Moxnes, "Asceticism and Christian Identity in Antiquity: A Dialogue with Foucault and Paul", *Journal for the Study of the New Testament* 26, no. 1 (2003): 22.

means when he speaks of being "called" (*klêtos* in Greek). Agamben's work is structured as a commentary in six chapters on the first verse in Romans, but it draws in fact on several of Paul's Letters, including First Corinthians. The centre of gravity throughout Agamben's reading of Paul can be said to lie in the passage that begins at 1 Cor. 7.20. These verses supply him with the prism for the apostle's thinking.[90] This is due, first of all, to the fact that Max Weber gives these verses a key role in his understanding of the background to the Protestant work ethic that makes early capitalism possible. Second, it is inspired by the prominent role this passage has in Jacob Taubes' lectures on Paul,[91] which also leads Agamben to read Paul as a precursor of Walter Benjamin. And third, Agamben notes how his former teacher, Martin Heidegger,[92] paid attention to this passage and interpreted it as an expression of the experience of being in the world (that is to say, the opposite of Weber).[93] This opens up interesting perspectives for new and original readings of the scriptural passage.

Giorgio Agamben: The call to remain where you are

Weber maintains that this section of the First Letter to the Corinthians played a prominent role in the contribution of Protestantism to the development of modern capitalism, and Agamben does not doubt that this hypothesis may be correct. Nor does he contradict the claim that Martin Luther appealed to Paul in order to make obedience to the state and the call from God two sides of the same coin. But he attacks Weber's reading of the text as an expression of Paul's indifference to the worldly dimension – an indifference due to the expectation that Christ would shortly return. Agamben does not take up Weber's idea that this expectation was, historically speaking, strongly present in the Corinthians. Instead, he replies with a philological argument.[94] For what

---

[90] Jayne Svenungsson, *Divining History: Prophetism, Messianism, and the Development of the Spirit* (New York: Berghahn, 2016), 169.
[91] Taubes, *The Political Theology of Paul*, 53-4, 73-6.
[92] Agamben took part in some of Heidegger's seminars in the 1960s.
[93] Agamben, *The Time That Remains: A Commentary on the Letter to the Romans*, 33-4. See also Heidegger, *The Phenomenology of Religious Life*, 84-5.
[94] It is typical of Agamben's style or procedure that he focuses on the meaning of individual words, as if this should be a principal concern of philosophy: "In the scholastic enumeration of transcendentals (. . .), the term that, remaining unthought in each, conditions the meaning of all the others is the adjective *quodlibet*." Giorgio Agamben, *The Coming Community* (Minneapolis: University of Minnesota Press, 1993), 1.

does the key concept that Paul employs in this passage (7.20) for "being called", *klêsis,* mean?

According to the Italian philosopher, this concept must be understood as a part of Paul's messianic vocabulary. It must be meaningful on the basis of the type of messianism that Paul upholds after the Messiah has come. The Greek noun *klêsis* means a special form of transformation of every juridical status or worldly condition under which one lives, according to Agamben.[95] This differs from Weber's reading, where the apostle was exhorting the Corinthians to live in indifference to the present time, thanks to their expectation of the divine intervention in the future. Nor can we appeal to Paul for support of an unambiguous division between the worldly sphere of the present day and the spiritual sphere of the future. The Corinthians are not to live for a time that will come in the future, but for "the time that remains" – the title of Agamben's commentary on the Letter to the Romans (*Il tempo che resta,* 2000).

If Paul is a messianic thinker who proclaims a transformation of some kind, one would expect that the apparently indifferent attitude to the question whether or not a person was a slave would pose challenges. For how can this be a messianic text that announces a form of transformation of the world, when Weber and others interpret it as reflecting an indifferent attitude to earthly realities – such as whether one is a slave or free? "Were you a slave when called? Do not be concerned about it" (7.21) These words do not sound revolutionary; they seem not to contain any criticism of power. It is not easy to translate the Greek *mallon khrêsai,* with which 7.21 closes. It means literally: "Rather, make use." This may mean that the slave should remain a slave and "make use of your present condition" (as in the translation above), but it can also signify the opposite, namely, that one should liberate oneself from slavery.[96] It can thus have two widely divergent and mutually exclusive meanings. And if we add that the historians assume that Corinth had many manumitted slaves in its population, alongside a population of slaves that always existed in the Roman Empire, we will understand that the reminder to potential hearers of the Letter

---

[95] *The Time That Remains: A Commentary on the Letter to the Romans,* 22.
[96] Laura Salah Nasrallah, "Grief in Corinth. The Roman City and Paul's Corinthian Correspondence", in *Contested Spaces: Houses and Temples in Roman Antiquity and the New Testament,* ed. David L. Balch and Annette Weissenrieder (Tübingen: Mohr Siebeck, 2012), 120. Martinsen Anders, "Oversettelsesprobelmatikk og slaveri", *Teologisk tidsskrift* 7, no. 2 (2018): 124.

that "You were bought with a price" (7.23) was not merely a metaphor.⁹⁷ The New Testament scholar Dale Martin maintains that Paul is challenging here the dominant hierarchical power structures in society at his time, by insisting that a slave who becomes a believer in Christ truly becomes a free person in Christ. Paul's countercultural universe of faith destabilizes the dominant hierarchies in Corinth. When Paul affirms that "whoever was called in the Lord as a slave is a freed person belonging to the Lord" (7.22), the apostle is, in reality, giving slaves who believe in Christ a position higher than their free non-believing owners. Martin argues that this destabilization of dominant societal hierarchies runs through the whole of First Corinthians.⁹⁸ He sums up his study of the Letter as follows:

> Throughout 1 Corinthians Paul attempts to undermine the hierarchical ideology of the body prevalent in Greco-Roman culture. He attempts to make the strong weak and the weak strong. He calls on Christians of higher status to please those of lower status. . . . Paul even implies that higher-status Christians should follows his example and lower themselves socially in order to identify themselves with those of lower status.⁹⁹

Paul not only attacks the hierarchy in the ancient world, which inter alia justified slavery as a basis of society; his Letters also give us an insight into this society from a standpoint that does not represent the elite. This is a rarity in the source material that survives from this epoch.¹⁰⁰ When we read Paul, therefore, we get glimpses of a lower-class standpoint. This may have sounded like a rare form of solidarity and identification with the poor, including slaves. But Agamben's philosophical interpretation is not interested in how those who heard these words in antiquity may have perceived the content of this Letter. Instead, he asks how it is that Paul defines a messianic life as if there are perennially valid structures or characteristics in an existence based on the coming of the Messiah.¹⁰¹

Agamben reduces the linguistic ambiguity in 7.21 by saying that the call in this passage does not have a specific content. No one is called to be specifically a slave or free in the situation in which Paul is writing. When he writes: "Let

---

⁹⁷ Nasrallah, "Grief in Corinth. The Roman City and Paul's Corinthian Correspondence", 115.
⁹⁸ Dale B. Martin, *The Corinthian Body* (New Haven: Yale University Press, 1995), 198.
⁹⁹ Ibid., 248.
¹⁰⁰ Ibid., xii.
¹⁰¹ Agamben, *The Time That Remains: A Commentary on the Letter to the Romans*.

each of you remain in the condition in which you were called" (7.20), the call entails a repetition of the de facto conditions in which one was called and in which one existed. It is a call to the call, that is to say, a revocation (a "calling back") that at the same time puts a question mark to the call, potentially giving it a new value, or opening the door to a new use of the call. The position one was in is relativized or reset, but one is not called to something radically new *in terms of content*.[102] The radicality lies in a very fine distinction between what one was called to before the Messiah came and what one is called to afterwards. And the radicality also means that everything in the world is encompassed by this difference.[103] The messianic life is a way of being in the world.[104] This is why the call is not the expression of indifference about the world and the position in which one is – irrespective of the form. While this commitment is not indeed an activism, nor is it a pure passivity:

> To live in the Messiah means precisely to revoke and render inoperative at each instant every aspect of the life that we live.... And in the inoperativity that takes place there is not mere inertia or rest; on the contrary, it is the messianic operation par excellence.[105]

The divine call transforms the human being into a messianic existence that consists in a new attentiveness to the life one leads, in which one almost rises above the role and position in which one has landed. This bestows a new type of freedom inside the same conditions that one lived under, as slave or free. Accordingly, one is not condemned by God either to be a slave (God forbid!) or to be free, nor is one destined for one particular professional role or sociocultural identity. To be called is not a profession, nor a defined task. Agamben claims that the call is empty of content. It gives no new identity but makes you identity-less in solidarity and fellowship with the others who are likewise called to a call without content – the others who likewise live with the fact that their conditions are undermined although the form of these conditions is not altered. Agamben writes that the new fellowship, the *ekklêsia*,

---

[102] Ibid., 23.
[103] Peter Forrás, "Kronos, Kairos Og Arché", *Agora* 29, no. 4 (2011): 36.
[104] Agamben is inspired here by his former teacher Martin Heidegger, who interpreted these verses in the sense of a new way of being in the world, a *de facto* experience in this world, not a flight from the world. Agamben, *The Time That Remains: A Commentary on the Letter to the Romans*, 33-4.
[105] *The Kingdom and the Glory: For a Theological Genealogy of Economy and Government (Homo Sacer Ii, 2)* (Stanford: Stanford University Press, 2011), 248-9.

is literally all the calls (in the plural: *klêseis*).¹⁰⁶ Remain where you are – this is the demand – but in a new relationship to what you are. This new relationship entails an inner tension between the old and the new in which you already exist, and from which you should not necessarily get out.

If we are to believe Agamben, the most precise definition of this messianic existence is found in a much-discussed passage in the seventh chapter of First Corinthians, where we encounter the expression *hôs mê*, which the NRSV translates as "as though":

> I mean, brothers and sisters, the appointed time has grown short; from now on, let even those who have wives be as though they had none, and those who mourn as though they were not mourning, and those who rejoice as though they were not mourning, and those who rejoice as though they were not rejoicing, and those who buy as though they had no possessions, and those who deal with the world as though they had no dealings with it. For the present form of this world is passing away. (7.29-32)

Paul draws attention to time. Agamben translates the words at the beginning of this passage (in 7.29) as "time contracted itself".¹⁰⁷ His concept of the messianic time is a variant of the model that Christian theologians have based their work on in modern theology.¹⁰⁸ Paul is speaking of a salvation that has already come, but not yet. This is why more time is needed. Agamben's understanding of Paul differs from that of many Christian theologians here, because he limits the "not yet" to our earthly existence.¹⁰⁹ With formulations such as: "... the life that begins on earth after the last day is simply human life",¹¹⁰ Agamben constructs with Paul an eschatology that is not in the least open to an eschatological reversal as the result of a divine intervention *ab extra*. The extra time for the "not yet" of the messianic kingdom is a time within our time, not something

---

¹⁰⁶ *The Time That Remains: A Commentary on the Letter to the Romans*, 22.
¹⁰⁷ Ibid., 68. Laura Nasrallah points out that Agamben is right in his insistence that the "living as not..." echoes a Jewish first-century text like 4 Ezra. She adds, however, that this detachment is also echoed in Stoicism: "We need to choose between a Stoic or Jewish eschatological 'background' for Paul's statements 'as not' in 1 Corinthians." Laura Salah Nasrallah, *Archaeology and the Letters of Paul* (Oxford: Oxford University Press, 2019), 176.
¹⁰⁸ The conventional character of this model means that Agamben's statements about the epochal aspect of his own interpretation sometimes appear in a rather strange light, as when he generalizes about theologians as follows: "now it may embarrass those theologians." ibid., 117.
¹⁰⁹ This is connected to Agamben's concept of God as "absolute immanence": "... rather, the *pure transcendent is the taking-place of every thing*. God or good or the place does not take place, but is the taking-place of the entities, their innermost exteriority." *The Coming Community*, 15.
¹¹⁰ Ibid., 7.

that comes chronologically after it. The messianic time is not the pure opposite of chronological time, but a time that is contracted within this time. When we count and objectify time as chronology, we remain passive onlookers at time, but the messianic time arises when we actively "take hold of time", so that we realize that this time is all we have.[111]

Time is getting shorter and shorter, but this does not mean for Agamben that this world is to be replaced by a new world. When Paul writes of "the present form of this world" (7.31), this means that it is the *form* of this world that is to disappear. This world is to be recreated when the "calling back" of "those who have wives", "those who mourn" or "those who rejoice" intervenes de facto in the world. The new creation takes place when the calling back posits the identities, actions, and positions in contradiction to themselves, in an inner tension. And the new creation is, for Agamben, the messianic reusing of the old life.[112] He finds evidence of this reusing in the Pauline expression *hôs mê, as though* or *as not*, in 7.30-32, which expresses the fact that the call both maintains and deactivates the societally created living conditions.

All earlier calls and roles are handed over to a new use but not in order that one may take possession of them. An essential point for Agamben is that the messianic call to live in the state of *hôs mê* consists in using and not possessing. He points out that Paul draws a contrast between possession and use when the apostle writes that, in the messianic time, "those who buy" live "as though they had no possessions, and those who deal with the world as though they had no dealings with it" (7.30-31). According to Agamben, there is a trajectory that runs from these words to the Franciscans' refusal to possess property.[113] The messianic relationship to the world means, not the possession of property, but a free use of belongings. What Paul has in mind is thus not a spiritual flight, as Nietzsche and Weber (each in his own way) supposed, but a new involvement on behalf of the material dimension here and now.

Agamben is also fully aware that interpreters have scratched their heads over the Greek expression *mallon khrêsai* in 7.21. Both the New Revised Standard Version (NRSV) and Agamben translate *khrêsai* as an imperative:

---

[111] *The Time That Remains: A Commentary on the Letter to the Romans,* 68. Forrás, "Kronos, Kairos, Og Arché", 39.
[112] Ibid.
[113] Ibid., 26-7.

"make use"; this tends to evoke associations of a temporary and messianic use, rather than of a definitive state of things.

Through translation choices and readings of this kind, Agamben makes Paul a more consistent thinker, who is also more in harmony with the philosophy that the Italian had constructed in the years prior to the publication of *Il tempo che resta* in 2000. When Agamben, with help from Taubes, comes to see Paul as a messianic thinker who undermines power rather than legitimating it, he already brings a number of presuppositions that are not equally clear in his readings of Paul. Several of these are already established in the book *La comunità che viene* (1990; "The Coming Community" in English), and they find their form in the subsequent publications.[114] Here, he presents the philosophical problems to which Paul's description of the messianic life *hôs mê* is an answer.[115]

Strong biopower versus the weak power of messianism

Giorgio Agamben describes our late-modern condition as the result of a hedonistic consumer society, on the one hand, and of a controlling biopower, on the other. Drawing inspiration from Michel Foucault (1926-84), Agamben claims that while the power of the state was directed in the past to the control of a territory, it has switched in the modern period to become the control of populations and the regulation of human life itself. The state not only watches over the national borders; it can also regulate the population in increasingly comprehensive ways. This biopolitical control of human life has demonstrated its appalling potential through modern totalitarianism, but Agamben sees something of the same logic as guiding the security regime in the aftermath of 9/11 and in the war against terror.[116] Agamben caused a sensation in 2004 when he refused to travel to New York for a lecture because the American

---

[114] The biblical scholar Alain Gignac claims that the commentary on Romans is "prefigured" precisely in this book. Alain Gignac, "Agamben's Paul. Thinker of the Messianic", in *Paul in the Grip of the Philosophers: The Apostle and Contemporary Continental Philosophy*, ed. Peter Frick, Paul in Critical Contexts (Minneapolis: Fortress Press, 2014), 171.
[115] "To oversimplify, one could say that *Time That Remains* is the answer to, or even the solution to the problem presented, in the trilogy *Homo Sacer*." Ibid.
[116] This is why Nazism and Fascism remain latent possibilities.

state had recently introduced fingerprint scanning for everyone who entered the country, and he found this state control unacceptable.

Giorgio Agamben is a philosopher who springs freely from one religious tradition and academic discipline to another in his texts, in order thereby to show the reader unexpected and provocative connections. At one moment, he refers to a character in Kafka's novels, at the next, to categories in mediaeval scholasticism and then to a rabbinic statement from the Talmud. Paul's thinking is certainly not the only inspiration Agamben draws from classical antiquity for the interpretation of the present day. Agamben the jurist finds in Roman legislation the figure of the *homo sacer*, the holy human being. The *homo sacer* in Roman law is a person who could not be put to death within the sacred precinct but could be killed outside it, without this being regarded as a murder. This forgotten figure unmasks for Agamben the violent core that is the basis of political power and sovereignty. The *homo sacer* was an exception in law, but the Italian philosopher argues that it is precisely such exceptions that unmask power and demonstrate where the human being is reduced to the "naked life". Concentration camps leave not the slightest doubt that the exceptional state of things has become the rule (Walter Benjamin),[117] but refugee camps too are contemporary examples of how the naked life is simultaneously excluded and integrated into the legal order. This is how what Agamben regards as the hidden fundament of all political systems finds expression. He points out that the revolutions of the past century failed because neither anarchism nor Marxism had grasped the fundamental structure of the state. This is why the strategy of conquering the state through a revolution did not succeed.

On the one hand, Agamben relies on a traditional ideological critique. He employs a Marxist vocabulary to maintain that "exchange value has completely eclipsed use value and can now achieve the status of absolute and irresponsible sovereignty over life in its entirety".[118] The fetishistic character of wares falsifies society in an even more comprehensive manner than in the past, now that the human body is reified as a ware, and advertising covers up this manipulation of life itself. This alienation knows no bounds and penetrates into what is the dwelling place of existence itself – our language: "Even more than economic

---

[117] "The tradition of the oppressed teaches us that the 'state of emergency' in which we live is not the exception but the rule." Benjamin, *Illuminations*, 257.
[118] Giorgio Agamben, *Means without End: Notes on Politics* (Minneapolis: University of Minnesota Press, 2000), 76.

necessity and technological development, what drives the nations of earth toward a single common destiny is the alienation from linguistic being, the uprooting of all peoples from their vital dwelling in language."[119]

On the other hand, Agamben breaks with Marxism when he claims that the differences between the political left wing and right wing are being continuously erased and that the old recipe, involving the conquest of the state, is not the solution. Agamben does not attempt to answer the question: "What must be done?", which would presuppose that the philosophical framework was ready to elaborate programs or hasten to action. The philosopher recognizes that he is content instead to prepare the ground for a new politics that has not yet been thought out, and he seeks potential answer to a more fundamental question: "How must something be done?"

Agamben secularizes Paul in a different way than Badiou. Agamben's philosophy with its Pauline inspiration has no more room than Badiou's for a supernatural intervention. Both philosophers champion a radical this-worldliness in Paul, and thus contradict Nietzsche. For Badiou, this ends up in a universalist philosophy about the truth event, without a content in faith in the risen Christ, while Agamben has a messianism without a Messiah with the proper name "Jesus".[120] Agamben maintains that he can sift out the messianic language and structure in Paul's thinking, much as Badiou maintains that he can extract a secular understanding of grace from it. But the implications of their readings of Paul are extremely divergent.

In Agamben, there are no truth events in the form of revolutions to which the acting subject can adhere in devoted loyalty, as in Badiou. While an optimistic Badiou provides inspiration for zealous activism in loyalty to an event, and reads Paul in order to establish a new universal subject, Agamben directly criticizes this idea in Badiou.[121] He writes in a polemical tone that there is no universal principle in Paul that overcomes all the differences. The

---

[119] *The Coming Community*, 83.
[120] A possible objection to Agamben's use of Paul arises here. He wants to formulate a messianism without a Messiah. But how is it possible to let go of the content in Paul's messianism, where it is specifically Jesus of Nazareth who is the Messiah? Boer, *Criticism of Religion: On Marxism and Theology*, Ii, 192.
[121] "For Paul, it is not a matter of 'tolerating' or getting past differences in order to pinpoint sameness or a universal lurking beyond. The universal is not a transcendent principle through which differences may be perceived – such a perspective of transcendence is not available to Paul. Rather, this 'transcendental' involves an operation that divides the divisions of the law themselves and renders them inoperative, without ever reaching any final ground. No universal man, no Christian can be found in the depths of the Jew or the Greek, neither as a principle nor as an end; all that is left is a

messianic call generates a tension in every existing call or identity (*klêsis*) – slave/free, man/woman, circumcised/uncircumcised – without ending up in a new identity. To live "as if" suspends the calls and the identities. But the messianic life in Agamben's version does not found any new call or identity. And this is why neither "universalist" nor "Christian" is an appropriate category for those who share the messianic experience.[122]

This is because Agamben reads out of passages such as "The day of the Lord will come like a thief in the night" (1 Thess. 5.2) and "The appointed time has grown short" (1 Cor. 7.29) a messianic experience of time that transforms us and that can be found also in texts by Walter Benjamin – a thinker who "perfectly understood Paul's meaning".[123] It is as if Agamben had heard Rudolf Bultmann's demythologizing paraphrase of the same passage from First Corinthians: "Let those who have the modern world-view live as though they had none."[124] The modern scientific world view is built on chronological time and objectifying knowledge; but according to Agamben's understanding, with its inspiration from Benjamin, the condensed or shrunk time that occurs in the believers' lives breaks into the chronological time. This messianic time is a present "which is shot through with chips of Messianic time".[125] Agamben finds another example of the overlapping meaning between Paul's and Benjamin's perspectives on the messianic time in Benjamin's statement: "for every second time was a strait gate through which the Messiah might enter."[126] In this experience of time, a weak messianic power is accessible, which may seem impotent and powerless.

While Badiou and Žižek point to Paul as the prototype of the militant activist who fights for revolutions that look dramatic from the outside, Agamben holds that Paul is rather the prototype of the human being who experiences a shift that is small, but nevertheless makes all the difference. While Badiou holds that it is decisively important to alter the state of things,

---

remnant and the impossibility of the Jew or the Greek to coincide with himself. Agamben, *The Time That Remains: A Commentary on the Letter to the Romans*, 52–3.

[122] Agamben, *The Time That Remains: A Commentary on the Letter to the Romans*, 52.
[123] *The Church and the Kingdom* (London: Seagull Books, 2012), 5.
[124] Bultmann, *Jesus Christ and Mythology*, 85. Although Agamben does not refer to this reading of 1 Cor. 7.29 by Bultmann, he displays knowledge of Bultmann's work in other parts of his commentary on Romans. Agamben, *The Time That Remains: A Commentary on the Letter to the Romans*, 72.
[125] Benjamin, *Illuminations*, 263.
[126] Ibid., 264.

Agamben maintains that the big difference "does not refer to the state of things, but to their sense and their limits".[127] He once again quotes Benjamin, who is said to have told a parable about the messianic kingdom to his friend Ernst Bloch:

> Benjamin's version of the story goes like this: "The *Hasidim* tell a story about the world to come that says everything there will be just as it is here. Just as our room is now, so it will be in the world to come; where our baby sleeps now, there too it will sleep in the other world. And the clothes we wear in this world, those too we will wear there. Everything will be as it is now, just a little different."[128]

A little different after the world is transformed after the coming of the Messiah through "every second of time" – this is the liberation that Agamben hopes for, on the basis of Paul's weak messianism. It can be ushered in at every moment, and its total transformation will leave everything "just a little different". The messianic dimension embraces everything, while at the same time altering little or nothing. It entails first and foremost a new way of seeing everything that presents itself.[129] So what kind of politics can be liberating in the encounter with the all-embracing biopolitical control and alienation that Agamben describes elsewhere in his political philosophy? What kind of politics can correspond to the messianic life *hôs mê*?

As far as proposing solutions or concretizing the praxis to which the messianic life leads, Agamben's writing can seem both evasive and resigned.[130] He regularly takes refuge in intellectual constructs about non-potentiality as a form of passivity that nevertheless is not completely passive and that contains an undefined potential. On the rare occasions when Agamben holds up political resistance as exemplary or obligatory for his political philosophy,

---

[127] Agamben, *The Coming Community*, 54.
[128] Ibid., 53.
[129] This new way of seeing things that the messianic transformation entails is expressed *inter alia* with the Heideggerian conceptual pair authentic-inauthentic. While the content is unchanged, the relationship to this content is different: "Ethics begins only when the good is revealed to consist in nothing other than a grasping of evil and when the authentic and the proper have no other content than the inauthentic and the improper." Ibid., 13.
[130] Agamben has been criticized for his lack of political solutions and ways out of the problems he himself raises. For a powerful criticism of Agamben's philosophy as political nihilism and exaggerated formalism, see Matthew Calarco and Steven DeCaroli, *Giorgio Agamben: Sovereignty and Life* (Stanford: Stanford University Press, 2007), 22, 27.

he tends to refer to the episode of the students on Tiananmen Square in China in 1989.¹³¹ He claims that this protest was characterized by the relative absence of specific demands put forward to the authorities, and by the ensuing disproportionate reaction of the state. This lack of proportion shows that the state regarded the diffuse demands for democracy and freedom as a threat. Here, what Agamben calls singularity in "any identity at all" was a source of genuine political resistance, especially because the state was taken by surprise by an opposition it was unable to identify.

The protest not only illustrates the fellowship of the recalled believers that Agamben finds in the First Letter to the Corinthians. The students can be said, not only to illustrate, but even more strongly, to incarnate this messianic fellowship when Agamben declares that the students on Tiananmen Square in 1989 formed a fellowship without demanding an identity. In other passages, he speaks of "the first inhabitants of a fellowship without presuppositions or a state", in messianic language that speaks of something promising that is to come.¹³² It is also in this form of indefinable political resistance that Agamben's attraction to Jacob Taubes' interpretation of the *hôs mê* passage may lie. Taubes defined the *hôs mê* attitude as nihilistic, in the sense that it contained an exhortation by Paul to engage in a strategic conformity and obedience to the law (obedience to the state, payment of taxes, etc.) on behalf of an underground movement that lacked any kind of political legitimacy. As Taubes writes: "[N]ow here comes a subterranean society, a little bit Jewish, a little bit Gentile, nobody knows, what sort of lowlifes are these anyway – for heaven's sake, don't stand out!"¹³³

An indefinable fellowship of believers who expressed their loyalty to the crucified Jesus could constitute a diffuse threat to the authorities in the Roman Empire. Like the students on Tiananmen Square, they stood on town squares and in synagogues while they spoke about the crucified one. What might this now mean?

---

[131] Agamben, *The Coming Community*, 85-7; *Means without End: Notes on Politics*, 88-9.
[132] These identity-less dwellers, according to Agamben with a reference to the Talmud, will be able to "enter the paradise of language and will come out of it injured". *Means without End: Notes on Politics*, 85. There is a soteriology in Agamben here that finds much of its meaning in the formulation of, and the refuge in, language. Agamben sounds the messianic note in the first sentence of his 1990 book: "The coming being is whatever being." *The Coming Community*.
[133] Taubes, *The Political Theology of Paul*, 54.

Platonism for the people?

As we have seen, Friedrich Nietzsche believed it was in ch. 15 of the First Letter to the Corinthians that a step was taken that was to have fatal consequences for Western history. It is here that Paul employs Jesus' message as a pretext for inventing a promise that the apostle knows can never be fulfilled for the human being. When he writes: "if Christ has not been raised, then our proclamation has been in vain" (15.14), Paul has in reality invented a new doctrine – "the doctrine of personal immortality".[134] This idea has remained and exerted pressure as part of the "millennial Christian-ecclesiastical pressure" against humanity that Nietzsche in *Jenseits von Gut und Böse* (1885) called "Platonism for the people".[135] According to Nietzsche, the Christianity invented by Paul had terrorized people's minds down through the centuries with a Christianized Platonism. Plato's thought was adapted to the masses through Christianity and turned into a religious popular property. In this way, the idea of the immortality of the soul – based on promises of heaven or hell in the afterlife – was cultivated alongside a Platonic-Christian contempt for the body and a distrust of the sensuous.

When Nietzsche sets out to tear into pieces Christianity's ideas about the afterlife, he hits the nail on the head when he attacks a verse in the penultimate chapter of First Corinthians, for no other Pauline text has contributed more than precisely this chapter to form the ideas of the Christian tradition about what awaits us after death. The problem that confronts Paul is that he has heard that some of the Corinthians contradict him by claiming that "there is no resurrection of the dead" (15.12).[136] His response here elaborates much of the basis for the theology of later church fathers concerning the possible existence of the human person after death. But does the apostle do so because of a form of Platonism? Is the author we meet in Paul's Letters a kind of popular Platonist, as Nietzsche understands this term?

---

[134] Nietzsche, *The Anti-Christ, Ecce Homo, Twilight of the Idols, and Other Writings*, 38.
[135] Nietsche, *The Essential Nietzsche: Beyond Good and Evil: The Genealogy of Morals*, 10.
[136] It is commonly claimed that Paul's primary concern in this chapter is to get the Corinthians to understand that the resurrection belongs to the future, rather than something that has taken place (he would thus be arguing here against an exaggerated realized eschatology). We need not take sides in this scholarly disagreement, because it is first and foremost the bodily aspect of the resurrection that is most relevant to the assessment of Nietzsche's reading of Paul's resurrection theology as "Platonism for the people".

In Plato, we encounter a sharp division between an immortal soul and a perishable body that keeps the soul a prisoner, with its sensuous experiences that have a blunting effect on the real perception by the soul. By liberating oneself from sense perception, the human being can remember what our soul saw in the past and can thereby reach a higher level of knowledge through the concepts and a more moral life.[137] We also find in Plato the idea of a judgement after this life, which leads either to punishment in an underground world or to reward in a heavenly existence, before the soul returns in an animal or a human form.[138] Very few people in classical antiquity read Plato, but dualistic ideas with a similar division between body and soul were probably widespread in places like Corinth in the first century, especially among the educated and prosperous. Dale Martin's hypothesis is that Paul met with resistance or ridicule because of his belief, with its Jewish inspiration, in the resurrection of the dead and because of every idea of a life after death that in some way included the bodily dimension.

> The mistake of the masses, according to the philosophical view, is not their belief that men may become gods but their unsophisticated notion that the lower-status aspect of human existence, the body, could possibly attain the high status reserved for the more subtle, purer substances of the self. Thus the idea of the resurrection of the body would indeed have struck some Greeks as ridiculous or incomprehensible. Specifically, the notion would have offended the educated – those exposed, at least minimally, to philosophical arguments and assumptions.[139]

The absence of Paul, and especially of First Corinthians, is striking in Michel Foucault's three-volume work *Histoire de la sexualité*, when we bear in mind that the French philosopher was so strongly interested in the Christian regulation of the self and of sexual morality in antiquity. Nevertheless, Foucault paints a picture of early Christianity, and especially of Christian asceticism, as a highly important contribution to an increasing turn towards the self and self-cultivation. There is little doubt that Paul's exaltation of a life without marriage (1 Corinthians 7) had a massive influence on later Christian ideals and on monastic movements that championed a strict asceticism. Foucault

---

[137] Plato, *Phaedrus*. Loeb Classical Library, 465–80.
[138] Ibid., 478–9.
[139] Martin, *The Corinthian Body*, 114.

completely confirms this picture of Christian asceticism as the renunciation of bodiliness, and especially of enjoyment, while choosing instead to cultivate the soul through a continuous self-examination for the sake of a higher ideal.[140]

In his reading of the First Letter to the Corinthians, with the emphasis on ch. 6, the New Testament scholar Halvor Moxnes points out that Foucault's one-sided pictures of early Christianity as an individual examination of the soul could have been nuanced if he had paid closer attention to Paul. For Paul, the main problem is not the body, but desire. Instead of narrowing the Christian life down to an ascetic relationship to oneself, on which a critical light is shed in a solitary room with a father confessor (Foucault's sources include mediaeval manuals for hearing confessions), the earliest Christian author highlights bodily praxis as the true adoration of God.[141] The body is involved through meals (later ritualized and standardized in the church's eucharistic praxis) and through a baptism that entailed complete immersion in water.

Paul against the Platonists

One of those in modern philosophy who come close to a reading of Paul that matches Nietzsche's reading is Giorgio Agamben, who describes the "machine" of Christian theology in ways that can suggest the picture of the church as an ideological juggernaut that rolls over human beings in the course of history. Agamben sees interpretations of Christianity that reduce the eternal and messianic life to a future condition, or to something that exists only after death, as manifestations of a theological machine that entrenches the biopower.[142] In this way, he comes close to Nietzsche's critique of Christianity. The big difference is that the Italian finds Paul not guilty. He lays the blame on later theologians,[143] for example, on those who reserved eternal life for

---

[140] Michel Foucault, *The History of Sexuality: 3: The Care of the Self*, vol. 3 (Harmondsworth: Penguin, 1988).
[141] Moxnes, "Asceticism and Christian Identity in Antiquity: A Dialogue with Foucault and Paul", 23.
[142] Agamben, *The Kingdom and the Glory: For a Theological Genealogy of Economy and Government (Homo Sacer Ii, 2)*, 1.
[143] Agamben identifies an epochal shift in Christian theology between Paul and later church fathers in an ideological accommodation of theology to the rule of the biopower. "[I]n Paul, there is an 'economy of the mystery' and not, as will be the case with Hippolytus and Tertullian, a 'mystery of the economy'." Ibid., 26.

"blessed ones" instead of interpreting it more "generally" as the resurrection of the just. In other words, Agamben sees something vital at stake here in the restriction of the scope of the resurrection.

> [I]n the future eon, when the just will enter into the inoperativity of God, the eternal life is, for Paul, placed decisively under the sign of glory. The celebrated passage in 1 Corinthians 15.35-55 – the interpretation of which is the source of so much endeavor for the theologians from Origen to Thomas Aquinas – in truth says nothing more than this: that the bodies of the just will be resurrected in glory and will be transformed into glory and into the incorruptible spirit. What in Paul is left intentionally indeterminate and generic . . . is articulated and developed into a doctrine of the glorious body of the blessed by the theologians. In accordance with an apparatus that has by now become familiar to us, a doctrine of glorious life that isolates eternal life and its inoperativity in a separate sphere comes to substitute that of the messianic life.[144]

Agamben points out that theologians subsequent to Paul have found it difficult to interpret "the celebrated passage". He can cut the Gordian knot because he holds that this passage "in truth" has only one meaning, which contradicts Nietzsche's claim that Paul, as the true founder of Christianity, is spreading a Platonic idea of the soul's immortality. In Agamben's reading, it is not, in a Christian-Platonic manner, an immortal soul that is held captive in a body and that is freed from the prison of its body after a resurrection beyond death. Nor is it a dead body that comes to life again, as if a dead corpse could simply be resuscitated in another world. Agamben maintains that Paul is referring to the bodies of just persons who rise again and at the same time are transformed into something else, "into glory and into the incorruptible spirit". That which rises again is something other than that which dies. Agamben thus reads a discontinuity out of Paul's belief in resurrection.

He thus points in the same direction as the Pauline scholar Jorunn Økland.[145] Paul intends to correct those Corinthians who hold that "there is no resurrection of the dead" (1 Cor. 15.12). We can say, with Alain Badiou, that the apostle faces the impossible task (given that resurrection is an impossibility) of

---

[144] Ibid., 249.
[145] The following exposition is inspired by Jorunn Økland's reading of the chapter in Økland, "Sjelløs lesning", in *Den levende kroppen* (Oslo: Vidarforlaget, 2016).

explaining to the Corinthians how the resurrection from the dead is possible. Paul's logic is that, if this is not possible, then Jesus too cannot have risen from the dead (15.13). But in that case, his entire faith is meaningless (15.14), the word about the cross (1.18) is nothing special, and Jesus' cross has no cosmic significance of any kind. He and the believers in Corinth are "found to be misrepresenting God" (15.15). In other words, faith in the resurrection is all-decisive. There is an inherent connection between Christ's individual resurrection and the collective resurrection of the dead, between the one and the many. Christ rises again first, and then come the others (15.20).

Paul writes as if there is one or other sceptical ancient Nietzschean in the community in Corinth (15.35). We do not know who it is that articulates the scepticism about Paul's belief in the resurrection, although one may be entitled to propose the hypothesis (as historians like Dale Martin do) that they were educated Greeks and Romans and their tirades against Paul may not have been any less mocking than Nietzsche's. But the philosophical premises that lead them to regard the apostle's message as foolishness (1.18) differ: whereas Nietzsche dethroned Paul on the basis of anti-Platonic premises, it can seem from First Corinthians that some in Corinth were trying to dethrone him on the basis of an anthropology that more strongly resembles Plato's dualist view. Against Nietzsche, and with Badiou (Paul exemplifies in a literary way the event of truth), we could also have emphasized that Paul does not reply by inventing a belief in resurrection, but by elaborating further a belief that already exists, since what he writes is based on "what I had turn had received" (15.3).

When Paul wishes to convince his hearers that resurrection from death is possible and to answer the question about what kind of body the risen human beings have, he resorts to a comparison with the only thing we have: life on earth. When he compares the resurrection with planting a seed in the earth, it is as if he is saying: "How stupid can people actually be?" (15.36) – for what comes up is a completely new plant, not a completely identical form with what was put in the soil. When God raises up the dead, therefore, this does not mean that the same body (*sôma*) that was buried will rise again. Above all, it is does not mean that it is the flesh (*sarx*) that rises again, because "flesh . . . cannot inherit the kingdom of God" (15.50), since all flesh, of human beings or of animals (15.39), rots and is therefore perishable. As Paul writes: "What is sown is perishable, what is raised is imperishable" (15.42). So what is it that is sown? Or what is it that dies? That which dies is "a body that had a soul" (*sôma phusikon*). And that which lives on, according to Paul, is not the soul. It is not a timeless and immutable soul that leaves the body behind and inherits an eternal life, but rather a "spiritual body" (*sôma pneumatikon*, 15.44). As Jorunn Økland writes:

"Paul thus employs the course of nature as evidence to demonstrate this sequence and consequently to demonstrate how the philosopher who thinks in Platonic terms is wrong. *First* the seed, *then* the plant. The emphasis on the sequence – first earth/dust, then spirit – as well as the fact that he appears to understand the spirit, *pneuma*, likewise in material terms, are further reasons for placing Paul among the materialists rather than among the Platonizing philosophers or those who speculated about the *logos*. . . . There is thus no soul in 1 Cor. 15 that could guarantee the continuity between the animated body (or flesh-body) and the spiritual body (or aura-body, that is to say, between different kinds of bodies on different cosmic levels)."[146]

This means that a structural element in Platonic thought, a soul that ensures continuity between what is on this earth and what lies beyond death, is absent from Paul. If we accept that neither Paul nor others among those to whom his Letter was read aloud shared the modern distinction (from Descartes onwards) that posits a radical difference between the immaterial and the material, between the spiritual and the physical,[147] he at once appears on the horizon of our understanding of the apostle as a materialist rather than a Platonist. It is materialism for the people, rather than Platonism for the people, that begins to take shape when our premise is that soul, body, spirit and flesh are not different types of material or of matter in Paul's thinking here. What contemporary Greeks found absurd was not, perhaps, the fact that Paul envisaged a state after death, for there were many ideas in folklore about what lay beyond death. For example, it might be a matter of dead persons who returned to this world.[148] But it appeared much more stupid to imagine that one of the lowest things in the societal hierarchy at that time, the bodily element, should live on. And it was presumably the stupidest idea of all to link this to a crucified man who had

---

[146] Brian McNeil's translation of ibid., 276.
[147] Martin, *The Corinthian Body*, 115.
[148] Ibid., 111.

been thrust by his humiliating death on a cross down to the very lowest rank in the societal hierarchy. This was indubitably "foolishness" (1.18).

For Paul, the bodily is more constant than the soul. This makes him a kind of materialist, as opposed to a Platonist who primarily linked the timeless and the constant to the existence of the soul. But certainly not everything was perpetual in the eyes of an apostle who does not avoid the recognition that human flesh and other flesh rot.[149] He surely knew the stench of a rotting corpse. But what is it in the person that lives on? Here, we encounter a boundary in Paul's conceptual world. What remains of the dead person after the resurrection is a mystery.[150] And this brings us back to Agamben's formulation. As he interprets Paul, there will come a resurrection of "the bodies of the just", and they will be "transformed" to "incorruptible spirit".[151] The resurrection entails a transformation (for the just, according to Agamben; so what about the rest?). Paul is not much more concrete than this.

To hell with the non-believers?

One central element in the Platonism for the people from which Nietzsche wants to liberate the human being was what he claimed as Paul's invention of "personal immortality". He depicts Paul as the brain behind the fear of the torment of hell and eternal pain in the next world, a fear that held sway for centuries, especially on the basis of the idea of predestination, which means that some people are damned in advance by God himself.

> Paul conceived the idea, and Calvin appropriated the idea, that countless numbers have from all eternity been condemned to damnation and that this lovely universal plan was thus instituted so that the glory of God might be revealed in it. Heaven and Hell and humanity are thus supposed to exist so as to – gratify the vanity of God! What a cruel and insatiable vanity must

---

[149] This is why Jorunn Økland insists that Paul speaks, not of the "resurrection of the bodies" (*sômatôn*), but of the "resurrection of the dead" (*nekrôn*). The Pauline formulation underlines discontinuity, while later dogmatic formulations underline continuity. The Pauline language leaves a greater unclarity about what it is that rises again; and this too is a hermeneutic strength. "The resurrection of the dead" calls for further interpretation.
[150] "Paul himself does not know this. He only calls it a mystery." Økland, "Sjelløs lesning".
[151] Agamben, *The Kingdom and the Glory: For a Theological Genealogy of Economy and Government (Homo Sacer Ii, 2)*, 249.

have flickered in the soul of him who first conceived or first appropriated such a thing!¹⁵²

Nietzsche claimed that for Paul, the resurrection is reserved to only a few,¹⁵³ some "elect" ones who themselves arrogantly look at the others with this feeling of an imaginary superiority.¹⁵⁴ They are in fact merely driven by a will to have power – a power that also enjoys imagining that others are damned.¹⁵⁵ Nietzsche maintains that more is involved here than damnation in the sense that one does not receive a share in the resurrection and eternal life, since Paul's idea of personal immortality entailed that those who did not believe and who therefore did not rise again were also immortal. This gave a new twist to the apostle's cunning strategy for controlling the masses.

> That heathen and not altogether un-Jewish addition of Hell became a welcome instrument in the hands of proselytisers: there arose the novel teaching of eternal damnation, and it was mightier than the idea of *definitive death*, which thereafter faded away.¹⁵⁶

A moral critique of the fear that could be generated by faith in divine promises or threats about punishment and reward in the next life was nothing new. More than a hundred years before this, David Hume in Scotland (1711-76) had put forward a similar critique of religion. He believed that he could trace a connection between the picture of a God who could demand anything at all of the believer, on the one hand, and the abandoning of the natural reason of the believer, on the other.

> The more tremendous the divinity is represented, the more tame and submissive do men become to his ministers; and the more unaccountable the measures of acceptance required by him, the more necessary it becomes

---

[152] Friedrich Nietzsche, *Human, All Too Human: A Book for Free Spirits*, 1993 ed. (Cambridge: Cambridge University Press, 1986), 331-2.
[153] *Daybreak: Thoughts on the Prejudices of Morality*, 44.
[154] According to Nietzsche, this contemplation or sight is also a part of Thomas Aquinas' vision of the next world, where the blessed in the kingdom of heaven are to see the punishment of the damned, in order that they may enjoy their own bliss even more strongly. Nietzsche, *The Essential Nietzsche: Beyond Good and Evil: The Genealogy of Morals*, 228.
[155] "What deliriums of the divine ascetic can be imagined when he creates sin and sinners and eternal damnation and a vast abode of eternal affliction and eternal groaning and sighing! – It is not altogether impossible that the souls of Dante, Paul, Calvin and their like may also once have penetrated the gruesome secrets of such voluptuousness of power." Nietzsche, *Daybreak: Thoughts on the Prejudices of Morality*, 114.
[156] Ibid., 73.

to abandon our natural reason, and yield to their ghostly guidance and direction.[157]

The picture of a deity who made irrational demands and threatened punishment if the human being did not obey him thus represented an interpretation of religion that justified a sharper distinction between faith and knowledge. The new element in Nietzsche's critique of religion was that he believed he could trace the origin of these ideas to the apostle Paul. But did they really come from Paul?

If we look for vivid pictures of the eternal torments that await the non-believers after death and that could have been the origin of the hateful and perverse enjoyment that Nietzsche believes he can identify in Paul and those like him, we will search in vain in the First Letter to the Corinthians, although ch. 15 is the most detailed exposition of what Paul believes will happen after death and in eternity. What we find here is his great cosmological vision of God's plan for the last times. But Nietzsche is not simply plucking things out of thin air. He finds aspects of the text on which he can base his speculations.

Paul's Letter is structured by a division between those who have received grace in Jesus Christ (1.4), who are called (1.9) and can stand without being accused when the end comes (1.8), on the one hand, and others, who will be lost (1.18). Those in Corinth who are called, who are not wise in the world's eyes and do not come from high-status families (1.26), can be understood as an election in keeping with God's plan to choose for himself the weak in order to "shame the strong" (1.27). This means that there is something incalculable in the choice God makes – an incalculability that Hume regarded with scepticism. And the picture of a deity who allows some to be lost can inspire fear. But the question of who is lost is not wholly arbitrary. "The message about the cross is foolishness to those who are perishing", and this can serve as a warning not to dismiss the whole message about a deeper meaning in Christ's cross. Accordingly, one is confronted by a choice; one is called to accept responsibility on the basis of a freedom. When Paul takes up anew the motif of perdition or condemnation, the divine judgment does not fall on anyone at random, but on "the rulers of this age". It is they who are "doomed to perish"

---

[157] David Hume, "The Natural History of Religion", in *Hume on Religion*, ed. Julian Baggini (London: Philosophy Press, 2010), 118.

(2.6). And they are not acting in a moral vacuum. On the contrary, they are guilty of the execution of one who was innocent, of Christ. "The rulers of this age" have "crucified the Lord of glory" (2.8). There is a thematic link from this passage to the description of the last times in 15.24, where Paul prophesies about God's final victory over his enemies, who include the rulers of this world who are responsible for Christ's crucifixion:

> Then comes the end, when he hands over the kingdom to God the Father, after he has destroyed every ruler and every authority and power. For he must reign until he has put all his enemies under his feet. The last enemy to be destroyed is death. For "God has put all things in subjection under his feet." But when it says, "All things are put in subjection," it is plain that this does not include the one who put all things in subjection under him. When all things are subjected to him, then the Son himself will also be subjected to the one who put all things in subjection under him, so that God may be all in all. (1 Cor. 15.24-28)

When the end comes, Christ, with the kingly power delegated to him by God, will wipe out powers and authorities, and hence also those who crucified him. Paul's God thus puts all these enemies "under his feet". He conquers them.[158]

Is Nietzsche right to allege that the idea of a definitive death fades away in Paul, in favour of a doctrine of the eternally damned, who are condemned to eternal tortures? In one word: No.[159] In this scenario, there is no eternal punishment of the damned. But there remains a final death, after death (so to speak) – quite to the contrary of Nietzsche's reading. And earlier on in the Letter, the apostle envisages a cleansing after death that will manifest what a human being has done on earth: this will come to light (1 Cor. 3.13). So does Nietzsche find this idea of eternal torment in other Letters?

Alan Badiou notes that the idea of hell plays no role in the Letters of Paul. Distributive or proportional justice in the legal sense, with a punishment for the sinners, is drowned out and suppressed by a motif of reconciliation that is

---

[158] "But what about those objects of God's wrath, both human and divine, against whom the apostle had also thundered? By the time that Paul reaches his paen of praise in Romans 11, the human sinners, whether pagans or Jews, seem excused: all humanity at the Parousia are saved." Paula Fredriksen, "The Question of Worship", in *Paul within Judaism: Restoring the First-Century Context to the Apostle*, ed. Magnus Zetterholm and Mark D. Nanos (Minneapolis: Fortress Press, 2015), 199.

[159] "The great chapter on the resurrection, 1 Corinthians 15, makes no mention at all of a judgment with a double outcome. Paul builds up his Adam-Christ typology on the same pattern." Jürgen Moltmann, *The Coming of God: Christian Eschatology* (London: SCM Press, 1996), 240-1.

governed by universal love.¹⁶⁰ Jacob Taubes points out that the Greek word for "everything" (*pas*) drives the argumentation throughout First Corinthians in the direction of the salvation of all things, which also include the non-believers in the people of Israel.¹⁶¹ Love will overcome all things (1 Corinthians 13). In this vision, God becomes "everything in everyone" (15.28), and no boundaries are posited for the world of salvation. There is thus a universal vision in Paul that is in tension with a message about exclusivity and the election of those who are called and believe. There is a perpetual tension in the Pauline argumentation, which is based on the existence of a small minority who believe in Christ ("you") and a religious revolution with universalist implications ("everything"), because the time has *now* come to integrate all the peoples into the salvation of history, which in the past was restricted to the election of the Jewish people. They are still enemies of God's will for the world: "Many live as enemies of the cross of Christ. Their end is destruction; their god is the belly; and their glory is in their shame; their minds are set on earthly things" (Phil. 3.18-19). Paul warns against the risk of perdition,¹⁶² but not because being lost entails eternal torment for a separate soul in a world after death. The apostle does not preach a Platonism for the people. But he preaches for the people. Indeed, believe it or not, Paul is purely a man of the people, or "idiotic", if one prefers that term.

Pauline idiocy

Alain Badiou presents Paul as an exemplary figure, because the apostle wages war for the truth without being armed with the artillery of rhetoric. Paul is described as an anti-philosopher because he brings explanations without relying on a philosophy that gives "wisdom" the priority as the central category

---

¹⁶⁰ Badiou, *Saint Paul: The Foundation of Universalism*, 94. Dale B. Martin, who is otherwise critical of aspects in Badiou's reading of Pauline universalism, agrees with the French philosopher on this point. Dale B. Martin, "The Promise of Teleology, the Constraints of Epistemology, and Universal Vision in Paul", in *St. Paul among the Philosophers*, ed. John D. Caputo and Linda Martín Alcoff (Bloomington: Indiana University Press, 2009), 93.

¹⁶¹ Taubes, *The Political Theology of Paul*, 25. Taubes' reading is based on a longer exposition of chs 9-11 in the Letter to the Romans. Like Taubes, the German theologian Jürgen Moltmann also points out that Rom 11:32 "embraces 'Jews and Gentiles' without abolishing the difference between them, or reducing it to uniformity". Moltmann, *The Coming of God: Christian Eschatology*, 241.

¹⁶² And as Moltmann writes, "... Paul also talks about a state of 'being lost' (apoleia) in Phil 3.19; I Cor 1.18; II Cor. 2.15, and elsewhere." *The Coming of God: Christian Eschatology*, 241.

and that is supported by rhetorical superiority.¹⁶³ And Paul makes it clear at the start of the Letter (1.17) that he is not sent to spread the message with the help of "eloquence" and "wisdom". The latter term denotes what he sees as an inadequate "wisdom of the world", as opposed to a saving "wisdom of God" (1.24). Paul emphasizes twice that he did not employ oratory when he preached to the Corinthians (2.1; 2.4), before saying that if anyone regards himself as wise, then let that person become a fool (*môros*), for it is only thus that one can become wise in the true sense (3.18). He goes even further in the Second Letter to the Corinthians, when he describes himself as an "idiot" (*idiôtês*) in speaking. When he describes himself in this way, he probably means that he is not an expert in the practical and public practice of rhetoric.¹⁶⁴ Paul was thus a completely ordinary person, since this expertise was reserved to the upper class in Corinth and other cities, where noble families could send their children to academies where rhetorical skills were practiced, especially with an eye to exercising influence in political assemblies and courtrooms. It was precisely the concern about this elite with its potentially seductive eloquence that led to the emergence at times of an alternative rhetorical strategy, where the speaker could accuse the opposite party of being unprincipled sophists who could not be trusted. But the speaker could also fight to get himself listened to, precisely as an ordinary man (*idiôtês*), by describing himself as an idiot with no training in rhetorical speaking techniques.¹⁶⁵ This made him (women were excluded from so-called democratic assemblies in antiquity) trustworthy, because he was not seducing the assembly – or simply because he was a man of the people (i.e. the free men). This helps us glimpse the contours of an ancient populism, a political discourse directed against the elite.

A recurrent theme in Plato is the dangerous and seductive rhetoric that can convince the people without championing the truth.¹⁶⁶ And in Badiou's interpretation, Paul becomes a Platonic hero who fights indefatigably for the truth without rhetorical tricks and who gives inspiration for the fight against the sophistry of our own time.¹⁶⁷ The scholar of Judaism Daniel

---

[163] Badiou, *Saint Paul: The Foundation of Universalism*, 27–8.
[164] Anna C. Miller, "Not with Eloquent Wisdom: Democratic Ekklesia Discourse in 1 Corinthians 1–4", *Journal for the Study of the New Testament* 35, no. 4 (2013): 333.
[165] Ibid.
[166] Plato, *Phaedrus*. Loeb Classical Library, 513–15.
[167] Vigdis Songe-Møller points to interesting similarities between Paul in Badiou's version and Plato. In Badiou's reading, Paul acquires Platonic traits. Vigdis Songe-Møller, "Metamorphosis and the

Boyarin reads Paul as an ancient sophist with a different premise than is customary in classical philosophy (which Badiou defends): sophistic rhetoric is not primarily a manipulative instrument.[168] Rhetoric is the unavoidable performative dimension in the articulation of every truth – and untruth. This is why its many forms can also be the expression of uncompromising fidelity to one's principles in the encounter with relativism.

Badiou does not see that positing an antithesis between foolishness and weakness, on the one hand, and wisdom and strength, on the other, is also a rhetorical maneuver from an unheard-of and shameful starting point, namely, the taboo language about the cross – in this case, the cross of Christ. When Paul admits that he is not especially eloquent, and then takes the role of a fool (*môros*), this need not be read as the invention of a new Christian discourse (as Badiou suggests) that is not indebted to Greek rhetoric. On the contrary, Paul's apparent admissions that he is an idiot in the general sense, and his declaration that he is a fool who is usually an object of ridicule, can be understood as a rhetorical strategy to break down the status of forms of wisdom that reject or laugh at the Pauline idea of the significance of the cross (1.18). At one moment, Paul takes the role of a fool (4.10), and at another moment, he rebukes the Corinthians (4.14) as if he possesses the authority to tell them how they are to think and to live. The admissions have nothing to do with an attitude of subjection. They display a hard-won charismatic authority that stands or falls with what he says in the epistolary form. The scriptural scholar Larry L. Welborn argues that the admissions contain a Socratic self-parody, a form known to intellectuals at that time that comes the closest to Paul's embrace of the role of a simple fool in First Corinthians.[169] Plato does little to hide the fact that Socrates (470-399) was sometimes regarded both by intellectuals and by ordinary people as a ridiculous fool, as for example in the *Gorgias*, where Callicles emphasizes how ridiculous Socrates appears in the eyes of the men of Athens.[170] The Socratic figure has taken the role of

---

Concept of Change", in *Metamorphoses: Resurrection, Body and Transformative Practices in Early Christianity*, ed. Turid Karlsen Seim and Jorunn Økland (Berlin: Walter de Gruyter, 2009), 120-1.

[168] Daniel Boyarin, "Paul among the Antiphilosophers; or, Saul among the Sophists", in *St. Paul among the Philosophers*, ed. John D. Caputo and Linda Martín Alcoff (Bloomington: Indiana University Press, 2009), 123.

[169] Larry L. Welborn, *Paul, the Fool of Christ: A Study of 1 Corinthians 1-4 in the Comic-Philosophic Tradition* (London and New York: T&T Clark International, 2005), 150.

[170] Plato, *Gorgias*. Loeb Classical Library, 391-3.

a naïve and ignorant man in order to bring out a greater self-awareness in his dialogue partners or to wrest from them their exaggerated pretensions to be already in possession of wisdom. There is a Socratic pedagogy in Paul's pedagogy, or something Pauline in the Socratic pedagogy. Something must be unlearnt in order to be learned. In the case of the apostle, this lesson is that the cross of Christ is not merely a grotesque meaninglessness. It is not merely a foolishness that one would be ashamed even to mention in a public context – as, for example, in a letter. It is indeed ridiculous to assert that the crucified one can save the world, and this is why the believers in Christ "have become a spectacle to the world" (4.9), where they play the role of "fools for the sake of Christ" (4.10). After stating that what appears to be foolishness in the eyes of the world is in reality the wisdom of God, Paul declares that he is a fool. A fool is a simple character who makes a fool of himself, and whom people therefore laugh at. He is ridiculous. But he is not wholly irrational, as if he were one who denied rational philosophy and science.

Welborn has shown how the reaction to the message about the crucified Christ slid from the original Pauline meaning, "foolishness" (*môria*), to a later meaning in the church fathers, namely "madness" (*mania*). For Greek speakers, the term used in First Corinthians had connotations of stupidity and ineptitude, rather than absurdity. The societal stigma entailed by the punishment inflicted on a slave meant that the message about the crucified Christ would sound in the ears of the intellectual elite more like a vulgar joke than as an idea that was inherently absurd or paradoxical.[171]

Conclusion: Philosophical perspectives on First Corinthians

So what contribution could Paul's ideas in the First Letter to the Corinthians make in modern philosophy?

For Nietzsche, Paul is useful as a target for his critique of religion, because the German philosopher assumes that the apostle is the great hindrance preventing the human being from taking on his or her new form as *Übermensch* and throwing Christianity onto the rubbish heap of history. The Pauline

---

[171] Welborn, *Paul, the Fool of Christ: A Study of 1 Corinthians 1-4 in the Comic-Philosophical Tradition*, 1-2.

exaltation of the weak, in the form of the crucified Jesus, is to be buried and forgotten once and for all. Taubes holds that the charges Nietzsche levels point to one of the most valuable elements in the inheritance from Paul. Through this new reading, Taubes leads Agamben to read Paul in the light of Walter Benjamin's messianism.

Alain Badiou regards Paul as the inspiration of a radically new politics. His reading of Paul does not take the form of a Platonism for the people – we recall that Nietzsche accused the apostle of being the origin of this – but the Frenchman's reading ends up in a Platonism for the radical elite on the extreme left wing. For Badiou, the true and the good can be cultivated in the subject's loyalty to the idea of the great event. Although Paul is meant to be the inspiration for a radical change of material circumstances, the outcome is nevertheless a strikingly idealistic philosophy of the subject. Badiou wants more class struggle in today's world, but he does not see any class conflict being played out in Paul's Letter to the Corinthians between the addressees of 1.26 (those who are neither wise, powerful, nor of noble birth) and the implicit addressees who regard the rhetorical eloquence acquired at upper-class schools as the most sublime sign of wisdom. Friedrich Nietzsche detected this conflict, and he took the side of the upper class against Paul.

Nietzsche's primary bone of contention with Paul's "invention" of the resurrection in 1 Corinthians 15 is that he employs this formula to erase the gospel's attentiveness to the earthly dimension and shifts the attention to a state after death.[172] Agamben accuses the church of having operated a similar shift down through the centuries by means of its theological machine. But according to philosophers such as Agamben, Critchley, Badiou and Žižek, Paul was not the brain behind this shift. On the contrary, the decline set in when the church became the official religion for an empire, and Platonism for the people could spread much more freely. But it is possible to look beyond this formerly powerful ecclesiastical institution and read Paul, who was critical of worldly power, as he expounds a line of thought that existed before a lid was put on the whole question.

---

[172] Nietzsche, *The Anti-Christ, Ecce Homo, Twilight of the Idols, and Other Writings*, 38.

3

The Letter to the Romans

Introspection and the quest for justice

The law was the cross to which he felt himself nailed:
how he hated it! How he had to drag it along!
How he sought for a means of destroying it –
and no longer fulfil it![1]

Friedrich Nietzsche in *Morgenröte* (1881)

Nietzsche describes Paul as a psychologically unstable type who before his conversion enforced the law more harshly than anyone else, while in reality he was exhausted by his attempt to observe the Jewish law. Paul switches from fanatical defence to the other extreme when he discovers that Jesus' death on the cross can become the pretext for release from observing the law – and indeed, for abolishing the law once and for all. This "notion" makes Paul "the happiest human being of all". He no longer needs to endeavour to observe the detailed prescriptions of the law; and best of all, he receives a power few can match. From now on, "the destiny of . . . all mankind" will be linked to his idea, which leads to a completely new doctrine.[2]

> From now on he is the teacher of the *destruction of the law*! To die to evil – that means also to exist in the law! To become one with Christ – that means also to become with him the destroyer of the law; to have died with him – that means also to have died to the law" (. . .) for the law existed so that sins might be committed, it continually brought sin forth as a sharp juice brings forth a disease.[3]

---

[1] *Daybreak: Thoughts on the Prejudices of Morality*, 40.
[2] *The Anti-Christ, Ecce Homo, Twilight of the Idols, and Other Writings*, 41.
[3] Ibid.

According to Nietzsche, Paul wants to eradicate the law, and this is why he preaches a message about an existence liberated from the flesh and hence free from the law. Through union with Christ, the Christian is to die to the law and abolish it with Christ. It is as if Nietzsche has read the proclamation in the Letter to the Romans: "You have died to the law through the body of Christ" (7.4). The idea that the law or the commandments cause sin, just as surely "as a sharp juice brings forth a disease", is also a logic that resembles what Paul in the same Letter describes as a tragic effect of a certain use of the law: "but when the commandment came, sin revived and I died" (7.9-10). Nietzsche never pokes fun at Paul's alleged wish to abolish the law or at the description of the relationship between the law and sin. The critic of religion seems to acknowledge the apostle's insights precisely on this point, and there is a certain admiration that is expressed in one of Nietzsche's writings: "All deeper people are of one mind about this – Luther, Augustine, Paul come to mind – that our morality and its events are not congruent with our *conscious will*."[4] Jacob Taubes remarks that Nietzsche arrives here at a point where he can see something of Paul's genius.[5] Moreover, on this exact point, Nietzsche's own utopian alternative to Paul's Christianity is uncannily similar to what the apostle declares. Nietzsche's *Übermensch* is to give free rein to his natural instincts, detached from every external law. His gospel is a message that emphasizes pleasure, for those who are "of a higher station" and today's "upper classes" who do not accept that concern for the weak should set any boundaries to what they want to do.

But the Nietzschean gospel about freedom from the law for the *Übermensch* is also an indication that, culturally speaking, Nietzsche remained a Protestant.

The introspection of the West and the climax of the Letter to the Romans

In 1963, Krister Stendahl published the essay "The Apostle Paul and the Introspective Conscience of the West" in the *Harvard Theological Review*.[6] The

---

[4] Nietzsche quoted in Taubes, *The Political Theology of Paul*, 87.
[5] "For what he [Nietzsche] finds horrifying, and this is a very humane concern, is the cruelty of the pang of conscience. The conscience that can't be evaded. Romans 7, right?" Ibid.
[6] The text was later reprinted in the collection of essays *Paul among Jews and Gentiles and Other Essays* (1976); page references are to this edition.

Swedish theologian argued against the general Protestant idea that the doctrine of justification by faith alone, which was Martin Luther's great discovery in Paul's Letter to the Romans, was the answer to the human being's problem when one turned one's gaze into one's own self. In this Protestant logic, the need for God's forgiveness would become urgent when the human being was completely honest and recognized his or her individual sins – which existed and were numerous. The more deeply one looked into oneself, the more quickly would one know that one was a sinner. This bad conscience would then prepare the unconverted person to accept Jesus' forgiveness, which was seen as the very core of Christian salvation.

Paul was a model for this introspection, the distressed conscience and the conversion to Christianity's God. Much of Protestant Christendom had learned that the apostle's conversion was a climax in a lengthy spiritual struggle in the inner life of his soul. This is reflected in ch. 7 as the climax in the drama Paul describes in the Letter to the Romans. This conversion came through the experience that no one could live up to the Jewish law. And this meant that every moral self-satisfaction was crushed by the law, which thereafter took on an exclusively negative meaning: the fact that the human being could not experience grace in the legal Jewish piety made him or her only all the more desperate for the Christian salvation in Jesus. The conversion to the Christian faith was thus interpreted as a definitive breach with a Jewish form of stiff ritualism and narrow-minded legalism, which had characterized a religion in spiritual decline. Paul had replaced a misunderstood Jewish obedience to the letter of the law with the Christian spirit of freedom.

As a Protestant clergyman, Stendahl knew this Christian train of thought from the inside. This made it all the more interesting that he, as a Lutheran theologian, obstinately claimed that something completely different was found in Paul's Letters. First of all, he maintained that there was nothing at all in those texts to support the idea that Paul himself had been tormented by a bad conscience for not observing the Jewish law.[7] Second, forgiveness was the metaphor or model for salvation that Paul employed with the least frequency in his Letters.[8] Third, in the case of the Jewish Pharisee, one cannot speak of

---

[7] Stendahl, *Paul among Jews and Gentiles and Other Essays*, 80.
[8] Ibid., 82.

a Christian conversion, but of a call like that of the Old Testament prophets.[9] And fourth, chs 9-11 are the climax of the Letter to the Romans – not ch. 7.[10] If one accepts this critique of Protestant readings of Paul, very central premises for parts of Protestant theology will collapse, and an almost new branch of research can arise. And this is what happened. In the wake of the Holocaust, Christian theologians entered into dialogue with Jewish theologians to a much greater extent than in the past, and the way lay open to understand Paul as a child of the Judaism of his period rather than a child of the Christianity of later periods. Few texts have had an influence on modern Pauline scholarship comparable to that of Stendahl's brief, fifteen-page essay.[11]

Paul's longest Letter, and probably his last, begins and closes with explanations of why the apostle has not come to Rome. This is thus a text that the author has written without knowing the addressees personally, and this may make it more important him to get them to understand the mission he hopes to carry out in Rome, and later in Spain (15.24). Accordingly, the argumentation is lengthier and more elaborate. The motif of Christ's death and resurrection, with a significance of cosmic proportions, is absolutely central. People have lived in profound unrighteousness, slaves of the power of sin; but through the death and resurrection of the Messiah, God's justice has been revealed (1.17), and it is given to the one who believes (3.22) that the crucified Jesus is the Messiah and that he has been raised from the dead. Paul describes this divine intervention as an act of supererogation in response to a sin that was great, an act that shows that grace is even greater (5.20). The believer is set free from the power of sin, in order to live in the Spirit. This new life leads to a righteousness (6.16) that is characterized as being "disclosed apart from the law" (3.21), that is to say, the law of the Jews. Although Jews and Greeks have lived under different circumstances (1.17), both the Jews and the non-Jewish peoples are equal before God (2.12-16). This divine impartiality is a leitmotiv in chs. 9-11 when Paul interprets the Christ event in the light of God's special history with his chosen people. In chs 12-15, Paul gives ethical instructions

---

[9] Ibid., 84-5.
[10] Ibid., 85.
[11] Representatives of the dominant scholarly currents "The New Perspective" and "Paul within Judaism" often pay tribute to Stendahl for initiating the paradigm shifts they claim to have developed further in Pauline scholarship. See, for example, Magnus Zetterholm and Mark D. Nanos, *Paul within Judaism: Restoring the First-Century Context to the Apostle* (Minneapolis: Fortress Press, 2015), 3.

to the believers, before the Letter closes with a summary of his travel plans (15.14-33) and personal greetings (16.23).

A wholly conventional rhetorical analysis of the Letter treats 1.16-17 as its principal thesis, backed up by three arguments. First, the righteousness of faith has been given by God's grace because of sin in the world (1.18-4.25). Second, the life in the Spirit of the believers in Christ bears witness to peace with God, who is the author of righteousness (5.1-8.39). And third, God's righteousness, to which the promises in the past pointed, has prevailed through the victory of the gospel among both Jews and non-Jews (9.1-11.36).[12]

According to Stendahl, Paul was misunderstood because he was read as if his writings were the expression of the apostle's perennially valid introspection into human nature. Instead of reading Paul's discussions of the meaning of the Jewish law as primarily anthropological insights, they ought to be understood as answers to much more restricted and historically conditioned questions: What is the status of the law of Moses, now that the Messiah has come? What does the coming of the Messiah mean for the relationship between Jews and Gentiles?[13]

Stendahl thus wants to restrict what Paul writes in ch. 7 to these more delimited historical problems, rather than have the Pauline formulations supply answers to timeless questions about the human being's nature or sinfulness. In order to explain why the history of reception has almost run wild and allowed the Letter to the Romans to be regarded as the gateway into the deepest and darkest sides of human nature, Stendahl offers a strange argument: Paul simply wrote too well![14] Expressions in ch. 7 such as "I do not do the good I want, but the evil I do not want is what I do" (7.19) are thus so well-written that later readers take them as expressions of a universal human experience – and thereby misunderstand. In such formulations, according to Stendahl, Paul wanted to say how badly things go with a Gentile (a non-Jew) who attempts to express obedience to Christ by obeying the law or so-called

---

[12] One of the most extensive commentaries on Romans in the past decades operates with this conventional division of the Letter. Robert Jewett, *Romans: A Commentary* (Minneapolis: Fortress Press, 2007).
[13] Stendahl, *Paul among Jews and Gentiles and Other Essays*, 84.
[14] "Unfortunately – or fortunately – Paul happened to express this supporting argument so well that what to him and his contemporaries was a common sense observation appeared to later interpreters to be the most penetrating insight into the nature of man and into the nature of sin." Ibid., 93.

"works prescribed by the law" (3.28).[15] The apostle is seeking to justify a set of regulations for persons who are not Jews and who join the fellowships of believers in Christ that have grown up in the Roman Empire – and now also in the very heart of the Empire.

This problem no longer exists today. The Christian churches do not see great numbers of believers in Christ without a Jewish background who want to follow the detailed commandments of the law of Moses! Does this then mean that Paul's well-written textual passages from the Letter to the Romans are now out of date?

If one chooses to ignore Stendahl's injunctions, reject his interpretations and see ch. 7 in the Letter as an expression of the perennial human problem in the encounter with the law as a universal (and not exclusively Jewish) phenomenon in every culture and society, it becomes possible to read Paul in completely different ways. And it is precisely this that some of the most prominent representatives of modern psychoanalysis have done.

The despairing "I" in ch. 7 who laments: "I do not do the good I want, but the evil I do not want is what I do" (7.19) is then read not only as Paul's depiction of a non-Jew in the first century who – quite unnecessarily, as Paul sees it – has got entangled in the prohibitions and commandments of the law of Moses – a law that is meant to apply only to Jews.[16] On the contrary, this "I" is read as a reflection of a universal human experience of the law. The experience of sin in this chapter points to an inclination to break the law that is transmitted from generation to generation, from father to son, from mother to child – in other words, an inherited inclination. In Christian dogmatics, this is called "original sin".

From Paul to Freud – and back

On one of the rare occasions when Nietzsche praises Paul as a man of deep thought, this is due to the apostle's insight that our moral conduct of life

---

[15] An influential scholar who maintains this view of ch. 7, and is inspired by Krister Stendahl, is Stanley Stowers.

[16] Many of the formulations in Paul's Letters, and especially in Romans, suggest that even Jews who came to belief in Christ ought (unlike the Gentile believers) to continue to follow the prescriptions of the law of Moses.

does not coincide with our conscious will. Nietzsche regarded this lack of convergence, not as sin in the Christian sense, but as the expression of instincts. Sigmund Freud took over this view of the human being as one governed by instincts and developed it into a theory about the human unconscious. Freud's wish to strengthen the ego through psychoanalytic therapy was due precisely to a supposition that unconscious forces, by means (for example) of the superego, controlled the human being more than was necessary and desirable. Psychoanalysis thus operated with a supposition that it was possible to attain a greater autonomy through therapy and that such a liberation of the human being was desirable as part of a modern progressive project in which the human being conquered a larger measure of control over nature – including human nature. But where Nietzsche's gospel of freedom from the law meant the expression of the natural instincts, Freud held that a certain amount of suppression of them was necessary for the ego and that persistent conflicts between nature (instinct) and culture (norm) were inevitable.[17] All the same, while it was Nietzsche who came in order to abolish the law, Freud's project consisted in suspending the law. And now, what was to be made inoperable was not the law of Moses, but demands that produced neuroses, as well as petit-bourgeois norms.

Freud has usually been regarded as an atheist,[18] but he had an ambivalent relationship to religion.[19] On the one hand, he writes like a typical modern critic of religion who regards religious ideas as illusions. Freud thought that he had uncovered the genesis of religion as the result of an infantile experience of helplessness and a subsequent need for protection by one's father.[20] This longing for a protective father figure was then projected onto the idea of a God the Father. If the human being could be treated for the neuroses that were the consequence of these childhood experiences, he or she could also get rid of numerous religious aberrations.

---

[17] Siri Erika Gullestad, "Arven Fra Freud", *Nytt norsk tidsskrift* 23, no. 4 (2006): 319.
[18] William B. Parsons, *Freud and Religion: Advancing the Dialogue* (Cambridge: Cambridge University Press, 2021), 105.
[19] For an interesting discussion of Freud's relationship to Judaism, see Jacques Derrida, *Archive Fever: A Freudian Impression,* trans. Eric Prenowitz (Chicago: University of Chicago Press, 1996), 33-81.
[20] "The derivation of religious needs from the infant's helplessness and the longing for the father aroused by it seems to me incontrovertible..." Sigmund Freud, *The Future of an Illusion: Civilization and Its Discontents, and Other Works: (1927-1931),* ed. James Strachey and Anna Freud, vol. 21, The Standard Edition of the Complete Psychological Works of Sigmund Freud (London: Hogarth Press and the Institute of Psycho-analysis, 1961), 72.

Human feelings of guilt often had their origin in an obsessional submission to the commandments and rituals of religion. The less religion, the fewer unhealthy guilt complexes would arise. On the other hand, Freud also claimed that there was a forgotten patricide in primeval times that had also generated an ineradicable guilt. In *Totem und Tabu* (1913), he had already shown his fascination with the Christian doctrine of original sin,[21] which he regarded as a distorted form of guilt feelings that arose after the original patricide in Freud's imagined primeval times. Behind such religious distortions, Freud saw more than merely worthless illusions. He also held that he could identify important progress in the history of religion. One such privileged moment is the appearance on the scene of the apostle Paul, which Freud describes in his book *Moses and Monotheism*:

> It seems that a growing feeling of guiltiness had seized the Jewish people and perhaps the whole of civilization of that time as a precursor of the return of the repressed material. This went on until a member of the Jewish people, in the guise of a political-religious agitator, founded a doctrine which – together with another one, the Christian religion – separated from the Jewish one. Paul, a Roman Jew from Tarsus, seized upon this feeling of guilt and correctly traced it back to its primaeval source. This he called original sin; it was a crime against God that could be expiated only through death. Death had come into the world through original sin. In reality this crime, deserving of death, had been the murder of the Father who later was deified. The murderous deed itself, however, was not remembered; in its place stood the phantasy of expiation and that is why this phantasy could be welcomed in the form of a gospel of salvation (Evangel). A Son of God, innocent himself, had sacrificed himself and had thereby taken over the guilt of the world.[22]

The expiation that Paul proclaimed in the death of Christ was thus a distortion that pointed to a real feeling of guilt, although the message about salvation was a fantasy. Paul derived the consciousness of guilt in the correct direction, from the patricide, although this happened through the return of the memory from the unconscious. And not least, Paul's confession was a veritable breakthrough for Freud. As long as the suppressed grudge against the father figure had

---

[21] *Totem and Taboo, and Other Works: (1913-1914)*, ed. James Strachey and Anna Freud, vol. 13, The Standard Edition of the Complete Psychological Works of Sigmund Freud (London: Hogarth Press and the Institute of Psycho-analysis, 1958), 153-4.
[22] *Moses and Monotheism*, 42.

no release, the guilt feeling simply accumulated new strata in the history of religion and caused new obsessional neuroses. While Judaism lacked an open channel for hatred of the primeval father figure, Paul shattered the parameters with his insight that the patricide must be openly confessed and expiated:

> Although food for the idea had been provided by many suggestive hints from various quarters, it was, nevertheless, in the mind of a Jew, Saul of Tarsus, who as a Roman citizen was called Paul, that the perception dawned: "it is because we killed God the Father that we are so unhappy." It is quite clear to us now why he could grasp this truth in no other form but in the delusional guise of the glad tidings: "we have been delivered from all guilt since one of us laid down his life to expiate our guilt."[23]

Paul's theology thus contained truths, in a distorted form, that Judaism had withheld. These are surprising assertions on the part of the father of psychoanalysis, who was himself a Jew and who had begun the book *Moses and Monotheism* after the Nazis took power in 1933. This work was meant as an answer to the questions why the Jews steadfastly retained throughout history their characteristics as an ethnic group, and why they had been the object of so much hatred.[24] Freud's psychoanalytical look at religion seldom resulted in an acknowledgment of religious authorities in history. On the contrary, his concern was to pull down the religious heroes from their throne, for example, by speculating that Moses was no Jew at all. But when the psychoanalyst comes to Paul, he cannot conceal his admiration for what he regards as the apostle's brutal honesty. The philosopher Jacob Taubes, who spent his childhood as a Jew in Freud's native city, Vienna in Austria, goes even further.[25] He has proposed the daring thesis that Freud

---

[23] Ibid., 65.
[24] Sigmund Freud's theory of the denial of the patricide and the apostle's contrasting honesty about the same murder are appallingly problematic in the light of the history of Anti-Semitism: "The poor Jewish people, who with its usual stiff-necked obduracy continued to deny the murder of their father, has dearly expiated this in the course of centuries. Over and over again they heard the reproach: you killed our God. And this reproach is true, if rightly interpreted. It says, in reference to the history of religion: you won't admit that you murdered God (the archetype of God, the primaeval Father and his reincarnations). Something should be added, namely: 'It is true, we did the same thing, but we admitted it, and since then we have been purified." Ibid., 44. Scholars have attempted to come to terms with the historical speculations about Moses in *Moses and Monotheism* by referring to the cultural pressure under which German-speaking Jews lived in the years prior to the publication of Freud's book in 1939. Santner, "Freud's Moses", 58.
[25] Taubes' family moved to Switzerland in 1935, after his father was appointed chief rabbi there. In this way, Jacob Taubes and his closest family escaped the Nazi persecutions and the gas chambers. Freud escaped to London shortly afterwards.

not only admired Paul, but also identified with him – especially thanks to a common endeavour to come to terms with the human guilt complex.[26] Taubes applied some of Freud's psychologization on Freud himself: "It is not a matter of sheer speculation that Freud conceived his work, his theory, and therapy, in analogy to the message Paul preached to the Gentiles",[27] Taubes claims, in his recognizably provocative manner, in the essay "Religion and the Future of Psychoanalysis" (1957).[28] Taubes is certainly aware that his comparison of Freud with Paul can provoke psychoanalysts who have a critical attitude to religion and want to keep Christianity and other religions at arm's length in order to legitimate psychoanalysis as a completely secular science. But if Freud's psychoanalysis is to be counted as a modern science, we must at any rate note that this scientific discipline has religious roots and operates with a secularized concept of sin. It then seems that psychoanalysis, which has been both praised and criticized for being "a Jewish science", most strongly resembles the pillars of Christianity, according to Taubes:

> Never since Paul and Augustine has a theologian taught a more radical doctrine of original guilt than Freud. No one since Paul has so clearly perceived and so strongly emphasized the urgent need to atone for the act of original guilt as has Freud.[29]

The Christian idea of original sin has largely been read out of the fifth chapter of the Letter to the Romans. When Paul writes that "sin came into the world through one man" (5.12), this evokes associations with the first human being who sinned: Adam in the Garden of Eden (Gen. 3.6). The apostle sets up the picture of Christ as the antitype to Adam: "for just as by one man's disobedience the many were made sinners, so by the one man's obedience the many will be made righteous" (5.19). The old Adam is contrasted with the new Adam through Christ's sinless example. The concept of sin in this passage can lead to differing understandings of the power of sin over human beings in the course of history. For example, it may be an original sin that is, as it were,

---

[26] "I want to defend the claim that Freud, who is involved with the basic experience of guilt, is a direct descendant of Paul." Taubes, *The Political Theology of Paul*, 89.
[27] *From Cult to Culture: Fragments Towards a Critique of Historical Reason*, 337.
[28] The essay is printed in its original (English-language) form in ibid., 334-41.
[29] Ibid., 337.

sin's *primus motor* or the emphasis may lie on the universal character of sin, both in terms of human beings' participation in sin and in terms of the reach of sin's destructive impact; but it can also be a question of an "original sin" more as Augustine understands it, which transmits the "contamination" in a biological sense.[30]

Taubes remarked that Freud's psychoanalysis encountered great resistance precisely because it was regarded as such a revolutionary theory. But many of the intellectuals who gladly looked forward to the social revolution that psychoanalysis would implement were disappointed. The belief in progress was dimmed when many grasped Freud's view of the human being: namely, that no one can escape the shadow of the past. Even if societal structures were to be transformed, the human being in Freud's picture would nevertheless be driven by forces with a destructive potential:

> Even in the new society man remained the old Adam possessed by his drives and instincts, unredeemed from his lusts, and therefore even more apt to stumble into barbarism when the conservative fences around the political order were removed.[31]

According to Taubes, therefore, there was also a conservative element in psychoanalysis that it shared with religion, namely, the pessimistic anthropology that was articulated in the ideas of each of these about an original guilt or original sin. This meant that the Pauline message was more optimistic than the Freudian, since the apostle claimed that human guilt could be expiated and overcome through the suffering of one human being. Freud rejected this positive message as an illusion and maintained instead that guilt could only be admitted. But Freud finds that, precisely in the implicit admission in Paul's message, there also lies a step in the right direction, towards liberation.[32] Both forms of therapy, the Pauline and the Freudian, presuppose (according to Taubes) that the human being must confront the

---

[30] In one of Paul's contemporaries, Philo of Alexandria, we encounter an anthropology that links the desire for pleasure with generation and therefore with the flesh – which, according to Gitte Buch-Hansen, may constitute a pre-conception of Augustine's doctrine of original sin. Anthropological ideas similar to those of Philo provide a relevant background for reading Paul's Letters – above all Romans 7 and Galatians 2. Gitte Buch-Hansen, "Beyond the New Perspective: Reclaiming Paul's Anthropology", *Studia Theologica* 71, no. 1 (2017): 139.
[31] Taubes, *From Cult to Culture: Fragments Towards a Critique of Historical Reason*, 335.
[32] Ibid., 338.

past. History must be worked upon, in order to come to true insights about oneself. It is simply not the case that the human being can contemplate eternal ideas, without taking the path through history.[33] This is why Taubes also sees both therapies as Jewish sciences. And as Kenneth Reinhard adds, Freud takes on Paul's role and continues the apostle's endeavours to lighten the burden of the law.[34] It is impossible to predict when the believer (that is, the one who believes in psychoanalysis or in the therapist) will experience the lightening of the burden. This can happen in a second, in an exceptional or miraculous awakening in a long stream of associations and stories from one's own life. Or, as Eric Santner puts it, if there is a Jewish element in psychoanalysis, it is that the healing or cure is an *exodus* that departs, not only from Pharaoh's Egypt but from every form of "Egyptomania".[35]

One effect of the miraculous moment in the treatment can be the loosening of knots in the patient's life. But there will always be other knots that are very tight in a human life. We always return to the evasions and the suppression of the underlying wishes that are buried deep in the unconscious. This is why this *exodus* from Egyptomania is not a triumphant march that can enter into a sinless Promised Land – the knots are too tight, the unconscious forces are too strong, and the power of the law is too great.

In ch. 6 of the Letter to the Romans, Paul proclaims: "now that you have been freed from sin" (6.22), as if the might of sin had been forced to capitulate to the power in the transformation of the old Adam into the new human being in Christ. But when the following chapter presents an ego that remains stuck in knots tightened by the grip of sin and the law on the human will, it does not seem that the liberation from sin is complete. The tragedy in the drama in Romans can appear perennial, even in the life of the believer, who must turn anew in desperation to Christ: "Wretched man that I am! Who will rescue me from this body of death? Thanks be to God through Jesus Christ our Lord!" (7.24-25).

---

[33] *The Political Theology of Paul*, 90. We should note that while Taubes emphasized the tragic and pessimistic aspects of psychoanalysis in his 1957 essay, his Heidelberg lectures thirty years later see more of the messianic potential for transformation in the same theory by Freud.

[34] Kenneth Reinhard, "Paul and the Political Love of the Neighbour", in *Paul and the Philosophers*, ed. Ward Blanton and Hent de Vries (New York: Fordham University Press, 2013), 461.

[35] Eric L. Santner, *On the Psychotherapy of Everyday Life: Reflections on Freud and Rosenzweig* (Chicago: University of Chicago Press, 2001), 45.

The name of the father – how the law is inscribed on the mind

Taubes mentioned the opposition that psychoanalysis encountered because of its radical character. The opposition came not least from religious circles, and it is perhaps not surprising that only a few Christian theologians entered into dialogue with a thinking that reduces faith to a reflex of an infantile feeling of impotence – a feeling that adults really ought to grow out of. One of the few theologians who saw the parallels between Paul and Freud to which Taubes refers was Paul Tillich (1886-1965), who held that the insights of psychoanalysis were a gift to theology, although he did not adopt Freud's postulates uncritically. Like Taubes, Tillich pointed to something of the unresolved tension between psychoanalysis' pessimistic view of human nature and its optimistic promise of offering treatment to the human person and to culture.[36] It is also interesting that Tillich's theological reflections on psychoanalysis occur when he reads the Letter to the Romans. When one draws on the insights of psychoanalysis, Paul's words about the relationship between flesh, law and spirit also have a place for modern psychological distinctions between the conscious and the unconscious, the ego and the superego, beginning already with childhood's early internalization of norms:

> If we receive a law which we must acknowledge and which, on the other hand, we cannot fulfill, our soul inevitably develops hatred against him who has given the law. The father, being the representative of the law which stands against the child's desire, necessarily becomes the object of the child's unconscious hate, which may become conscious and may appear with tremendous force. This would not be so if the law against its unordered and unrestricted desire were felt by the child to be arbitrary and unjustified. But it is felt to be justified. It has become part of the child's "super-ego," as recent psychology would say.[37]

If a law is imposed upon us, Tillich writes – with the reservation that human beings' situations are very diverse. But according to the psychoanalysts, this law is imposed upon us whether we like it or not, whether or not we even think about it. One of Freud's most significant and innovative successors was the Frenchman Jacques Lacan (1901-80). For Lacan, the Law is the sum total

---

[36] Paul Tillich, *Theology of Culture* (Oxford and London: Oxford University Press, 1959), 120.
[37] *The Shaking of the Foundations* (London: SCM Press, 1949), 133-4.

of the commandments and prohibitions of a society. A child is socialized into this Law when it enters into language between the ages of two and three.[38] When the child enters into this linguistic fellowship, it is subjected to the Law in the form both of the conditions that make communication possible and of the values of its culture. This means that the Law has us in its grip at an earlier stage than our memory can take us back to.

Like the theologian Tillich, the psychoanalyst Lacan saw that there is a father figure who represents the Law. Although Lacan's theory is not dependent on a traditional nuclear family for the description of the dynamic, there is a third party that takes its place between mother and child and represents the law of societal ordering. The entrance of this third party coincides with the child's subjection in language. The "father" establishes the law through a repeated "No!" that sets limits to the child's desire and shatters the pre-linguistic symbiosis between mother and child, in which the child does not experience any difference between its own self and the breast or the mother's body. This means that the effect of the Law is separation and alienation for every human being.

While Freud's ideas were spread through his writings, Lacan had a great influence through his seminars. In his seminar in 1959, about what he called the ethics of psychoanalysis, he included the apostle Paul in his canon of thinkers who could shed light on Freud's mysterious discoveries about the human mind. Instead of taking the route via Freud's interpretation of Paul in *Moses and Monotheism,* Lacan goes straight to the source. He was reasonably certain that the participants in the seminar would know whose voice he was borrowing, when he began to paraphrase Paul:

> Is the Law the Thing? Certainly not. Yet I can only know of the Thing by means of the Law. In effect, I would not have had the idea to covet it if the Law hadn't said: "Thou shalt not covet it." But the Thing finds a way of producing in me all kinds of covetousness thanks to the commandment, for without the Law the Thing is dead. But even without the Law, I was once alive. But when the commandment appeared, the Thing flared up, returned once again, I met my death. And for me, the commandment that was supposed to lead to life turned out to lead to death, for the Thing found

---

[38] Svein Haugsgjerd, *Å møte psykisk smerte* (Oslo: Gyldendal, 2018), 183.

a way and thanks to the commandment seduced me; through it I came to desire death.

> I believe that for a little while now some of you at least have begun to suspect that it is no longer I who have been speaking. In fact, with one small change, namely, "Thing" for "sin", this is the speech of Saint Paul on the subject of the relations between the law and sin in the Epistle to the Romans, Chapter 7, paragraph 7. . . . The relationship between the Thing and the Law could not be better defined than in these terms. . . The dialectical relationship between desire and the Law causes our desire to flare up only in relation to the Law, through which it becomes the desire for death. It is only because of the Law that sin . . . takes on an excessive, hyperbolic character. Freud's discovery – the ethics of psychoanalysis – does it leave us clinging to that dialectic?[39]

First of all, Lacan recommends the students to study in-depth religious texts – that is to say, those that are good (for not all religious texts are good).[40] Among these, Paul occupies a special position: "Saint Paul's Epistle is a work that I recommend to you for your vacation reading; you will find it a very good company."[41] Second, Lacan believes that there is no better definition or exposition of the relationship between the "Thing" and the Law than ch. 7 of the Letter to the Romans. And third, Lacan replaces the Pauline "sin" with the "Thing", a concept from his own psychoanalytic vocabulary. To borrow the language of the literary scholar Roland Barthes, Lacan constructs in this way an "intertext" in which another text is present. Barthes claims that all texts are intertexts of this kind, where old texts are present in new ones in ways that are more or less recognizable. With his light paraphrase, Lacan has created "a new web of past quotations".[42]

The passage that Lacan paraphrases here is a break in style in Romans, because Paul switches from the second-personal plural to the singular: "I". He displays an "I" who undergoes various experiences. Against the background of these genuine or fictitious experiences, the "I" reflects on complicated and contradictory relationships between law, desire and sin. "What then should we say? That the law is sin? By no means!" (7.7) is a recapitulation of the motif

---

[39] Jacques Lacan, *The Ethics of Psychoanalysis, 1959-1960: The Seminar of Jacques Lacan*, vol. VII (London and New York: Routledge, 2008), 102-3.
[40] Ibid., 102.
[41] Ibid., 103.
[42] Barthes, quoted in Prafulla C. Kar and Paul St-Pierre, *In Translation: Reflections, Refractions, Transformations* (Amsterdam: Benjamins, 2007), 125.

expounded earlier in the Letter, with an almost identical rhetorical form, of the relationship between the believer in Christ and the law: "Do we then overthrow the law by this faith? By no means! On the contrary, we uphold the law" (3.31). Faith leads to righteousness, which is a divine righteousness "disclosed...apart from law" (3.21), but although the value of the law is relative in relation to God's righteousness, Paul confirms that the law is to remain. However, the apostle has hinted in 5.20 that there is a strange relationship between sin and law, when he writes: "Law came in, with the result that the trespass multiplied." And just before the verses that fascinate Lacan, Paul has taken this logic between law and sin one step deeper: "While we were living in the flesh, our sinful passions, aroused by the law, were at work in our members to bear fruit for death" (7.5).[43]

The "Thing" is one of the most enigmatic concepts in Lacan. It is striking to note that it is replaced, later in his reading of the Letter to the Romans, by "desire", which gives a clue to what Lacan means. He operates with three different openings onto reality for the human being. The "imaginary" is the pre-linguistic level on which we mirror things, imagine them and picture them to ourselves without words or a linguistic fellowship. While "the name of the father" is an aspect of the societal ordering, and thus belongs to what Lacan calls the "symbolic", the "Thing" belongs to another and less tangible dimension that he calls the real. There are thus three levels: the imaginary, the symbolic, and the real.[44]

If the "Thing" is the same as "sin" in the Pauline sense, and this term can be replaced by "desire", an obvious interpretation of the "Thing" that Lacan reads into the Letter to the Romans is to see it as a sphere of transgressions of the Law, or as things that we seize in our desire without letting ourselves be stopped by moral considerations. But if we accept both that we cannot actually "grasp" the "Thing" (since the real lies outside language), and that it cannot be tied down empirically to any place or time, since the real is just as inaccessible as the Kantian *Ding an sich*, it follows that desire must be something that has not been experienced hitherto. Or else there must be a desire that is antecedent to memory and language, something we have lost en route to our entry into the symbolic and into the underlying subjection to the law that alienates us

---

[43] Jennings, *Outlaw Justice: The Messianic Politics of Paul*, 111.
[44] Svein Haugsgjerd, *Lidelsens karakter i ny psykiatri* (Oslo: Pax, 1990), 43-8.

from our original desire. The pre-linguistic needs-oriented desire is, in turn, inseparably linked to the Other's desire: in other words, what the child has perceived as the mother's desire, which continues to cast shadows in the child's life. The desire that is awakened in us when the law says: "You shall not desire" can lie behind us in the past and ahead of us in the future, but we have no direct access to it. It is a part of the often disturbing reality around us that affects our psyche, although we cannot remember it (the past) or predict it (the future) – the real. As the Norwegian psychiatrist Svein Haugsgjerd puts it, psychoanalytic therapy is meant to open up what he calls the room of desire.

Haugsgjerd describes this as a room where the patient grasps that a complete satisfaction of desire will never be attained in this life. It is therefore important to grasp that this is the case, and to enjoy the freedom that lies in the movement through life, always driven by something unattainable. As Haugsgjerd interprets Lacan, the goal of analysis is to get in contact with one's desire. What Lacan has in mind is not the realization that one has one determined, fixed, instinctive wish, which is one's own psychological signature, but rather the hope that the one who begins psychoanalysis will be able to put words to his or her wishes and recognize that the desire, in this sense, will never come to an end. The instinct moves *towards* its goal and then circles *around it*, without ever hitting the target. One moves from the domain of illusions to the realm where one speaks, and where "the goal is the way". In other words, the truth about the desire comes to light when one "crosses the fantasies". This means talking one's way through the wilderness of the illusions into clarity about oneself as free and responsible.[45]

If we do not know the Thing without the law, it is reasonable to think that the Lacanian psychoanalyst who is speaking in ch. 7 of the Letter to the Romans is telling us that all the prohibitions and commandments in the ordering of society quite simply make us aware that we are beings who desire. We then come into what Lacan calls a dialectical relationship between desire and law, where we break the law because something in the law wakens in us the desire to break it. And sin thereby assumes such exaggerated forms that it becomes a "desire unto death", that is to say, a desire that lies beyond the pleasure principle that Freud taught us about when he said that the human

---

[45] *Å møte psykisk smerte*, 187.

being usually lived in accordance with this principle, in order to maximize the experience of pleasure and minimize unpleasure.[46] Lacan's Paul is describing here a psychological dynamic that is less primitive and less hedonistic than the dynamic that leads us quite simply to break laws and rules for our own gain or our survival: this is a psychological logic that leads us into a desire to break the law, a desire that does not really profit us, and a desire over which we do not have full control. This is no longer a transgression of the law for our own egotistic benefit, but a potentially self-destructive pattern generated by a "desire unto death" or (to use Freud's concept) the "death drive". For the Thing seduced me thanks to the commandment, and through the commandment I came to desire death, says Lacan with Paul.

First of all, therefore, the ego became aware of its desire through being confronted by the law. Next, a desire that cannot be reduced to the satisfaction of needs was awakened. Then this was driven into a dialectical movement between law and desire. This can be understood as a psychoanalytic elaboration of a psychological logic that this Pauline passage invites us to enter into. And this means that Lacan's reading of Paul can also be interpreted as a hypothesis about the apostle as a precursor of psychoanalysis, a modern science that is based on a methodological atheism. For where is God in Lacan's reading? God plays no role, for what Lacan draws out of the Pauline theology in the Letter to the Romans is the psychological logic. Not unlike Alain Badiou, Lacan reads Paul in a secular manner – as if Bultmann was correct to say that Paul was particularly suited to demythologization. Lacan reads Paul as if the Frenchman was an atheist, thereby confirming the picture that what we have in Paul is an apostle for atheists. But for Lacan, God is not dead, but subconscious. If we dare to lie down on the couch and pour forth a stream of words, it can happen that we let the cat out of the bag, or forget what we wanted to say – and that we reveal that we reckon with God or do not do so, whether we believe or do not do so. True confession can thus manifest itself as a slip of the tongue. Belief in God can be inhibited in a secularized culture where religion is less able to sustain the light of day and sinks down into the subconscious.

To interpret the law in the Letter to the Romans as Jacques Lacan does has two far-reaching consequences. First, what Paul says about the law will apply,

---

[46] Sigmund Freud, *Beyond the Pleasure Principle*, trans, C. J. M. Hubback (DigiReads, 2009).

not only to the Jewish law or a religious law but to the sum total of all the norms that the name of the father inscribes upon our mind in the culture in which we grow up. But we must liberate ourselves, or at least take our distance from, the law that we have more or consciously accepted, in order to attain a greater measure of real freedom and autonomy. Second, Protestantism's message about Christian freedom becomes much less realistic, since psychoanalysis shows how difficult it is to detach oneself from the law. Our learning egos may perhaps romp around in ideology critique, but the psychoanalytic truth is that none of us can erase from our subconscious the traces left by the values of our culture.

Julia Kristeva

Julia Kristeva (born 1941) is another psychoanalyst who has discovered Paul as a philosophical resource. She is a Bulgarian literary scholar and a self-declared atheist.[47] Nevertheless, she laments that modern people, as children of the Enlightenment age, too easily celebrate the death of God, since both believers and non-believers can find sources of a deeper knowledge in religious ideas, especially if one wears the spectacles of psychoanalysis. Kristeva trained as a psychoanalyst in Paris in the post-Lacan tradition, and she continues to employ fundamental Lacanian categories such as the imaginary, the symbolic, and the real. But unlike Lacan, Kristeva does not centre her readings of Paul on the relationship to the law and to the name of the father on the symbolic level. She is interested in the imaginary in Paul's thinking, and she asks: Is this message relevant in a post-Christian situation?[48]

In her book *Black Sun: Depression and Melancholia* (1987), Kristeva's starting point is the painting *The Body of the Dead Christ in the Tomb* by Hans Holbein (1497-1543). She interprets the painting's unadorned and realistic depiction of Christ's body as an encounter with the human being's own death. She sees the special value of Christianity in the way in which it confronts us, through the picture of this suffering, with an earthly suffering that lacks any heavenly redress. This religion inflicts imaginary confrontations and encounters on

---

[47] Julia Kristeva, *Passions of Our Time* (New York: Columbia University Press, 2018), 86.
[48] "Is there a Post-christian Actuality?" *Tales of Love* (New York: Columbia University Press, 1987), 140.

the human being, without expectations of a divine transcendence, by means of the picture of the crucified Jesus without a resurrection: and it is these confrontations and encounters that communicate true insights into our own selves. In the suffering of the crucified Jesus in Christianity, there lies a seed of "humanization" or secularization, for the more we accept human pain, the more quickly does the dream of a supernatural God and a life beyond death evaporate, according to Kristeva: "The unadorned representation of human death, the well-nigh anatomical stripping for the corpse to convey to viewers an unbearable anguish before the death of God, here blended with our own, since there is not the slightest suggestion of transcendency."[49] By means of the figure of God's death, Christianity takes the human being to the uttermost boundary of faith, where it can dissolve, and hurls him or her into a meaninglessness that abandons one in fear in face of one's own death. Kristeva emphasizes that this is a moment in the believer's life *before* the idea of life after death and resurrection calms the believer with a fantasy about salvation. Although religion offers space only for a brief encounter with this tormenting fear, Kristeva believes that the encounter points to something real: it is a mythical depiction of the genesis of the subject, a genesis that in a psychoanalytic sense always takes form through a series of separations, such as birth, weaning, frustration and castration.[50]

> The break, brief as it might have been, in the bond linking Christ to his Father and to life introduces into the mythical representation of the Subject a fundamental and psychically necessary discontinuity. Such a caesura ... provides an image, at the same time as a narrative, for many separations that build up the psychic life of individuals. ... In addition to displaying a dramatic diachrony, the death of Christ offers imaginary support to the nonrepresentable catastrophic anguish distinctive of melancholy persons.[51]

The idea of Christ's death gives the human being an imaginary support as a dramatization of the loss and separation that one experiences from childhood

---

[49] *Black Sun: Depression and Melancholia* (New York: Columbia University Press, 1989), 110.
[50] Castration in the Lacanian sense should not be understood as a phenomenon that only has to do with the penis, but rather with the loss or renunciation of enjoyment (*jouissance*). The claim is related to Freud's description of the Oedipus complex where the child's identification with the father is precisely linked to a form of symbolic castration as the child discovers that it is not the object of the mother's desires. Bruce Fink, *The Lacanian Subject: Between Language and Jouissance* (Princeton: Princeton University Press, 1995), 99.
[51] Kristeva, *Black Sun: Depression and Melancholia*, 132-3.

onwards. In faith, the believer is united in an imaginary manner with the crucified Jesus. Kristeva claims that this gives the believer a great strength to live one's own death, and in this way to process what one has lost in the various separations. The image is a myth, but the effect on the subject is real.

If Christianity can have this effect on people, this is due not least to what Kristeva calls the Pauline "revolution".[52] She claims that it was Paul who clarified the radically unconditional love that is expressed in the gospels. Through the idea of the Christian as one loved by God independently of works, Paul defined love (or *agapê*) as a selfless gift. And Kristeva finds the expression of God's supreme gift through the Son's sacrifice on the cross in ch. 5 of the Letter to the Romans:[53]

> For while we were still weak, at the right time Christ died for the ungodly. Indeed, rarely will anyone die for a righteous person – though perhaps for a good person someone might actually dare to die. But God proves his love for us in that while we still were sinners Christ died for us. Much more surely then, now that we have been justified by his blood, will we be saved through him from the wrath of God. For if while we were enemies, we were reconciled to God through the death of his Son, much more surely, having been reconciled, will we be saved by his life! (Rom. 5.6-10)

Kristeva finds here in Paul an idea about divine love for the godless. She sees this as a radically Pauline idea, because it breaks with every concept of divine retribution. This is not a deity who safeguards only those who believe in him. No matter what the human being does, Paul's God offers a gift, a new possibility – an invitation to reconciliation and reunion. The human being comes to faith through identifying with the crucified Jesus, the one who in his person is the Sacrifice, and by offering his or her old ego – the desiring and erotic body – by means of this identification. Eros is replaced by *agapê*, and the new body devotes itself totally to the ideal of love.

As a psychoanalyst inspired by Freud, Kristeva has the critique of religion in her very bones, and it is unsurprising that she has some objections to Paul. He envisages the killing of one's old ego; is this, in reality, masochism? Is this Pauline idea, with its orientation to sacrifice, a concealed eroticizing of maximum physical and moral pain? No, says Kristeva. Paul moves the

---

[52] *Tales of Love*, 139.
[53] Ibid., 140.

believer's psyche far beyond a masochistic logic, because the apostle makes logic analogous, rather than real, for the believer's life. The believer does not have to inflict pain on oneself in order to imitate Christ's pain. This prevents one from being obsessed by this type of destructive enjoyment.[54] Instead, the believer is to identify with the one who suffers. Through this identification, he or she will be cured of another illness, namely narcissism. The Pauline message twists the focus from my own death to the death of the Other, namely Christ, and thus my gaze is turned away from my own self. And this overcoming of narcissism is accomplished through the love of neighbour in the same message.[55] But through the identification with Christ – also as the dead Christ – I am confronted with my own death. In this way, the Pauline fixation with Christ counteracts the suppression of death. Nor is this all: when the story of the suffering of the crucified Christ is exalted to become the universal narrative for the subject, the fantasy is neutralized, because this story forbids the believer to confuse oneself with Christ as the midpoint of the world.[56] In other words, as Kristeva understands it, the Pauline message is a remedy for a number of psychological diagnoses or pathologies.

Like Badiou, she underlines that the institution Paul builds up is of a political nature. But Kristeva insists more strongly than Badiou that the successful building of the institution is based on the apostle's psychological insights. The Pauline groups offer not a fellowship for the militant universalists but rather what Kristeva calls "the therapy of exile" for foreigners and strangers in the Greco-Roman world. Paul replaces the foreigners' feeling of being split between two worlds with a cosmopolitics constructed on a separation between psychological states, between body and soul. In this way, the foreigner's melancholy suffering is eased, because the split that is experienced is no longer interpreted as a mistake, but rather as the expression of a spiritual journey. Just as Christ is a foreigner in the world, so too those who are made foreigners by a forced exile find a new belonging in the world, in union with the Foreigner. And it is this identification with the subject's own split that leads Kristeva to call this Pauline therapy an overcoming of psychosis.[57] How can Paul be a pill against psychosis?

---

[54] Ibid., 143.
[55] Ibid., 145.
[56] Ibid., 144.
[57] *Strangers to Ourselves* (New York: Columbia University Press, 1991), 82.

Kristeva builds on Lacan. In everyday language, psychosis refers simply to a person's total breach with reality, but Lacan's more precise point is that the psychotic person has broken with the intersubjectively and linguistically conditioned interpretation of a reality to which we have no access outside the language we human beings share. According to Lacan, the psychotic person has done the opposite of what Paul invites us to do (on Kristeva's reading). Paul builds his fellowships on the fact that those who join them recognize their own subjective split, whereas the psychotic person, as Lacan (and thereby also Kristeva) understand it, has rejected the split and refused to welcome it into oneself. The child who becomes a subject, who submits to the law that is woven into language, loses the wordless, inseparable unity with the world in the pre-linguistic existence. The psychotic person rejects the loss and the deficiency that the splits and separations entail.[58] He or she rejects the existence to which Paul (according to Kristeva) invites the human being.

From a feminist standpoint, Kristeva's interpretation of Paul can appear uncritical of aspects in Pauline thinking that seem to legitimate the subordination of women or a gender-based hierarchy of cosmic proportions. We encounter here again a limit to Kristeva's self-declared feminism. She criticizes Western culture for suppressing and excluding the mother's body – which nonetheless is strikingly absent in the Bulgarian philosopher's readings of Paul. She cites the Letter to the Galatians, but she fails to notice that Paul depicts himself as a mother giving birth: "My little children, for whom I am again in the pain of childbirth until Christ is born in you" (Gal. 4.19).[59]

In a similar way as with art, Kristeva sees a powerful force in this identification with Christ. It is also interesting that she refers to the Letter to the Romans more frequently than to any other Pauline Letter, since it is especially in Romans that Paul's metaphors for the new life in Christ express a mystical uniting by means of Christ's death and resurrection. Whereas traditional Christian theology has largely emphasized the more juridically oriented doctrine of justification as the central element in Paul, Kristeva points instead to this mystical uniting.[60]

---

[58] Haugsgjerd, Å møte psykisk smerte, 184-6.
[59] For several critical perspectives on Kristeva's readings of Paul, see Roland Boer, "Julia Kristeva, Marx and the Singularity of Paul", in *Marxist Feminist Criticism of the Bible*, ed. Jorunn Økland and Roland Boer (Sheffield: Sheffield Phoenix Press, 2008).
[60] Pauline scholars such as Albert Schweitzer and later E. P. Sanders have emphasized this too. Schweitzer claimed in his 1930 book that the doctrine of justification could not be detached from the Pauline mysticism, and the uniting with Christ was at the very centre of the Pauline

She then constructs a picture of a cosmopolitical alliance between Pauline Christianity and modern psychoanalysis, by postulating that the Pauline fellowships are psychoanalytically therapeutic and culturally inclusive. She makes connections between Paul and cosmopolitics in a similar way to Jacques Derrida, who calls cosmopolitanism "the great tradition . . . passed down from Stoicism or Pauline Christianity to the Enlightenment and Kant".[61]

With Kristeva, yet another psychoanalyst has interpreted Paul as an introspective thinker. Against Stendahl's reading, Paul is interpreted once again in anthropological terms and as an apostle who to a special degree has understood universal traits in the human psyche. Kristeva shares this way of looking at Paul with another psychoanalyst in the French psychoanalytical tradition after Lacan: Slavoj Žižek.

Alain Badiou's reading of Romans 7

Žižek discovers Paul through Alain Badiou's reading. It was through his fascination with Badiou's reading that the Slovenian philosopher also was reminded that Lacan had recommended his students to read Paul. Both Lacan and Badiou lead Žižek in the direction of ch. 7 of the Letter to the Romans, a scriptural passage to which Žižek returns again and again in his philosophical writings.

In his reading of Romans 7, Žižek adopts several premises from Badiou, whose interpretation of the chapter as an expression of Paul's thinking contains a theory about the unconscious; seen in this light, it overlaps with modern psychoanalysis. Badiou discovers in Paul two possibilities of existence. Either the human being lives under grace, or else the human being lives under the law. The former is life-giving and the latter brings death. The human being must choose. The problem is that one does not manage to see clearly and to

---

understanding of salvation. Albert Schweitzer, *The Mysticism of Paul the Apostle,* trans. William Montgomery, 1998 ed. (Baltimore: Johns Hopkins University Press, 1931), 226. – Or, as E. P. Sanders writes: "The normally juristic, forensic or ethical language of righteousness is forced to bear the meaning of 'life by participation in the body of Christ.' But this reversal of meaning never works the other way round." E. P. Sanders, *Paul and Palestinian Judaism: A Comparison of Patterns of Religion* (Philadelphia: Fortress Press, 1977), 504.

[61] Jacques Derrida, *Adieu to Emmanuel Levinas,* trans. Pascale-Anne Brault and Michael Naas (Stanford: Stanford University Press, 1999), 88.

choose consciously when life is on the path of death, when it is no longer the ego that acts, but rather the sin that dwells in the ego (Rom. 7.17). In that case, the thinking of the ego is rendered powerless, and the human being is a split self.[62] The subject no longer acts as it truly desires, because unproconscious powers have taken possession of it. Accordingly, the subject lives without freedom under the law, in what Paul calls "sin". But how has this occurred? And what is sin?

Badiou's understanding has its origin in a link Paul makes between law and sin – a link that has fascinated a number of philosophers. As Paul Ricoeur writes, "[t]he great discovery of Paul is that the law itself is a source of sin."[63] According to Badiou, the subjective existence under the law that Paul describes is a very complicated state,[64] since it entails that it is the law that gives sin its origin. Badiou employs Paul's idea of a state prior to the coming of the law (Rom. 7.8) to describe a kind of state of innocent in which the human being's desire was not awakened, so that one could do neither evil nor good. The desire could not be a part of salvation or the solution. But with the law, desire is awakened and determines the objects of desire, that towards which the desire is directed. The human being under the law desires what which the law forbids, irrespective of what the human being's genuine will or desire is. Desire begins to lead a life of its own, and directs itself time and again towards what the law forbids. In this way, the subject does not live as it truly wills; it lives in sin, which is an unconscious automatism. And this brings death for the subject. Badiou finds this expressed in Rom. 7.11: "For sin, seizing an opportunity in the commandment, deceived me and through it killed me." This is why he writes that sin is the life of desire as an unconscious autonomy.[65] And this means, according to Badiou, that in Paul's thinking, it is not the breach of the law per se that is sin. Sin is something that goes deeper than simple infringements of religious rules.

Desire circles around the commandment and its transgression in a circular destructiveness, and this (according to Badiou) makes it evident to Paul that it is necessary to break with the law. The human being must get out of the domain of the law and cross over into the domain of grace, where desire can

---

[62] Badiou, *Saint Paul: The Foundation of Universalism*, 75-80.
[63] Paul Ricoeur, *The Symbolism of Evil* (Boston: Beacon, 1969), 140.
[64] Badiou, *Saint Paul: The Foundation of Universalism*, 79.
[65] Ibid.

be set free to practice loyalty to the truth event and to its creative universalism. In freedom from the law, the commandment can no longer seduce one, and human thinking rediscovers itself in its hard-won control over action. The split between thinking and acting is overcome. What Paul describes as "the evil I do not want" (7.19) has lost control over the ego. The unconscious no longer governs what happens. What Paul describes as a way out of sin with the help of God (Rom. 7.25) is described by the atheist Badiou as a secular salvation in the subject's overcoming of the legal and of the unconscious. The subject has freed itself in the encounter with the truth event. It has become capable of expressing love.

Žižek's reading of Romans 7

Slavoj Žižek develops further this reading of ch. 7 of Romans. Like Ricoeur and Badiou, Žižek focuses on the close link that Paul posits between law and sin. Like Badiou, Žižek holds that Paul is not a moralist who deplores human beings' lack of religious self-discipline, as if the observance of religious commandments would give genuine freedom. Friedrich Nietzsche writes: "[w]herever the religious neurosis has appeared on the earth so far, we find it connected with three dangerous prescriptions as to regimen: solitude, fasting, and sexual abstinence."[66] But Paul is not speaking in favour of a life-denying religious asceticism, according to Žižek. Nor does Paul think that to yield to the temptations of the flesh simply means abandoning oneself to earthly pleasures and dissipations that are contrary to a moral law.[67] On this point, therefore, Nietzsche's criticism does not affect Žižek's Paul.

The sinful existence that Žižek's Paul describes is an existential crisis that must be understood with the conceptual apparatus of modern psychoanalysis and in the light of the modern criticism of ideology. This leads him to bring Paul into an even larger arena than Alain Badiou does. Žižek agrees with Badiou that one direct consequence of the law is the splitting of the subject and that this split introduces a morbid confusion in the Pauline subject, so that one can no longer distinguish between that which leads to life and that which

---

[66] Nietzsche, *The Essential Nietzsche: Beyond Good and Evil*, 51.
[67] Žižek, *The Ticklish Subject: The Absent Centre of Political Ontology*, 171.

leads to death, between a conscious obedience to the law and an unconscious desire to transgress it – a desire generated by the prohibitions of the law.[68] But Žižek employs the diagnoses of psychoanalysis to describe the split in Romans 7 and the way out of it. These diagnoses are clinical structures or types that can be encountered in therapeutic rooms and that always involve various forms of the superego. Žižek claims that there is a special dynamic in the superego that unfolds in the inner drama expressed in Romans 7. This is a matter of the superego's dialectic between the law and its transgression:

> The dialectic of Law and its transgression does not reside only in the fact that Law itself solicits its own transgression, that it generates the desire for its own violation; our obedience to the Law itself is not "natural," spontaneous, but always-already mediated by the (repression of the) desire to transgress it. When we obey the law, we do it as part of a desperate strategy to fight against our desire to transgress it, so the more rigorously we obey the Law, the more we bear witness to the fact that, deep within ourselves, we feel the pressure of the desire to indulge in sin. The superego feeling of guilt is therefore right: the more we obey the Law, the more we are guilty, because this obedience is in effect a defense against our sinful desire.[69]

This human being who attempts to live "normally" and to follow the law can come to be hunted by a ghostlike doppelgänger, that is, by a will in the superego to transgress the law out of a perverse lust. As in Lacan, the law in Žižek must be understood as the sum of higher norms that regulate a human being's place in the world, and that are legitimated by ideologies. But this law is split between the official legal text and the law's obscene superego.

A perverse person is not defined on the basis of promiscuous sexual actions, as our everyday use of language tends to suppose. For Žižek, the perverse person is defined on the basis of his or her relationship to the law. Such a subject takes delight in breaking the law, and no longer asks about the name of the father or the meaning of the law, since he or she claims to know the will of the Other. According to Žižek, this perverse logic in relation to the law is a trap that Paul at all costs wants to avoid in Romans 7.[70] He understands the rhetorical question in Rom. 3.8, "Let us do evil so that good may come?", as the most

---

[68] Ibid., 173.
[69] Slavoj Žižek, *The Parallax View* (Cambridge, MA: MIT Press, 2006), 90.
[70] "In the whole of this part of the Epistle, the problem St Paul struggles with is how to avoid the trap of *perversion*." Žižek, *The Ticklish Subject: The Absent Centre of Political Ontology*, 171-2.

exact definition of the perverse diagnosis or position that a subject takes.[71] Paul puts this question against the background of his claim in the Letter that human injustice has made God's righteousness visible for the world. The implied logic might be that human beings ought to commit more injustice, because the more injustice they commit, the more clearly will God's righteousness stand forth (3.5-8). But although Paul is not a moralist, he maintains throughout the Letter moral distinctions between good and evil. And the problem for Paul in ch. 7 is that, although the ego who speaks is capable of distinguishing between good and evil, this ego is not capable of doing what is good (7.19): "For I do not do the good I want, but the evil I do not want is what I do." For Žižek, this ego is stuck fast in a Gordian knot caused by the dialectic of the superego. At the same time, the desperate tone and the honesty in the lament of the ego in Romans 7 bear witness to hysterics. On Žižek's reading, the one who speaks here is a hysterical person.[72] Such a person has an ambivalent position vis-à-vis the law, but his indomitable search for truth gives him a great value: at the point where the perverse person has stopped asking questions, the intense challenge to the law continues to be made in the hysterical person's constant questioning of it. And while the perverse position is in fact conservative, the hysterical position contains a considerable potential for change.[73] At the very least, the hysterical person can unmask the lack of knowledge on the part of the authority and can thereby demonstrate the need for new authorities.[74] Moreover, the hysterical person's discourse is productive, because it is never content with current knowledge or with answers that are apparently complete. It knocks holes in these answers by a demanding insistence on new questions; and this also has a political significance, since the speech of the hysterical person is not only uttered in the closed and confidential therapy room but can also find expression through debates in society and through ideologies.

This means that Žižek finds an intelligent diagnosis of the subject in Romans 7. Paul's ideas possess a perennial relevance in Žižek's eyes, since the prohibitions and commandments of the law take on ever new forms in what he calls a postmodern age, where even the ideal of self-realization becomes

---

[71] Ibid., 172.
[72] Paul V. Axton, *The Psychotheology of Sin and Salvation: An Analysis of the Meaning of the Death of Christ in Light of the Psychoanalytical Reading of Paul* (London: Bloomsbury T&T Clark, 2015), 75.
[73] Žižek, *The Puppet and the Dwarf*, 53.
[74] Ibid., 43.

a new and crushing law for the subject. But Žižek also affirms that no one has surpassed Paul's description of the destructive dialectic of the superego in Romans 7. This description remains the finest in the history of philosophy.[75]

Camouflaged masochism in the Letter to the Romans?

Like Badiou, Žižek too reads the apostle in the light of Nietzsche. This means that Žižek approaches Paul with a hermeneutic of suspicion. He reads a religious figure like Paul through the lens of the modern criticism of religion, and he is therefore inclined to dismiss the Pauline love of neighbour on the basis of a psychoanalytic suspicion that behind religion's pious talk about love there lie concealed oppressive mechanisms that control the human being through his or her superego, killing natural spontaneity by means of religious obligations:

> What many people find problematic in the Pauline *agape* is that it seems to *superegotize* love, conceiving it in an almost Kantian way – not as a spontaneous overflow of generosity, not as a self-assertive stance, but as a self-suppressing *duty* to love neighbours and care for them, as hard *work*, as something to be accomplished through the strenuous effort of fighting and inhibiting one's spontaneous "pathological inclinations."[76]

This consistent suspicion vis-à-vis religious thinkers like Paul is based inter alia on the psychoanalytic insight that instincts and inclinations cannot be suppressed in such a way that they will not return in another form in the human being's psyche. The return of the suppressed always remains a possibility. This is one reason why Žižek was initially somewhat sceptical to Badiou's philosophical embrace of Paul.

As I have mentioned, one of the accusations levelled against Paul by the neo-atheists was that he was a fanatic, one who was hostile to life and glorified human suffering. Michel Onfray echoed Nietzsche by claiming that Paul was a masochist who propagated hatred of the body and was subject to the death

---

[75] "Paul provided an unsurpassable description of this entanglement." Žižek, *Living in the End Times*, 153. *Trouble in Paradise. From the End of History to the End of Capitalism* (London: Allen Lane, 2014), 99.
[76] Žižek, *The Fragile Absolute*, 92.

drive. As we have seen, Julia Kristeva too took up the question of masochism in her discussion of Paul. Her conclusion, however, was that the consequence of Paul's thinking was the opposite of masochism, because it made suffering for the one who followed Christ analogical rather than real. In a similar manner, Nietzsche's criticism of Paul's contempt for the natural human life and of his promotion of suffering plays a role when Badiou seeks to evaluate Paul critically as a thinker. The French philosopher explicitly asks whether Nietzsche was correct to say that Paul's thinking is in reality the expression of a hatred of life.[77]

One of Badiou's strategies to defend Paul against the accusation that the apostle's message was sheer unadulterated masochistic propaganda is that death plays no role whatever in Paul's idea of salvation. The Pauline truth event, which functions for Badiou as the prototype of his own concept of truth event (e.g. political and scientific revolutions), is based exclusively on the resurrection. For Paul, according to Badiou, the cross exists, but not the path to the cross. In Paul's thinking, suffering has no positive effects. In Paul, "death" is merely a name for an existential blind alley for the subject who belongs on the side of the flesh and the law. Death is not the basis of the Christ event in Paul – it is a stage that has been left behind after the resurrection.[78] Badiou appears confident that, by rejecting the idea that there is any kind of relationship or dialectic in the Letter to the Romans between Jesus' death and Jesus' resurrection, he can acquit Paul of Nietzsche's accusation.

Badiou's Paul is not only exonerated from Nietzsche's criticism. Badiou also goes a long way towards making Paul a Nietzschean who proclaims a radical freedom from the law, on the one hand, and proclaims the gospel of hitherto undiscovered possibilities for the new Übermensch, on the other. A striking downplaying of the human being's limitations and finitude leads Badiou to depict Paul as an apostle for the new human being – beyond good and evil, and not least, beyond rites and priests.[79] In reality, according to Badiou, what Paul wanted was to replace nihilism's "no" to life with a life-affirming "yes".[80] In this way, Badiou confirms Taubes' intuition about Nietzsche's identification with Paul and his jealousy of Paul. Nietzsche's philosophical project was more

---

[77] Badiou, *Saint Paul: The Foundation of Universalism*, 65.
[78] Ibid., 67-8.
[79] Ibid., 72.
[80] Ibid., 71.

Pauline than his polemic against the apostle would suggest. And there are two central premises from Nietzsche's reading of the Letter to the Romans that are preserved in Alain Badiou's reading of Paul. First, he interprets Paul as saying that the law is the cause of sin, because, as Nietzsche puts it, "it continually brought sin forth as a sharp juice brings forth a disease".[81] Second, he agrees with Nietzsche's understanding of Paul as a man who wanted to eradicate and abolish the law ("The law was the cross to which he felt himself nailed", Nietzsche claims). In this way, both Nietzsche and Badiou can be called Protestants, both in their reading of Paul and in the form taken by their own philosophy with regard to a radical freedom from the law. Although Slavoj Žižek adopts these two premises in his reading of Paul, he does not accommodate Nietzsche's criticism to the same extent as Badiou. Unlike Badiou, Žižek does not deny that the suffering of the cross and death play positive roles in Paul's soteriology. He writes that when Paul unmasks the morbid entanglement of law and sin in Romans 7, he has already avoided the masochistic logic of which the neo-atheists accuse the apostle – since masochism is a particularly prominent form of perversion, and Paul's entire argument in Romans 7 is intended to avoid the trap of perversion. It follows that this masochistic attitude to the self remains within the limitations of the law, and is thus not on the same level as the specifically Pauline understanding of love.[82]

The moment of negativity – preparing the ground for the new life

Žižek insists that while Paul does not glorify human suffering through a form of death cult around the crucified Jesus, the apostle nevertheless sees death in his philosophy as a necessary step on the path to the secular salvation of the subject. Žižek cannot accept the move that Badiou takes in order to understand Paul's relevance today, namely, the French philosopher's dismissal of Freud's idea of the death drive and of Hegel's negative moment in dialectics. When Badiou dismisses the death drive as "a morbid obsession with death",

---

[81] *Daybreak: Thoughts on the Prejudices of Morality*, 41.
[82] Žižek, *The Ticklish Subject: The Absent Centre of Political Ontology*, 169.

Žižek maintains that Badiou has simply stopped thinking.[83] And when Badiou radically detaches Jesus' resurrection from Jesus' crucifixion and claims that the resurrection is the only basis for the truth event in Paul, the truth event simply becomes a new beginning for the subject, who in an almost magical manner passes from life under the law (the path of death) to life under grace (the path of life). The subject simply decides to be loyal to the truth event. This demands, more than anything else, determination.[84]

According to Žižek, Badiou's obvious anti-Hegelianism means that finitude, suffering and negativity in human existence are neglected, both in the understanding of Paul and in the construction of philosophy. Death is not merely the end of life on earth: for Žižek, it stands for the negativity in human existence that is described by Hegel in *The Phenomenology of Spirit*:

> Death, if that is what we to call that non-actuality, is the most fearful thing of all, and to keep and hold fast to what is dead requires only the greatest force. Powerless beauty detests the understanding because the understanding expects of her what she cannot do. However, the life of spirit is not a life that is fearing death and austerely saving itself from ruin; rather, it bears death calmly, and in death, it sustains itself. Spirit only wins its truth by finding its feet in its absolute disruption . . . spirit is this power only by looking the negative in the face and lingering with it.[85]

Badiou recognizes that this corresponds to a Christian tradition that is several centuries old, but he denies that these ideas have roots in Paul.[86] Žižek takes a different view, and it is easy to agree with the Slovenian philosopher, given that Paul speaks in the Letter to the Romans about a death in a metaphorical sense, a death that takes place in the believer's life. When Paul writes about dying to the law or being dead to the law (7.4), Žižek understands this to mean that the subject goes through a symbolic death in which it is detached from all the inherited rules and norms that define a person's place in society.[87] At the same

---

[83] Ibid., 168.
[84] Although Žižek does not criticize this, Simon Critchley's criticism of this aspect of Badiou's philosophy is worth mentioning. Critchley aptly calls this a "heroism of the decision". Simon Critchley, *Infinitely Demanding. Ethics of Commitment, Politics of Resistance* (London: Verso, 2007), 48. This heroism of the decision also contains a problematic form of decisionism. Ole Jakob Løland, *Reception of Paul the Apostle in the Works of Slavoj Žižek* (London: Palgrave Macmillan, 2018), 160-7.
[85] Georg Wilhelm Friedrich Hegel, *The Phenomenology of Spirit*, Cambridge Hegel Translations (Cambridge: Cambridge University Press, 2018), 20-1.
[86] Badiou, *Saint Paul: The Foundation of Universalism*, 65.
[87] Žižek, *The Fragile Absolute*, 118.

time, Žižek emphasizes that, for Paul, it is *both* the death *and* the resurrection of Jesus that constitute the fundamental element in the Christ event.[88]

It follows that, for Paul, death is a state in which the believer can share in Christ's death, in order then to share in his resurrection. The believers share not only in Christ's death, but also in Christ's crucifixion, in that the "old human being" is crucified along with him. In this way, the believer becomes as one dead for sin, but alive for God (Rom. 6.1-11). For Žižek, there is no God for whom one can be alive. It would thus be a question of "the big Other" in Lacan's sense, whom one must get rid of in order to take genuine responsibility for an autonomous life with no illusory metaphysical guarantees. But death in the Hegelian sense is a reality that the subject can put up with and absorb into oneself; indeed, it is only by passing through destruction and inner laceration that the subject finds itself. One name for the willingness to risk painful psychological processes in which the self is unmasked and stripped naked is the death drive, which is a dimension of radical negativity in Žižek's philosophy. And according to Žižek, this is precisely what the "I"-person undergoes in Romans 7, and that the patient in psychoanalysis can undergo. The symbolic order that constitutes the law is not a systematic whole, one large and consistent narrative or ideology. But in order to compensate for its fragmentary form and its meaninglessness, we create fantasies that structure our desire. It is by confronting the utter lack of meaning, and passing through the fantasies that support desire, that it becomes possible for a sphere to open up in which we can die to the law through the inner laceration of subjectivity and its death in a moment of negativity that "wipes the slate clean".[89] At the same time, through the way in which he reads Paul, Badiou fails to see an important contribution from psychoanalysis: by "wiping the slate" of the

---

[88] In the words of the Pauline scholar John Barclay: ". . . so much is lost by this concentration on only one side of the cross-resurrection dialectic in Paul, not least his remarkable theology of suffering and the specific shape given to the Christ-event by its association with the love and self-giving of God." Barclay, "Paul and the Philosophers: Alain Badiou and the Event", 182. Simon Critchley accepts the premise from Badiou: "Of course, for Paul, this event is the resurrection of Christ." Critchley, *Infinitely Demanding. Ethics of Commitment, Politics of Resistance*, 45. L. L. Welborn sides with Žižek against Badiou in this discussion. Larry L. Welborn, "The Culture of Crucifixion", in *Paul and the Philosophers*, ed. Ward Blanton and Hent de Vries (New York: Fordham University Press, 2013), 139-40. The downplaying of the cross of Jesus in the radical left-wing political philosopher Badiou also leads to a paradox: a philosopher who asserts that he takes his stand on an atheistic materialism spiritualizes a historical crucifixion that has its roots in the class struggles of antiquity. The harsh reality of slavery, such as death on a cross or the threat of such a death, is reduced in Badiou's philosophy to a chance place where the truth event comes into view.

[89] Žižek, *The Ticklish Subject: The Absent Centre of Political Ontology*, 179.

subject's life, psychoanalysis can prepare the ground for a new beginning in which the subject's desire is restructured and the relationship to the law is completely new. For psychoanalysis does not give any new truths. Instead, it gets rid of old delusions and strips fantasies naked.

As Badiou reads him, Paul demands that the believer puts the domain of the law completely behind oneself and lives in fidelity to the truth event. For Žižek, on the other hand, it is in fact impossible for the new human being to put this fidelity into practice without relating to the law as the sum of norms, regulations and expectations. The law always seeks to structure social reality, and this is why a life totally independent of the law cannot be a goal. It is only psychotic persons who lead a life totally independent of the law, in the broad sense of the term. What Žižek's philosophy envisages is rather that one submits to the law with a new freedom: being capable of observing the law without actually being bound by it,[90] being capable of obeying the law without being a hostage to the psychological violence of the superego. In this new freedom, the ego has arrived at a new consciousness and has become able to live in love: "Once we become fully aware of the dimension of love in its radical difference from the Law, love has, in a way, already won, since this difference is visible only when one already dwells in love, from the standpoint of love."[91]

When the ego in Romans 7 emerges from the radical moment of negativity in which it experiences the profoundly tragic character of doing the opposite of what it truly wants ("the good that I want, I do not do"), it has been set free by God (Rom. 7.25). However, Žižek's atheistic reading means that the human being has freed his or her own self. And while, in Paul, the painful path taken by this ego has made the believer conscious of being deeply dependent on God, in Žižek, the same Pauline ego has become conscious of its own freedom. It has become more autonomous. It has not crushed its desire, but it has come to terms with it and given it a new orientation.

---

[90] "I use symbolic obligations, but I am not performatively *bound* by them." *The Puppet and the Dwarf*, 112. This is why Jayne Svenungsson is correct to sum up as follows the difference between the understanding of the law in the two philosophers: "By constructing the relation between law and grace in dialectical terms, Žižek ends up, to my mind, with a considerably more dynamic and complex perspective than Badiou's." Svenungsson, *Divining History: Prophetism, Messianism, and the Development of the Spirit*, 182-3.

[91] *Living in the End Times*, 154.

The Letter to the Romans as criticism of ideology

Alain Badiou reads Romans 7 as an account of Paul's own individual experience, which corresponds to universal traits in the human being.[92] Žižek does not claim that the ego in Romans 7 corresponds to Paul's own experience; his assertion is rather that Paul has uncovered universally valid aspects of the human being's relationship to the law. This does not apply only to an individual's relationship to one's environment, and it is certainly not restricted to the therapy room. His interpretation of psychoanalysis means that the boundaries of the therapy room are broken down, and that every reader of Žižek's texts is a potential patient. The philosopher thus aims to analyse a whole throng of readers – this throng is his clinic.[93] He also argues that the logic uncovered by Paul in Romans 7 can be applied directly to the contemporary age as a criticism of ideology. This Pauline logic gives insight into human beings, not only on the individual level, but also on a higher societal level. For Žižek, this applies especially to the Gordian knot that liberalism and fundamentalism form together:

> [T]he opposition of liberalism and fundamentalism is structured in exactly the same way as the one between Law and sin in Paul, i.e., liberalism itself generates its opposite. So what about the core values of liberalism: freedom, equality, etc.? The paradox is that liberalism itself is not strong enough to save them – i.e., its own core – against the fundamentalist onslaught. Why? The problem with liberalism is that it cannot stand on its own: there is something missing in the liberal edifice; liberalism is in its very notion "parasitic," relying on a presupposed network of communal values that is itself undermining its own development. Fundamentalism is a reaction – a false, mystifying reaction, of course – against the real flaw of liberalism, and that is why it is again and again generated by liberalism. Left to itself, liberalism will slowly undermine itself – the only thing that can save its core is a renewed left. Or, to put it in the well-known terms from 1968, in order for its key legacy to survive, liberalism needs the brotherly help of the radical left.[94]

If liberalism is the dominant ideology in the West, this is not because people are naïve liberals who have not yet grasped the true state of affairs in society.

---

[92] Badiou, *Saint Paul: The Foundation of Universalism*, 81.
[93] Sarah Kay, *Žižek: A Critical Introduction* (Cambridge: Polity, 2003), 15.
[94] Žižek, *Living in the End Times*, 154. "The Jew is within You, but You, You are in the Jew", 172.

Žižek argues against the classical criticism of ideology that is summarized in Karl Marx's words: "They don't know it, but they are doing it", as if ideology were merely a mask that could be removed in order to unmask reality as it truly is. In Žižek's eyes, the liberals are fully aware of the distance between the ideological mask and the societal reality, but they nevertheless want to keep the mask, since they are cynical sceptics who do not really believe in liberalism as an ideology. Žižek turns Marx upside down and claims instead that the attitude behind the dominant ideology and the cynical representatives of the law is: "They know very well how things really are, but still they are doing it as if they did not know."[95] The liberals do not really believe in liberalism as an overarching truth; they relativize all truths in the name of liberal tolerance, thereby provoking the counter-reaction on the part of fundamentalists who claim to possess the absolute truth. Fundamentalism is the clear break with liberalism as the law in today's world. The fundamentalists do the opposite of what liberalism commands them to do, but this means (according to Žižek) that they too are held captive in the vicious circle where liberalism generates its own antithesis or transgression, in the form of fundamentalism. And religious fundamentalists are excellent examples of the perverse type, since they claim to have direct access to the will of the "big Other" – to God's will. They act out of the supposition that what they do is directly guided by a divine will, as if they have a factual basis that lays down what is correct to do.[96]

In reality, however, says Žižek, they are living in sin, for they do not actually possess any knowledge base for their religious fundamentalism. On the contrary, they are captives of the circular logic of the law and its obscene demand that they transgress the liberal norms and ideals. The good news is that the circle can be breached. There is a love beyond the law of liberalism and the sinful antithesis. There is a love beyond the law. It is not Paul's God that rescues an ego from this intricate tangle. This is done by the radical political left wing – whoever this may be, since Žižek does not supply any particularly concrete definition. In any case, the atheist has removed God and has employed the apostle's criticism of the law to point to a renewed and radical political left wing as the rescuer. Besides this, the Slovenian atheist has made Paul's words

---

[95] *The Sublime Object of Ideology*, 2008 ed. (London: Verso, 1989), 30.
[96] Slavoj Žižek, *How to Read Lacan* (New York: W.W. Norton & Co., 2006), 116.

about the law relevant to what many regard as a much more powerful ideology than religion in relatively secularized countries, namely, liberalism.

As Žižek sees it, the liberals and the fundamentalists share one central characteristic: they are incapable of believing, in the sense that the atheist gives to this word.[97] Both types are unable to conceive of an action that is performed without a reason, the human decision that is taken without camouflaging oneself behind facts or postulating direct access to a super-individual will such as God, History or the Nation. In other words, the hysterical person whom Žižek hears speaking in Romans 7 is an atheist who has punctured all delusions and misunderstandings without replacing these with anything, and who in this way has arrived at an authentic belief.[98] And it is not primarily a hysterical individual, but a hysterical humankind that is capable of loving beyond the law.

The ambiguity of the law

Žižek's reading of Romans 7 as the description of a destructive entanglement of liberalism and fundamentalism is interesting for another reason too. Ever since his first book (*The Sublime Object of Ideology*), Žižek's interpretation of the law has been coloured by the many examples he presents of the irrationality of the law and of the oppression under communism behind the Iron Curtain in Eastern Europe. At rarer moments, he has also underlined the law as a liberation of the child from being entirely in the custody of its mother and totally abandoned to her desire. While the law alienates us, it also sets us free, through the distance it causes, from the desire and the arbitrary will of the Other (the mother).[99] Only rarely, as in the example above, has Žižek pointed out that the law has another core than to get us to obey, or that it aims at anything other than its own self. Time and again, he has pointed out

---

[97] Ibid., 117.
[98] "Authentic belief is to be opposed to the reliance on (or reference to) a(nother) subject supposed to believe: in an authentic act/decision of belief, I myself fully assume my belief, and thus have no need of any figure of the Other to guarantee my belief." Žižek, *Less Than Nothing: Hegel and the Shadow of Dialectical Materialism*, 118.
[99] *For They Know Not What They Do: Enjoyment as a Political Factor* (London: Verso, 1991), 265.

Paul's one-sided criticism of the law and has asserted that Paul is "clear and unambiguous" in his disparagement of it.[100]

When Žižek criticizes liberalism for undermining its own core values – which he understands as freedom and equality – it is possible that he is letting his tongue get away with him in his zeal to show that the radical left wing will rescue liberalism, since he thereby confirms that the core of liberalism, and its inalienable inheritance, is precisely freedom and equality. He concedes that liberalism *qua* law points beyond itself towards the realization of these values. This reading shows the outlines of a more complex understanding of law in the Letter to the Romans than Žižek had been willing to accept earlier on. Time and again, he has referred to the text of Romans 7, and each time, he has omitted to quote verse 12: "So the law is holy, and the commandment is holy and just and good." It is difficult to maintain that this is a "clear and unambiguous" disparagement of the law – since the opposite is true. Paul maintains that the law is just and good – after he has stated that the same law led to deception and death for the "I"-person in this chapter (7.10-11). It is contrasts of this kind, and apparently incoherent descriptions of the law, that have made it highly problematic for Paul's readers to understand what he means. As Paula Fredriksen writes, "[t]he Law's rhetorical valence varies wildly in Paul's epistles."[101] A brief look at Paul's Letter to the Galatians can confirm a divergence with regard to the significance of the law after Jesus' coming. Here too, Paul can describe the law as a curse (Gal. 3.13), and then go on to affirm that the law is not in conflict with God's promises (Gal. 3.21). The apostle can describe the circumcision of those who are not Jews as slavery, and the new existence of non-Jews who do not accept circumcision as freedom (Gal. 5.1-2). In the Letter to the Romans, Paul describes the law in even more complex and potentially self-contradictory terms. This is one reason for scepticism with regard to the reading of Romans 7 in Badiou and Žižek. One can ask: How is it possible that the law is the direct cause of sin, if the law is simultaneously holy, just and good? Are there central aspects of Paul's understanding of the law that Badiou and Žižek have omitted?

Although Žižek is marginally open to a law in Romans 7 that aims at freedom and equality, the Slovenian philosopher largely reads Paul within Alain Badiou's

---

[100] "Paul's negative appreciation of law is clear and unambiguous." *The Puppet and the Dwarf*, 117.
[101] Fredriksen, *Paul: The Pagans' Apostle*, 108.

interpretative framework. In this paradigm, it was the law that was the origin of the problem in Romans 7, namely, sin. This is, in other words, a law that, taken as a whole, imposes a burden on the subject, without having a clear connection to ethics. And although Badiou and Žižek linked freedom from the law to universalism, they virtually never interpreted the law in the light of one of the central themes in the Letter to the Romans: justice. Žižek, in particular, has shown something of the psychoanalytic potential of meaning in Romans, but we shall let the French philosopher Jacques Derrida do the same with regard to the relationship between law and justice. Since this is primarily a book about the readings of Paul in *atheist* philosophers, we should note that although Derrida is known for the religious turn in the course of his writings, he regarded himself as living a form of atheism. Perhaps his strongest confession of a certain form of atheism came in his declaration that he could "rightly pass for an atheist".[102]

Žižek's reading of Paul, inspired by Badiou, is possible, but it is not a necessary reading. Besides this, we do need to choose or reject philosophical readings. The fact that Žižek has demonstrated a psychoanalytic potential of meaning in the Letter to the Romans does not mean that this entire potential is exhausted, nor that the Letter has no other dimensions of meaning than this one potential.

We can appreciate Žižek's criticism of religion, which leads him to warn against the Pauline love of neighbour, and we can build further on the insight of psychoanalysis that love of neighbour quickly takes the form of a law that is made into a part of the superego that terrorizes the subject with guilt. At the same time, psychoanalysis has no other ethic than Lacan's categorical imperative that the subject must not give up its own desire. The strength of psychoanalysis is that it can cut through fantasy, liberate the subject from the tyranny of the superego that engender guilt and thereby strengthen the autonomy of the subject. Simon Critchley sums this up well: "[i]n psychoanalysis, the hateful watchful presence of the super-ego is exchanged for the more benign and trusted presence of the analyst."[103] The desire is cleansed, and the subject can recreate his or her relationship to the name of the Father and to the law. Greater autonomy gives new possibilities of authentic involvement in the world, but for

---

[102] Geoffrey Bennington, *Jacques Derrida*, ed. Jacques Derrida (Chicago: University of Chicago Press, 1993), 155. At the same time, Derrida was a French-Algerian Jew who went to the synagogue to pray. He was, in a certain sense, a man of prayer ("a man of prayer and tears"). Yvonne M. Sherwood and Kevin Hart, *Derrida and Religion: Other Testaments* (New York: Routledge, 2005), 27-50.
[103] Critchley, *Infinitely Demanding. Ethics of Commitment, Politics of Resistance*, 83.

what purpose? For one's own self-development? Or to assuage the sufferings of others? For the ego, or for the other? And it is here that questions about guilt and the conscience come in.

Not letting go of desire (as Lacan understands this term) means never refusing to accept the demand made by the unconscious desire in the work of interpreting this desire. The superego is the origin of much of the ego's suffering, through its bombarding the ego with the prohibitions and commandments of the law. In order to transform the suffering, the destructive relationship to the superego must be replaced by a healthier relation to the guilt one has inherited or to the shame one has experienced. But this does not mean that all guilt and shame are invariably oppressive or that they lack traces of a conscience that is rooted in an authentic moral experience. A bad conscience can also be a remnant of the self's utterly basic moral experience in the encounter with other persons or with societal injustice. A bad conscience or the experience of moral failure can also be the expression of a psychological realism and perceptiveness that cannot be reduced to the superego's morbid obsession or to its oppressive bombardment of the ego. This is why Simon Critchley links guilt to an ethical experience when he reads Romans 7:

> As will be familiar to many of us, the affect or emotion that accompanies this experience is *guilt*. Guilt is the affect that produces a certain splitting or division in the subject, something that Saint Paul understood rather well, "For the good that I would I do not: but the evil which I would not, that I do." [. . .] the phenomenon of guilty conscience reveals – negatively – the fundamentally moral articulation of the self. Namely, that ethical subjectivity is not just an aspect or dimension of subjective life, it is rather the fundamental feature of what we think of as a self, repository of our deepest commitments and values.[104]

Before the law – from Kafka to Paul

In an essay based on a lecture he held in 1982, the French philosopher Jacques Derrida writes about Kafa's short story "Before the Law",[105] which tells about

---

[104] Ibid., 22.
[105] Jacques Derrida, "Before the Law", in *Acts of Literature,* ed. Derek Attridge (New York: Routledge, 1992).

a doorkeeper who stands in front of a door that leads into the law and about a man who wants to enter. The doorkeeper tells him that it is possible to go into the law, but not at this precise moment. Accordingly, the man waits for the right moment, which never comes. For the man waits and waits without being allowed to go in. And as his life is nearing its end, the man asks how it is possible that in all these years, no one other than he himself has requested to be allowed to go into the law, although "Everyone strives to reach the Law." The doorkeeper replies: "No one else could ever be admitted here, since this gate was made only for you. I am now going to shut it."[106]

In his exegesis of this short story, Derrida emphasizes that the door was open for the man and that the doorkeeper employed no violence to block the way. For Derrida, it is the doorkeeper's speech that operates on the border, for the man has the physical freedom to move, even if not to move into the law. This is why the man must forbid himself to go into the law, in order to obey the law there where he stands, directly in front of the law that says: "Do not come to me – yet." The man thus wants to submit to the law for as long as he has no access to it, for the law is a prohibition and a forbidden area. In Derrida's exegesis, however, this does not mean that the law forbids, but that the law is per se a forbidden zone. It forbids itself and contradicts itself. And the man is located within the law's own contradiction.[107] As we shall see, he is located in a Pauline landscape, for it is at this point in Derrida's explanation of Kafka that Paul makes his entrance into the text of the French philosopher, albeit in a cryptic manner by means of a lengthy footnote:

> This contradiction probably is not simply that of a law, which in itself supposes and therefore produces transgression, the active or actual relationship to sin, to the fault. Before the Law perhaps gives rise to, in a kind of movement or trembling between the Old and the New Testament, a text which is both archived and altered, such as the Epistle to the Romans 7. More time needs to be devoted to the relationship between these two texts. Paul reminds his brothers, "people who know the law," that "the law exercises its power over man as along as he lives." And the death of Christ would be the death of this old law by which we "know" sin: dead along with Christ, we are released, absolved from this law, we are dead to this law, to the great age of its "letter,"

---

[106] *Acts of Literature* (New York: Routledge, 1992), 184.
[107] "Before the Law", 203.

in any case, and we serve it in a new "spirit." And Paul adds that when he was without law, he lived; and when, along with the law, the commandment came, he died.[108]

"Before the Law" supplies the origin of texts like Romans 7, Derrida writes, as if Kafka's story is describing a situation or an existential condition with a validity that goes far back in time, all the way to Paul. Something of the law's self-contradiction in Kafka's story can be found in Paul's description of a law that forbids transgression and thereby also presupposes and causes the transgression. Derrida writes that more time is needed to study Kafka's text and Paul's Letter to the Romans; this is either an encouragement to others or perhaps a promise that he will do so at a later date. This makes it possible for the reader to employ both Kafka and Paul to interpret his thinking about law and justice.

Further on in the essay, Derrida comments on ch. 9 of Kafka's novel *The Trial*. In this concluding part of the novel, the protagonist Josef K. meets a clergyman who tells him a version of the short story "Before the Law". Up to this point, the reader has followed Josef F. all the way since he was arrested on his thirtieth birthday for a crime, the contents of which he has never learned. Despite persistent and repeated attempts to know what he is accused of, the legal body that has condemned Josef K. remains both anonymous and in control of everything as the plot of the novel unfolds. In ch. 9, the clergyman tells him the story of the doorkeeper and the man before the law, expounding it in a way that leads Josef K. to identify himself with and defend the doorkeeper who refuses to let the man go into the law and who closes the door in his face.[109] Derrida describes this episode as an incredible scene with a Talmudic exegesis. He relates his own experience of being before the law when he visited members of the opposition behind the Iron Curtain and was arrested by the police in Prague,[110] before he returns to Kafka's character, the clergyman,

---

[108] Ibid.

[109] "'You know the story better than I do, and you have known it for longer,' said K. They were silent for a while. Then K. said: 'So you believe that the man was not misled?' 'Do not misunderstand me,' said the clergyman, 'I am only showing you the opinions about this matter. You ought not to pay too much attention to opinions. The writing [*Schrift*] cannot be changed, and the opinions are often merely an expression of despair at this. In this case, there even exists an opinion that the one who is misled is the doorkeeper.'" Franz Kafka, *Der Prozess* ([Berlin: Die Schmiede, 1925] Munich: Anaconda Verlag, 2021), 199-200.

[110] Derrida, "Before the Law", 218.

whom Derrida regards as a fusion of a priest, abbot, a rabbi and the apostle who wrote the Letter to the Romans:

> So we get a second exegetico-Talmudic wave from the priest, who is both, in some way, an abbot and a rabbi, a kind of Saint Paul, the Paul of the Epistle to the Romans who speaks according to the law, of the law and against the law, "whose letter has aged"; he is also the one says that "apart from the law sin lies dead": "I was once alive apart from the law, but when the commandment came, sin revived and I died." (Romans 7)[111]

According to Derrida, the rabbinic Paul in the shape of a kind of abbot (Jew, Protestant and Catholic?) is one who speaks in accordance with the law, about the law, and against the law; and the letter of the law has grown old. When he quotes Rom. 7.9-10a, Derrida is clearly attracted by the Pauline idea of a sinless state without the dominion of the law or its coming into existence. If there were parallels between Romans 7 and Kafka's *The Trial,* an understanding of the desperate "ego" in Romans as autobiographical could lead one to interpret Kafka's protagonist as a modern Paul who is persecuted by questions of guilt. Nor is Derrida the only one to have read Paul in the light of Kafka. Jacob Taubes comes close to such an understanding when he affirms that Paul feels accused in the same way as the protagonist in Kafka's novel.[112] But it is interesting to see that Derrida's reading points in another direction, which is staked out once again in the last part of his essay on Kafka, when he quotes from the episode with the clergyman:

> K. kept close to the clergyman in the darkness, without knowing where he was. The lamp in his hand had long gone out. Once, a silver statue of a saint gleamed before him, but only with the sheen of the silver, and immediately it passed over into the gloom.[113]

"Paul, perhaps?" asks Derrida here, in a way that creates a rapprochement between Paul and Kafka, the biblical and the literary, the ancient and the modern. He identifies Josef K. not with Paul but with the enigmatic figure emitted by "a silver statue of a saint" – that is to say, with the clergyman in *The Trial.* This means that Paul is identified with the interpretation of the law,

---

[111] Ibid., 219.
[112] Taubes, *The Political Theology of Paul,* 26.
[113] Translation of Kafka, *Der Prozess,* 203.

rather than with the individual who is plagued by a boundless, unexplained guilt until he dies (Josef K. is finally executed). At the same time, Derrida's 1982 exegesis of Kafka anticipates the reflections about law and justice that are found a number of times in his writings in the 1990s.

Paul and justice – with Derrida as magnifying glass

When we read Jacques Derrida's philosophy about law and justice against the background of the Pauline canvas that he himself sketched at the beginning of the 1980s, it becomes possible to read him as a kind of Pauline atheist. As Theodore W. Jennings Jr. demonstrated in his pioneering work on Paul and Derrida, many striking similarities emerge when one juxtaposes texts from the two writers.[114] A new potential of meaning is uncovered in Paul's Letters when the apostle is read via Derrida. In particular, it has proved fruitful to interpret the Letter to the Romans with the help of Derrida's philosophy, perhaps especially because such an interpretation takes into consideration another complexity in Paul's thinking about the law than the complexity indicated by Agamben, Badiou, Taubes and Žižek.[115] For it is perfectly possible to read Paul on this question is a manner almost diametrically different from Žižek's reading of Paul's view of the law as unambiguously negative. Indeed, Derrida can help to hold together the criticism of the law in Paul's thinking and his piety vis-à-vis the law, where Žižek consistently excludes the piety or obedience to the law. All readings are selective, but some readings are more selective than others in what they exclude. Nietzsche sums up Paul's awakening as follows: "From now on he is the teacher of the *destruction of the law*!"[116] He has caught the critical aspect of Paul's thinking about the law, without taking in the new obedience to the law that Paul seems to be promoting – especially in Romans. It seems to be above all the freedom from the law and the universalism that philosophers such as Nietzsche or Badiou have found interesting in Paul;

---

[114] Theodore W. Jennings, *Reading Derrida/Thinking Paul: On Justice* (Stanford: Stanford University Press, 2006); *Outlaw Justice: The Messianic Politics of Paul*.
[115] As Agata Bielik-Robson points out, all these four philosophers deny that the law can have a saving character, while they associate messianism (and thus also Paul) with antinomianism. Agata Bielik-Robson, "Tarrying with the Apocalypse: The Wary Messianism of Rosenzweig and Levinas", *Journal for Cultural Research* 13, nos. 3-4 (2009): 249-66.
[116] *Daybreak: Thoughts on the Prejudices of Morality*, 41.

but this means that a central motif, perhaps even the most central motif, in the Letter to the Romans has never found a place in their readings: justice. At the same time, many have identified the law in Paul's Letters with Torah, thereby making the specifically Jewish law the target of Paul's criticism of the law. Slavoj Žižek reads Paul with the same presupposition as many theologians and biblical exegetes when he assumes that the law Paul is criticizing is the Jewish law.[117] However, not all are convinced that the law Paul discusses can be reduced to Torah.[118] The fact that the examples he presents are drawn from Torah does not mean that his reflections on the law are not discussing law as a more general philosophical problem, and this is why there may be good reasons to reflect on law in Romans in a philosophical perspective, as a universal phenomenon in human societies. This justifies reading Paul with psychoanalytical interpretations (as above), and also with approaches more strongly drawn from the philosophy of law (as in Derrida below).

There may be several reasons why modern philosophers have only to a small extent discovered Paul as a thinker about justice who is relevant to political philosophy. First of all, translators in various languages have rendered the Greek expression *hê dikaiosunê tou theou* in words that lack connotations to justice. For example, Protestant translators have understood Paul's message as a settling of accounts with what has been seen as a misunderstood righteousness by works in Catholic Christianity, and not least in Judaism. Second, when translators and interpreters have perceived Paul's message to be righteousness by faith alone, *hê dikaiosunê tou theou* and similar expressions in Paul's Letters have sometimes been translated with concepts more suited to express the individual believer's religious relationship to God than secular circumstances that affect peoples and societies.[119] In English, for example, "righteousness" has quite different associations than "justice".[120] In this way, the justice of God was understood as something wholly different or completely detached from societal and political justice. Third, the modern differentiation,

---

[117] Žižek, *The Puppet and the Dwarf*, 113.
[118] Jewett, *Romans: A Commentary*, 274. Alan F. Segal, *The Other Judaisms of Late Antiquity*, Brown Judaic Studies (Atlanta: Scholars Press, 1987), 131-45.
[119] Miranda José Porfirio, *Marx and the Bible* (New York: Orbis Books, 1974), 173-83.
[120] For arguments that "justice" is a more appropriate translation than "righteousness", see Neil Elliott, *The Arrogance of Nations: Reading Romans in the Shadow of Empire* (Minneapolis: Fortress Press, 2008), 75-6. Fredriksen, *Paul: The Pagans' Apostle*, 120-1. Jennings, *Reading Derrida / Thinking Paul: On Justice*, 5.

with its ideals of stronger separations between the religious and the political spheres, has strengthened the tendency to read Paul's Letters apolitically, without grasping how much the religious and the political were interwoven in antiquity. And a modern ideal that religion ought to be a private matter for the individual has done nothing to modify this tendency. If, however, we look instead at justice from a philosophical perspective, we shift the problem taken up in Romans from traditional theology into political theory, so that Paul is actualized as a political thinker. Our starting point is that every reading is a reading experiment. For where is the boundary between interpretative skill and a reading experiment? It is difficult to define where it lies.

The justice that is manifest/revealed

This reading experiment will be coloured to a large extent by Derrida's texts from the first half of the 1990s, not least the revision of a lecture held by the philosopher at Cardozo Law School in the United States, which was published in 1990.[121] Here Derrida problematizes the foundations of law, morality and politics in a way that he believes is more at home in faculties of law and theology than of philosophy, although he is quick to dismiss the idea that such a question is in fact at home in one particular place. The question is too overarching to be assigned to only one academic branch or discipline.[122] Derrida wishes to approach the question of the foundation of law on the basis of the problem of justice. He believes that law is radically different in its nature from justice. Whereas a right, a legal entitlement, or the law can in principle be deconstructed, justice cannot be deconstructed or criticized in the same way. Criticism in the form of what Derrida calls deconstruction can analyse, dislocate or dissolve the law, either because it is founded by means of texts that can be interpreted or because there is no sufficient foundation. But this is not the case with justice; Derrida also expresses a reservation about whether it exists: "Justice in itself, if such a thing exists, outside or beyond law, is not deconstructible."[123] In other words, it is harder to approach justice

---

[121] Jacques Derrida, "Force of Law: The 'Mystical Foundation of Authority.'" (Deconstruction and the Possibility of Justice)", *Cardozo Law Review* 11, nos. 5-6 (1990): 920-1045. (See also n. 134 below.)
[122] Ibid., 931.
[123] Ibid., 945.

than law. Derrida explains that he has done this obliquely. It is difficult for him to tackle justice directly, and he has to do this in an oblique manner, that is to say, from a slanting position: "Obliquely, as at this very moment, in which I'm preparing to demonstrate that one cannot speak directly about justice, thematize or objectivize justice, say 'this is just' and even less 'I am just,' without immediately betraying justice, if not law (droit)."[124] Justice cannot be thematized or objectified in the same way as a right or law. And if it is not possible here and now to describe something as just, the concept of justice must be reserved for something else, something that is not completely present. For if one localizes justice in something that is present and human, such as a political party or a political program or a legal verdict, one betrays it. As Derrida writes: "Of justice where it is not yet, not yet *there*, where it is no longer, let us understand where it is no longer *present*, and where it will never be, no more than the law, reducible to laws or rights."[125]

Derrida's concept of justice recalls Paul's concept. In the first chapter of Romans, when he launches what can be called the principal thesis of the Letter (1.16-17), the apostle describes justice as manifest. In order to affirm that justice does not derive from human beings, but comes into the world of human beings from the outside, through a divine intervention, Paul employs the verb in a passive form: justice is manifested.[126] And it is manifested through the gospel, which is a dynamic power for the one who believes (1.16). This is not just any justice – it is God's justice. In the course of the Letter, Paul wants to present this justice as a contrast and antithesis to the law, although this is not a pure antithesis. And instead of giving concrete examples of justice, Paul gives tangible examples of injustice, first in non-Jewish societies (1.18-32) and then in Jewish societies (2.17-3.20). God's wrath smites injustice, because injustice "stifles" the truth (1.18). This is why justice is always on the side of truth. However, Paul cannot simply give examples of justice. The apostle never identifies justice with concrete actions or human works; he never writes: "this is just." Instead, he approaches justice indirectly, as a phenomenon or an idea that must be made manifest. As God's revelation, in a manner that cannot be thematized, justice is a knowledge in which human beings can receive a share

---

[124] Ibid., 935.
[125] Derrida, *Specters of Marx: The State of the Debt, the Work of Mourning and the New International*, xix.
[126] Jewett, *Romans: A Commentary*, 146.

by means of fragments. Since justice is God's, it remains a complete reality to which sinful human beings can receive an access that is incomplete before the last day.

Retributive justice – or was it the law?

A more complex picture of justice is gradually outlined in the Letter to the Romans. Paul states that because God is just or, perhaps more correctly, because God is like justice, his judgement is also just. All stand alike before the judgement of God: "For God shows no partiality" (2.11). And no one can present excuses in order to escape this judgement (2.1). In one way or another, everyone will either be smitten by God's wrath or rewarded by God's justice. Paul writes:

> For he will repay according to each one's deeds: to those who by patiently doing good seek for glory and honor and immortality, he will give eternal life; while for those who are self-seeking and who obey not the truth but wickedness, there will be wrath and fury. (Rom. 2.6-8)

A divine verdict is pronounced here on the basis of an idea of justice that is constructed on retributive principles. God repays good and evil deeds in keeping with a justice based on a kind of fairness and proportionality. If one does what is good, one receives in turn the good in the judgement, but if one does what is evil, the evil is returned through a kind of divine accounting. The punishment is in accordance with the transgression. This is thus a foreseeable religious and moral economy where the books can be balanced all the time by a just judgement from God. All that is askew in human lives will be adjusted by a God who, according to Paul, guarantees that the judgement will come. God's wrath is "storing up" (2.5) in relation to those who do what is evil, while eternal life waits for those who do what is good (2.7). Up to this point, there is a simple division between those who do good and those who do evil (2.1-11). In Derrida's words, we can call this form of justice a kind of "*rendering justice that would be limited to sanctioning, to restituting, and to doing right*".[127] But what if one has no knowledge of the law and its criteria for the good?

---

[127] Derrida, *Specters of Marx: The State of the Debt, the Work of Mourning and the New International*, 23.

There is equality before the law, in the sense that each one who knows the law is to be judged in accordance with it. Accordingly, those who have both known the law and broken it perish outside the law. The essential point is what one has done, irrespective of whether one had access to the prohibitions and commandments of the law. Besides this, the law cannot be restricted to explicit paragraphs or prescriptions that are written down and interpreted, because when Paul highlights non-Jews who nevertheless do what the law says, the apostle explains that "what the law requires is written on their hearts" (2.15). The law is therefore something greater. The law has an imprint on the conscience and a link with it – a conscience that is universal. Earlier on in the Letter, Paul has declares that "since the creation of the world", even those who are not Jews have been able to know something of what God intends with the world (1.20). Human beings have a kind of predisposition to know justice, because they have the demands of the law in their heart. They are receptive to what morality means. They have a conscience: "their conflicting thoughts will accuse or perhaps excuse them" (2.15). This resembles what we in everyday speech call "a bad conscience". We have a bad conscience when we live with a moral dilemma that we cannot shake off. But if we want to live more in accordance with justice, according to Derrida, and the alternative to a bad conscience is "a good conscience", the former is far more preferable.[128]

Paul emphasizes works when he writes that "the doers of the law . . . will be justified" (2.13). In other passages in the Letter, he contrasts law and justice, but here the two elements are closely linked. When Derrida writes that "it is just that there be law",[129] he is pointing to the intention of the law, namely, justice. This does not necessarily mean that the right or the law is just, but that the law aims at justice, and that justice needs the law. The law is the necessary medium or expression of justice, and justice cannot do without it. Without the law, and indeed without the coercive power of the law, it is difficult for justice to be either genuine or effective: "But it turns out that droit claims to exercise itself in the name of justice and that justice is required to establish itself in the name of a law that must be 'enforced.'"[130] Paul never yields ground on the demand for justice, which remains a perennial requirement for human

---

[128] *The Gift of Death*, 67, 85.
[129] "Force of Law: The 'Mystical Foundation of Authority' (Deconstruction and the Possibility of Justice)", 947.
[130] Ibid., 959-61.

beings. When he links justice to the law, Paul can be read as a thinker who has perceived that the law is necessary, if justice is ever to exist. But, as both Paul and Derrida have recognized, things are more complicated than this.

The usefulness and uselessness of religion

For Paul, the fact that the law is necessary for justice does not mean that it secures justice. Since the law embraces a totality, it is always possible for individual parts of it to acquire a priority for human beings and for their societies at the cost of other parts. One aspect of the almost ineluctable tragedy of the law is that its external expressions can retain their status as supremely important, and yet can be reduced to a justification of human beings' moral status and authority. When Paul addresses a "you" who calls himself "a Jew" and states that this person is convinced that he can be a guide and teacher for others (2.17-24), he is shining a critical light on precisely this moral superiority. This does not mean that Paul is against moral leaders. What he does is to put them on the spot, in order to show the importance of an inner piety vis-à-vis the law that cannot be reduced to merely external expressions: it must be lived, not just preached. In this way, he is putting a question mark against the power of these persons. His words are based on an ideal of being a "true Jew" (2.28), and this remains a title of honor for Paul. He is and remains a Jew, but a Jew who believes in Christ.

If we follow Karl Barth's interpretation, the figure of "the Jew" can be read as the self-declared believer or religious person, in view of the fact that circumcision is a religious ritual that makes religion something external, in various senses of the term.[131] Externalization is an insoluble problem with religiosity, in that, if religion is to find expression through human beings, even the most internalized religion must be turned into something external. But when the depth becomes the surface, this need not mean superficiality, and still less something even worse, such as insincerity. Derrida writes, "Religion is responsibility or it is nothing at all."[132] A morally irresponsible religiosity has no value, from his perspective. Paul makes a similar claim when he writes,

---

[131] Karl Barth, *The Epistle to the Romans,* 6 ed. (London: Oxford University Press, 1968), 40.
[132] Derrida, *The Gift of Death,* 2.

"Circumcision indeed is of value if you obey the law" (2.25). Since the goal of the law is justice, this entails that a fundamental religious mark of this kind is worthless unless it makes a contribution to a more moral existence or a more just world. This is why an internal relationship, perhaps a kind of awakening, to the original meaning of the ritual is required, to prevent it from being reduced to something purely physical and external:

> For a person is not a Jew who is one outwardly, nor is true circumcision something external and physical. Rather, a person is a Jew who is one inwardly, and real circumcision is a matter of the heart – it is spiritual and not literal. Such a person receives praise not from others but from God. (2.28-29)

The philosophical work of Derrida, who grew up in Algerian Judaism, where people usually said "baptism" instead of circumcision and "eucharist" instead of bar mitzvah,[133] suggests that Paul's admonitory words about circumcision should be addressed to more widespread religious rituals in today's Europe, such as "baptism" and "eucharist":[134] it is not enough to be baptized externally with water. You must also be baptized internally, with Spirit. You must to some degree live as a baptized person, if baptism is to have any value. And this may be a particularly urgent issue, given that much of the responsibility for Christianity's historical breach with Judaism has been ascribed to the apostle, not least thanks to later interpretations of his words about circumcision. In this historically important reception of Pauline texts about circumcision, the underlying premise in 2.28-29 has often been overlooked: Paul's argumentation about the relative value of circumcision is anchored in the premise that both being a "true Jew" and being circumcised have a high value in the apostle's thinking. This implicit premise is made explicit in the words that immediately follow:

> Then what advantage has the Jew? Or what is the value of circumcision? Much, in every way. For in the first place the Jews were entrusted with the oracles of God. (Rom. 3.1-2)

---

[133] Bennington, *Jacques Derrida*, 72-3.
[134] Here, Rom. 2.28-29 is consciously read partly in accordance with and partly in conflict with Derrida's own reading of this pericope. Derrida, "A Silkworm of One's Own", 344-5.

When the Jew becomes the illustration of the religious person, with all the problems that religion entails and raises, justice, as the goal of the law, becomes the criterion of religion's value. Paul becomes in this way a critic of religion who relativizes religion's exalted value from the critical perspective of the divine justice. Later ages see Paul as the author of the Christian religion, but he initiates its secularization: he almost empties religious ritual of its meaning in his eagerness to attribute the deepest meaning to the observance of the law and the fulfillment of justice, since it is utterly pointless to be baptized, if you do not live for justice. Paul thus appears to be secularizing religion in the name of piety vis-à-vis the law, and hence in the name of ethics – a religion that can degenerate into closed societies of enthusiasts who cultivate the secret and the mystical. In Paul's spirit, Derrida cannot envisage a religion in which the ethical has been expunged by the mystical; but he can acknowledge the value of a religion that has succeeded in taming the mystical at the service of ethics and of moral responsibility: "In the proper sense of the word, religion exists once the secret of the sacred, orgiastic, or demonic mystery has been, if not destroyed, at least integrated, and finally subjected to the sphere of responsibility."[135]

Justice as a gift in faith

Paul has insisted on justice as fairness and proportionality. God's wrath does not smite arbitrarily; it mounts up until the Day of Judgement (2.5). Given the serious character of human injustice, it is not unreasonable that the God of justice reacts and inflicts a punishment that is appropriate to the acts of wickedness. Here, we find a form of applied justice as proportionality, which resembles what Derrida describes as "the exercise of justice as law or right, legitimacy or legality, stabilizable and statutory, calculable, a system of regulated and coded prescriptions".[136] If justice is to be fair, it must necessary be articulated in a legal system. But how can one be sure whether a legal system is ultimately just, whether the coded regulations do justice to justice itself?

---

[135] *The Gift of Death*, 2.
[136] "Force of Law: The 'Mystical Foundation of Authority.' (Deconstruction and the Possibility of Justice)", 923.

Even the most honest conscience can encounter here an abyss between law and justice, precisely because the law is not experienced as a guarantor or as a pure image of justice. And there are no definite criteria that enable one to distinguish with complete certainty law or right, on the one hand, and justice, on the other: "The 'sufferance' of deconstruction, and what makes it suffer and what makes those it torments to suffer, is perhaps the absence of rules and definitive criteria that would allow one to distinguish unequivocally between droit and justice."[137] But it is an intellectual suffering of this kind, or an existential trial, that brings one nearer to a distinction between the two. The "father" of deconstructionism insists that justice is radically different from proportionality, the calculated administering of justice in accordance with the law and through the law. The philosopher describes justice as "rebellious to rule" and "foreign to symmetry".[138] For if the punishment is to be proportionate, law and right always involve in some sense revenge or retribution. As Derrida writes: "If right or law stems from vengeance, as Hamlet seems to complain that it does – before Nietzsche, before Heidegger, before Benjamin – can one not yearn for a justice that one day, a day belonging no longer to history, a quasi-messianic day, would finally be removed from the fatality of vengeance?"[139] He longs for an almost messianic day when justice has no longer made itself dependent upon retribution.

Paul has already proclaimed this day in the Letter to the Romans, when he describes a messianic present age in contrast to a period of time mentioned earlier. After describing the moral decadence of the pagans in 1.18-32 and stating in 2.17-19 that the Jews bear the same responsibility before the judgement of God, Paul emphasizes in 3.1-20 that sin is universal and that the entire world is guilty vis-à-vis the divine justice. Nothing measures up to the demands of justice, not even actions carried out in accordance with the law: "For 'no human being will be justified in his sight' by deeds prescribed by the law, for through the law comes the knowledge of sin" (3.20). In 3.21, Paul returns to the principal theme in Romans: God's justice, which has now become manifest. The messianic day has now come – through the Christ event:

---

[137] Ibid.
[138] Ibid., 959.
[139] Derrida, *Specters of Marx: The State of the Debt, the Work of Mourning and the New International*, 21.

> But now, apart from law, the righteousness of God has been disclosed, and is attested by the law and the prophets, the righteousness of God through faith in Jesus Christ for all who believe. For there is no distinction, since all have sinned and fall short of the glory of God; they are now justified by his grace as a gift, through the redemption that is in Christ Jesus, whom God put forward as a sacrifice of atonement by his blood, effective through faith. He did this to show his righteousness, because in his divine forbearance he had passed over the sins previously committed; it was to prove at the present time that he himself is righteous and that he justifies the one who has faith in Jesus. (3.21-26)

This is a compact textual passage in which what the apostle has described as a profound human injustice, followed by righteous wrath, is intercepted and interrupted. Paul maintains the close link between law and justice by underlining that the law "bears witness" to justice. "The law and the prophets" can be understood here to mean the whole of scripture, or the sacred texts of the Jews that contain the law. The fact that the law has pointed to justice means that it was not given without a reason. Its relationship to justice in the past was not purely arbitrary; but now, justice has emerged more clearly or definitively, and it is wholly obvious that this is "apart from law". This is a justice that is given through faith in Jesus Christ, either by believing in Christ or by believing like Christ (imitating Christ's faith or his faithfulness to justice).[140] Since all have sinned, each one who receives a share in this justice does so out of grace, without meriting it. When Paul postulates that all who believe in Christ become just, as persons who are "redeemed", he touches on both the legal and the economic spheres.[141] When this happens "as a gift", the legal logic and the retribution by righteous wrath are annulled, and the believers are given justice as a gift. The "gift" comes in here as an idea that breaks with the preceding idea that God is obligated and bound by human deeds to exercise a justice that is proportionate and has its place in a book-keeping that serves to re-establish the equilibrium.

---

[140] The Greek genitive expression underlying the translation "faith in Jesus Christ" is open to both interpretations. Halvor Moxnes, "Abrahams Gud for jøder og hedninger (Rom 3,21-4,25)", in *Paulusevangeliet: Nye perspektiver på Romerbrevet*, ed. Troels Engberg-Pedersen and Kasper Bro Larsen (Copenhagen: Anis, 2015), 93.

[141] Jewett, *Romans: A Commentary*, 282-3.

The way in which Paul here links the idea of an undeserved gift to justice appears to touch upon a link that is also articulated by the philosophy of Derrida, who declares that "discourses on double affirmation, the gift beyond exchange and distribution, the undecidable, the incommensurable or the incalculable, or on singularity, difference and heterogeneity are also, through and through, at least obliquely discourses on justice".[142] Up to this passage, Paul has emphasized the just judgement as the result of a type of exchange where good deeds (both with and outside the law) are cashed in for a good reward and evil deeds are paid back with a harsh penalty, whereas the idea of the gift has illustrated another dimension in Paul's concept of justice. This does not mean that the measuring of punishment and reward in accordance with the law is now superseded in Paul's eyes, or that this dimension of justice as a kind of economic balancing act is completely abolished. As he writes: "Do we then overthrow the law by this faith? By no means! On the contrary, we uphold the law" (3.31). The law's logic of calculation and computation remains valid, but it is relativized or secondary in relation to the justice that is now given as a gift. After the Christ event, it is as if benefits had been showered on human beings through hitherto undiscovered divine "surplus stock". Thanks to this surplus, justice has shed its light over the law and renewed the world from the outside. And from now on, justice in the Letter to the Romans has an overtone of something disproportionate, as when Paul writes: "But law came in, with the result that the trespass multiplied; but where sin increased, grace abounded all the more" (5.20). Grace or the gift becomes a surplus that is shared and given out of sheer generosity. The Pauline image of justice has thereby become more complex: legal retribution or economic distribution has been supplemented or surpassed by a justice that overflows all its banks.

What then does it mean to say that the human being is declared "justified" by grace (3.24)? The affirmation that some are declared just undeniably sounds somewhat formal and empty. Does a divine declaration actually produce more justice? The New Testament scholar Halvor Moxnes has pointed out that a traditional Protestant interpretation of this passage, as it was understood by the Reformer Martin Luther (*simul iustus et peccator*), scarcely succeeds in grasping the entire meaning in Paul's words here, since the driving force in

---

[142] Derrida, "Force of Law: The 'Mystical Foundation of Authority.' (Deconstruction and the Possibility of Justice)", 929.

Paul's argument in this passage concerns the effect of the declaration that a person is just through Christ. Moxnes refers to the scriptural scholar Philip Esler, who has coined a new English verb, "to righteous", in order to bring out this effect.[143] But how are we to understand this neologism?

Once again, our reading can be informed by Jacques Derrida,[144] since he too was attracted by this verbal form – not in order to read Paul, but in order to think through justice on a general philosophical basis:

> [T]o *justice, justicing,* the act of doing justice, of justi*fying* justice, of *putting* justice to *work,* operating a justice that, by rendering justice outside, in the world and for others, remains itself, remains the justice it is, carrying itself out in the world without going out of itself. *To justice* is intransitive even if justice, *by justicing,* does something, although it does nothing that is an object. Justice shines forth, it radiates and so does the just (Emphasis in original).[145]

We can therefore say that, for Paul, the effect of the Christ event is that the one who believes "is righteoused". Justice as a gift shines forth for the believer who is filled with justice through its gift. This transcendent action out of pure grace therefore has the effect, not only that justice is given to a person, but that this person puts it into action, in praxis, although this does not make justice an object in the world, in such a way that someone can say: "It is just", without thereby betraying it. This is why Derrida is attracted by the neologism "to justice" as an intransitive verb (that is to say, a verb that performs and works without a direct object). This allows us to understand Rom. 3.24 as more than a simple explanation. Rather, it is an effective spreading of justice among human beings who are made just. The point must be that there is in fact to be more justice in the world – with the help of human beings.

Romans 7: Sin takes the law hostage – not the other way round

Many people want to be nice. Many would like to contribute to the good in society. In particular, in the Scandinavian countries where corruption is low and trust in institutions is great, people want to obey the law in order to

---

[143] Moxnes, "Abrahams Gud for jøder og hedninger (Rom 3,21-4,25)", 93.
[144] Jennings, *Outlaw Justice: The Messianic Politics of Paul*, 117.
[145] Jacques Derrida, "Justices", *Critical Inquiry* 31, no. 3 (2005): 3.

do what is good. Some Scandinavians like to think of their own societies as exceptionally egalitarian and just in a global context, and there is doubtless much that is true in this self-image. But not even in these societal contexts, where obedience to the law indubitably results in much good, is obedience to law sufficient to ensure that the societies are just. Not even this social-democratic obedience to the law is capable of creating perfect justice, and fidelity to social-democratic laws and rights seems to fall short with regard to justice. The works of the law are not enough – more is needed. As Derrida writes, "Every time that something comes to pass or turns out well, every time that we placidly apply a good rule to a particular case, to a correctly subsumed example, according to a determinant judgment, we can be sure that law (droit) may find itself accounted for, but certainly not justice."[146] The law on its own, even in the form of modern human rights, does not provide access to justice. The law is not able to bring forth justice.

For Paul, the law is not only inadequate in relation to justice; under certain circumstances, it can even make the situation worse and strengthen injustice. In Romans 7, he describes a disastrous process whereby the law ends up as an instrument of injustice. The law that bore witness to justice has the opposite effect. And this is not merely a simple wrong interpretation or a misuse of the law. The law is taken hostage in order that injustice may be practiced. Nor is this a matter of individual instances. For Paul, this hostage-taking is a structural possibility with a fatal consequence, namely, that sin takes the law hostage and it is impossible to tell the difference between the law itself and sin, since they appear to be one. They cannot be distinguished, and this inseparability makes the law even more vulnerable to abuse:

> What then should we say? That the law is sin? By no means! Yet, if it had been for the law, I would not have known sin. I would not have known what it is to covet if the law had not said, "You shall not covet." But sin, seizing an opportunity in the commandment, produced in me all kinds of covetousness. Apart from the law sin lies dead. I was once alive apart from the law, but when the commandment came, sin revived and I died, and the very commandment that promised life proved to be death to me. For sin, seizing an opportunity in the commandment, deceived me and through it

---

[146] "Force of Law: The 'Mystical Foundation of Authority.' (Deconstruction and the Possibility of Justice)", 947.

> killed me. So the law is holy, and the commandment is holy and just and good. Did what is good, then, bring death to me? By no means! It was sin, working death in me through what is good, in order that sin might be shown to be sin, and through the commandment might become sinful beyond measure. For we know that the law is spiritual; but I am of the flesh, sold into slavery under sin. I do not understand my own actions. For I do not do what I want, but I do the very thing I hate. (7.7-15)

The "I"-person struggles to keep sin and law apart from each other, in order once again to be able to distinguish between what gives death and what gives life. It is possible to read such a struggle along the lines sketched by Žižek: there is a sincere "I" in search of truth. In other words, the "I" who undergoes these experiences has the best intentions.[147] This "I" represents something of the best in the human being: sincerity. But the encounter with the law under the conditions of sin is brutal, because sin exploits a law that in principle is holy, and misuses a commandment that Paul insists is "holy and just and good" (7.12). Sin comes from the outside and takes possession of the law in a way that leads to death.

Nietzsche claimed that Paul wanted to abolish the law, but the apostle's argument here surely aims to save the law from its misuse by sin. And unlike the readings by Badiou and Žižek, the origin of sin seems not to lie in the law. This becomes even clearer when, unlike Žižek, we include and emphasize verse 12. The boundless or transgressive desire can then be said to be caused by sin, which makes use of the commandment in the law. The law can expose what sin is ("I would not have known what it is to covet if the law had not said . . ."), and its criteria for right and wrong can therefore unmask a desire that poses a threat to one's self-control. In other words, the law can provide a knowledge that can lead to greater self-awareness and controlled behaviour. But the law also possesses a more destructive potential. In a tragic manner, it can waken sin to new life in a way that leads to a kind of psychological and moral death, on the individual or the societal level. We end up in a situation where we no longer do what we truly want. We do what is evil, although we want what is good (7.19). It is as if, through the law, sin institutionalizes itself. Sin becomes structural. Injustice is institutionalized, and this spiral of evil

---

[147] "Here it is crucial that we are not dealing with the worst of human beings but the best . . ." Jennings, *Outlaw Justice: The Messianic Politics of Paul*, 120.

alienates people more and more from their own selves. Sin rules structurally, and injustice escalates.

Derrida has pointed out how the laws and structures of the global world order literally kill innocent people, without any court ever calling to account the moral discourse of this world order or its exercise. Millions have died of hunger as a consequence of the law and its structures – not because the law has been broken.[148] Both Paul and Derrida, therefore, each in his own way, can be said to have drawn attention to the catastrophe of the law or, perhaps more correctly, to the tragedy of obedience to the law. This is why societal structures and legal systems must continually be revised, and sometimes revolutionized, if anything is ever to become more just.

The eschatological and ethical dimension of justice

The tragedy that the "I" undergoes in Romans 7 is great, but the proportions of God's restorating and reconciling justice in the Letter are even greater, since the justice that has been revealed independently of the law in order to redeem the created order "waits with eager longing" (8.19) and has a cosmic and eschatological significance: "We know that the whole creation has been groaning in labor pains until now" (8.22). The messianic day when justice comes can renew all things – on the basis of a past that lies behind us and a future that lies ahead. But both past and future are given a new meaning on the basis of the new justice of the messianic age, which irrupts into an intense and creative present day. Indeed, justice can be revealed – that is to say, justice is at all conceivable – only in relation to the sacrifices caused by injustice in the past and in an obligation vis-à-vis the coming generations in the future. Derrida maintains that justice necessarily has an eschatological dimension,[149]

---

[148] "... the smooth functioning of such a society, the monotonous complacency of its discourses on morality, politics, and the law, and the exercise of its rights ... are in no way impaired by the fact that, because of the structure of the laws of the market that society has instituted and controls, because of the mechanisms of external debt and other similar inequities, that same 'society' *puts to* death or (...) *allows* to die of hunger and disease tens of millions of children (...) without any moral or legal tribunal ever being considered competent to judge such a sacrifice, the sacrifice of others to avoid being sacrificed oneself." Derrida, *The Gift of Death*, 85–6.

[149] "Justice – or justice as it promises to be, beyond what it actually is – always has an eschatological dimension." Jacques Derrida and Maurizio Ferraris, *A Taste for the Secret*, trans. Giacomo Donis (Cambridge: Polity, 2001), 20.

and here there is a common denominator in Paul and Derrida – and in Walter Benjamin. To paraphrase Benjamin, we may say that the greatest strength we have received is the weak messianic power in justice, to which the past is entitled. This is what we owe to the past, although the extent of this guilt is not in any way made clear. Perhaps the most apt name for this unclarified guilt is responsibility. For Jacques Derrida, this responsibility is linked to our relation both to past and to future generations and is indissolubly linked to everything we say about justice:

> No justice – let us say no law and once again we are not speaking here of laws – seems possible or thinkable without the principle of some *responsibility*, beyond all living present, within that which disjoins the living present, before the ghosts of those who are not yet born or are already dead, be they victims of wars, political or other kinds of violence, nationalist, racist, colonialist, sexist, or other kinds of exterminations, victims of the oppressions of capitalist imperialism or any of the forms of totalitarianism.[150]

The atheist's belief in spirits is articulated here. The responsibility that justice entails concerns the spirits of those who have gone before us and to that which comes after us, and this is why Derrida interprets ethics eschatologically – on the basis of that which can come or must come – if justice is to occur. "[J]ustice is incalculable, it requires us to calculate with the incalculable", writes Derrida.[151] Eschatology here is no teleology;[152] it is neither predetermined nor predestined. It is entrusted to the human being's free (and potentially fatal) choices in the present day. But this is an eschatology that lives in a hopeful expectation of justice, because it can do nothing else, given the incalculability of justice. And it does not wait around passively, but acts actively, on the basis of the boundless responsibility.

It is especially in the dialogue with the philosopher Emmanuel Levinas that Derrida links this eschatological justice to the ethical responsibility. In the book *Adieu to Emmanuel Levinas,* Derrida explains his intellectual dependence on Levinas, whom he calls his teacher.[153] He gives a new reading of Levinas' book

---

[150] Derrida, *Specters of Marx: The State of the Debt, the Work of Mourning and the New International*, xix.
[151] "Force of Law: The 'Mystical Foundation of Authority.' (Deconstruction and the Possibility of Justice)", 947.
[152] *Specters of Marx: The State of the Debt, the Work of Mourning and the New International*, 37.
[153] *Adieu to Emmanuel Levinas*, 17. "I cannot, nor would I even try to, measure in a few words the oeuvre of Emmanuel Levinas. It is so large that one can no longer glimpse its edges." ibid., 3.

Totality and Infinity, the source of an idea that is particularly important for Derrida, and to which he refers many times in his own writings:[154] Levinas defines justice as the "equitable honoring of faces".[155] For Levinas, the "face" denotes the fundamental ethical experience of the vulnerability of the other human being. He claims that this is "the experience of the appearing of the absolutely other, where the face is the Other who addresses me and gives an order directly out of his nakedness, out of his strippedness".[156] This calls on me to take responsibility for the Other. It is not a dialogical relationship in which the Other tells me what I am to do. Rather, the order is a wordless command that speaks only from the face of the Other – from this human being's poverty, suffering or vulnerability. The vulnerability speaks as an injunction to respond. Responsibility demands a response in the form of action on my part, as an ethical subject. I must make a response without knowing beforehand what response I am to make. It is my responsibility to decide what I am to do, and there is in principle no limit to this responsibility. It is unlimited.[157] To the extent that I owe the Other something, this comes into being in the experience of this person's vulnerability, which speaks to me and calls upon me. Derrida calls this ethical obligation, which is generated by responsibility, "a guilt without fault and without debt".[158] We could also say that this responsibility is a debt that binds us although we have never taken a loan from the bank. It has nothing to do with a bank credit, and this is why it can never be paid down – for the responsibility we are given has no limitation in relation to the Other. Nor have we ever signed a contract on a promissory note in relation to the Other, because the ethical responsibility is anterior to my freedom. I have not signed anything, but I am requested to pay with all my compassion and mercy. The debt relationship consists in the fact that the Other's suffering affects me and calls upon me. There is no reciprocity, nor a fair distribution in the ethical relationship to the Other: there is asymmetry and unlimited debt. And all the religious language about submission and obedience is given

---

[154] Ibid., 29. See also Derrida, *Specters of Marx: The State of the Debt, the Work of Mourning and the New International*, 23.

[155] Levinas quoted in "Force of Law: The 'Mystical Foundation of Authority.' (Deconstruction and the Possibility of Justice)", 959.

[156] I translate "l'Autre" as "the Other". I retain the capital letter in order to underline the asymmetry, or the high moral position or supremacy of the Other; I do so also in order to emphasize the foreignness of the Other in relation to my own self.

[157] Derrida, *Adieu to Emmanuel Levinas*, 3.

[158] Ibid., 6.

a new ethical meaning.[159] For now, I am to submit to the call from the Other's suffering, in order to become an ethical subject and make a contribution to a more just world.

Like Derrida, Levinas had a Jewish background, but he was much more active as an interpreter of Jewish religious texts through his writings. In many ways, Derrida read his own Jewish inheritance through Levinas, for example, when he quoted one of Levinas' Talmud commentaries about justice and uprightness.[160] Derrida points out that in one of these commentaries, Levinas defines the uprightness that defines the attitude to myself, when I am receptive for what the Other says, as "an innocence without naivete, an uprightness without stupidity, an absolute uprightness which is also absolute self-criticism, read in the eyes of the one who is the goal of my uprightness and whose look calls me into question".[161] Uprightness thus entails a clear-sighted openness and a radical willingness to listen, in the passive reception of the challenging look of the Other. Justice *is* this receptivity. The Other's face affects me and is given to me. It cannot be calculated beforehand. We cannot calculate how the Other's suffering is to speak to us, what it is to say, and how we are to pose question marks against our own existence. It is and remains unpredictable – like the gift and like the responsibility in Derrida's philosophy. In other words, there are close similarities between what happens in the encounter with the face of the Other and justice as a gift in Derrida's philosophy.

At the same time, there are important links between the justice that has its origin in the encounter with the face of the Other and eschatology. Derrida refers to the foreword to *Totality and Infinity*, in which Levinas "removes the concept of prophetic eschatology from its usual philosophical applicability, from the horizon of history or of an end of history".[162] This is why Levinas posits "the eschatology of messianic peace" as a contrast to "the war of ontology" or the totality of existence. Eschatology thus becomes a kind of philosophy about

---

[159] "Metaphysics is enacted in ethical relations. Without the signification they draw from ethics theological concepts remain empty and formal frameworks." Emmanuel Levinas, *Totality and Infinity: An Essay on Exteriority*, trans. Alphonso Lingis, 2016 ed. (Pittsburgh: Duquesne University Press, 1969), 79.
[160] See the Talmud commentary "On the Tractate Shabbath". Derrida, *Adieu to Emmanuel Levinas*, 2.
[161] Ibid., 3.
[162] Ibid., 49.

how this totality ruptures and is broken up through the appearing of the face of the Other in a decisive and compact form of the present day.[163]

Derrida builds on an eschatology, and on an idea about what is to come, that does not depend on the existence of God. He develops further Levinas' idea that it is exclusively in the face of the Other that a divine dimension can become visible, and that it is only this appearing that can give a meaning to the word "God".[164] He seems to sympathize with Levinas' philosophical project of investigating what kind of meaning the word "God" can have in our modern world – without taking a position about whether or not God exists.[165] And to the extent that Derrida is an atheist, he professes an atheism that is very far from resting securely in a completely certain self-sufficiency. On the contrary, he speaks about an atheism that ends up in despair, and not least in alertness vis-à-vis what the Other says.[166] This is not an atheism that celebrates its own triumph, but rather a *sober* atheism that is radically open to being dislocated and turned upside down in the ethical event that is called "the face". The principal fear of a sober atheist is not that he or she might become a believer. The primary fear concerns the well-being of the Other.

The loving debt vis-à-vis the Other

Before he sends greetings to specific persons in Rome in the closing chapter of his Letter, Paul gives instructions in what modern editions of the Bible enumerate as chs 12-15 about how the addressees ought to live in the time ahead. These admonitions include a little passage that has attracted the special attention of some modern philosophers. Here, Paul also communicates his form of the commandment of love of neighbour, about which Sigmund Freud expressed such strong scepticism.[167] Paul writes about guilt and love

---

[163] Levinas, *Totality and Infinity: An Essay on Exteriority*, 21-30.
[164] "The dimension of the divine opens forth from the human face. A relation with the Transcendent free from all captivation by the Transcendent is a social relation." ibid., 78. Derrida writes: "God without being, God uncontaminated by being – is this not the most rigorous definition of the Face of the Wholly Other?" Derrida, *Adieu to Emmanuel Levinas*, 112.
[165] "This investigation was carried out independently of the problem of the existence or nonexistence of God." Emmanuel Levinas, *Of God Who Comes to Mind* (Stanford: Stanford University Press, 1998), xi.
[166] Derrida, *Adieu to Emmanuel Levinas*, 104-5.
[167] Sigmund Freud, "Civilization and Its Discontents", in *The Standard Edition of the Complete Psychological Works of Sigmund Freud: Vol. 21: The Future of an Illusion; Civilization and Its*

of neighbour in relation to the law, and then gives this an eschatological framework:

> Owe no one anything, except to love one another; for the one who loves another has fulfilled the law. The commandments, "You shall not commit adultery; You shall not murder; You shall not steal; You shall not covet"; and any other commandment, are summed up in this word, "Love your neighbor as yourself." Love does no wrong to a neighbor; therefore, love is the fulfilling of the law. Besides this, you know what time it is, how it is now the moment for you to wake from sleep. For salvation is nearer to us now that when we became believers; the night is far gone, the day is near. Let us then lay aside the works of darkness and put on the armor of light. (13.8-12)

Up to this point in the Letter, Paul has written in greater detail about God's love for human beings, and he has mentioned the human love for God (8.28); now, he turns to human beings' love for each other.[168] The perspective on this interpersonal love is strange, because it is presented as something the human person "owes", as a debt incumbent upon one. The underlying Greek verb has associations with economic, legal and societal obligations.[169] The society in which Paul and the Letter's addressees lived was a pyramid of obligations, with the Roman emperor at the top. In the Roman world, people entered into obligations in patron-client relationships that were very far from egalitarian, for example, between master and slave. If Paul's exhortation is interpreted to mean that the believers must disconnect themselves from this hierarchical network of obligations, where people constantly owe other persons services and goods, this can sound hopelessly utopian.[170] It is so radical. But it seems that Paul is serious about this admonition, which is presented in a part of the Letter where the instructions are strikingly concrete and practical.

The Pauline love of neighbour is based on equality and reciprocity, since it is addressed to all human beings as a radical form of universalism. When Paul expresses his injunction to love using the Greek pronoun *allêlous* ("each other"), one might think that it is restricted to those to whom he is writing,

---

Discontents, and Other Works: (1927-1931), ed. James Strachey and Anna Freud (London: Hogarth Press and the Institute of Psycho-analysis, 1961), 109-12.

[168] Joseph A. Fitzmyer, *Romans: A New Translation with Introduction and Commentary* (New York: Doubleday, 1993), 877.

[169] Jewett, *Romans: A Commentary*, 805-6.

[170] L. L. Welborn, *Paul's Summons to Messianic Life: Political Theology and the Coming Awakening* (New York: Columbia University Press, 2015), 56.

and concerns only their fellowship as believers in Christ. However, the very next sentence employs the Greek word *ton heteron* in declaring that the law is fulfilled by the one who loves one's fellow human being. A direct translation is "another", "the other" or "the one who is different", and this gives the Pauline love of neighbour a vast range.[171] The New Testament scholar L. L. Welborn notes that Paul's choice of the Greek term for "fellow human being" here in 13.8b is surprising, because the object that tends to follow the Greek verb *agapaô* is "brother" or "neighbor". When Paul summarizes the law with the commandment "Love your neighbor as yourself" (13.9), he appears to be quoting, or at least alluding to, Lev 19.18,[172] where we read: "You shall not take vengeance or bear a grudge against any of your people, but you shall love your neighbor as yourself: I am the LORD." If we give Paul's declaration in the Letter to the Galatians that "There is no longer Jew or Greek, there is no longer slave or free, there is no longer male and female" (Gal. 3.28) its due weight, we can assume that the ethnic limitation of "any of your people" in Leviticus is transcended here in Romans 13 by a love that embraces everyone, irrespective of ethnicity, status or gender.

This is a love of neighbour that both accords with the law and transcends the law. Like the justice that is manifested independently of the law (3.21) and is given to human beings without merits on their part, this is a love that is spread from a divine surplus that neither corresponds to what human beings have deserved nor is restricted by the calculating measurement and reckoning of the law. This love of neighbour is something much larger. Nor is it to be limited to a mutual obligation that reduces it to an equal exchange of kindness from one to another. Paul exhorts: "Owe no one anything" and then adds: ". . . except to love one another". The picture we are left with is of addressees who have a debt or liability in the matter of loving their fellow human being. Since the exhortation to love is boundless and unconditional, the words are also an injunction to live in a perennial debt or liability. And when we attach weight to the fact that one's fellow human being is a *ton heteron,* the consequence is that the one who is to be loved is different from our own selves.

---

[171] Fitzmyer, *Romans: A New Translation with Introduction and Commentary,* 678. Jewett, *Romans: A Commentary,* 808.
[172] Welborn, *Paul's Summons to Messianic Life: Political Theology and the Coming Awakening,* 58.

If love means that we are always in debt or liability vis-à-vis a figure that can be translated very literally as "the other", this puts us on the track of yet another trait shared by Paul and Derrida, since Derrida's ethics inspired by Levinas makes it easier to understand Paul's unexpected use of the term *ton heteron* for one's fellow human being and the Pauline idea of a loving debt or a debt that comes into existence in love of one's neighbour. Paul exhorts us to remain in this guilt, which we have incurred, not because of something we have done, but exclusively because of the ethical demand made by the Other. This ethical debt is a powerful Pauline image of the relationship between myself and the Other, where I am "in the dock" because the suffering of the Other poses fundamental questions about my way of life and my ego. The accusation is made, not against the background of my deeds, but exclusively from the face of the Other. This is an accusation or a guilt without content, so to speak; or more correctly, it is a movement out of my ego towards the Other. Because the guilt has no content, Paul links it exclusively to love for the neighbour who is different from me, for *ton heteron*. He emphasizes that the fellow human being whom I am to love is different, dissimilar or foreign. But *ton heteron* is not to be understood as "different" because this person belongs to another ethnic group, has a lower status in society or is of a different gender. The differentness cannot be read in sociological terms, but only ethically. The otherness or the ethical weight of the Other, which means that I must approach him or her with an almost religious reverence, does not consist in the fact that I am a woman and the other a man (or vice versa). Nor does it lie in a different skin colour or membership of a different social class. The ethical differentness that Paul designates as *ton heteron* lies exclusively in the vulnerability or suffering of the Other, which gives me an unbounded responsibility, to which I must then set boundaries in order to be able to act and achieve something for the Other. Earlier in the Letter, Paul has affirmed that Christ is the *telos* of the law (10.4), and this means that the goal of the law is ethics as fulfillment of the justice revealed in Christ.[173] In a similar way, Emmanuel Levinas insisted on

---

[173] "Assuming that ancient Judaism really was a legalistic religion, without any chance for individuals to experience grace, mercy, or love, it follows that any decent person, including Paul, would naturally fight against such an ideology, and thus, attribute a negative value to the Torah. According to the NRSV, Paul states that (. . .) "Christ is the end of the law" (Rom. 10.4). . . Translated in these terms, Paul seems to oppose the Jewish way of life based on Torah." Magnus Zetterholm og Nanos, *Paul within Judaism*, 42. "The law itself points to Christ as the linchpin of God's plan to extend his righteous mercy to the whole world." Stanley K. Stowers, *A Rereading of Romans: Justice, Jews, and*

the *telos* of Torah as ethics in the sense of the realization of justice. Both Paul and Levinas want to translate the Hebrew inheritance for the Gentiles, thereby proclaiming the ethical meaning of the revelation to all who are willing to accept it.[174]

Feuerbach in the Letter to the Romans?

It is striking to note that all the commandments from the Decalogue that Paul lists in Romans 13 are those that seek to regulate interpersonal relationships, for he writes: "The commandments, 'You shall not commit adultery; You shall not murder; You shall not steal; You shall not covet'; and any other commandment, are summed up in this word, 'Love your neighbor as yourself'" (13.9). The apostle does not mention the commandments that concern the relationship to God when he exemplifies and sums up the law in the new perspective in which it is located through the Christ event. One of those who noticed this was Jacob Taubes, who wanted to challenge the impression that the Christian idea of love in Romans 13 was in some way a sentimental emotionalism. According to Taubes, the opposite is true, since this scriptural passage is polemic against the Jesus of the gospels, who proclaimed love of neighbour as inseparably linked to love for God: "You shall love the Lord your God with all your heart, and with all your soul, and with all your mind, and with all your strength. The second is this, 'You shall love your neighbor as yourself'" (Mk 12.30-31a). In this way, Paul had removed the divine or vertical dimension from love of neighbour, and made it a purely human concern. Taubes held that this was nothing less than revolutionary:

> This sounds sentimental and so on, but it really isn't at all. This is a highly polemical text, polemical against Jesus . . . Paul doesn't issue a dual commandment, but rather makes them equivocal; I almost want to say, following Kojève, that he pulls a Feuerbach here. Forgive me, Feuerbach doesn't deserve to be mentioned in this context, but it is the love not of the

---

Gentiles (New Haven: Yale University Press, 1994), 308. See also Elliott, *Liberating Paul: The Justice of God and the Politics of the Apostle*, 177.

[174] Michael Fagenblat, *A Covenant of Creatures: Levinas's Philosophy of Judaism* (Stanford: Stanford University Press, 2010), 20-7.

Lord, but of the neighbor that is the focus here. No dual commandment, but rather *one commandment*. I regard this as an absolutely revolutionary act.[175]

Taubes' claim is that Paul consciously omits Jesus' commandment to love the Lord God, and thus "what emerges is a Feuerbach".[176] Taubes compares Paul to the left-wing Hegelian Ludwig Feuerbach (1804-72), who claimed that God was a human creation, and the worship of God little more than a worship of the human person's own being. Taubes insists that what Paul does in Rom. 13.9 is to limit God's role by reducing two commandments in Jesus' message to one commandment in his own. It is possible that Taubes became aware of this Pauline reduction thanks to the attention Spinoza had paid to it.[177] A germ of secularization may perhaps lie in this conscious or unconscious omission of the commandment to love God, but is it not an exaggeration to affirm that the Pauline version of the commandment to love one's neighbour is a revolution?

To omit Jesus' commandment to love God and instead emphasize love for one's neighbour need not be interpreted as a criticism of Jesus. This can instead be an emphasis that is in accord with Jesus' own intention – at the very least, with Jesus' attention to the Other in the preaching that finds expression in the gospels. We find an example of this kind of turning from love for God to love for one's fellow human being in Jesus' parable about the Good Samaritan (Lk. 10.25-37). The episode in which Jesus expounds the commandment to love God with all one's heart (10.27) goes in the same direction as Paul's "reduction" in Romans: Jesus' parable ends with a concentrated focus on the interpersonal relationship and on mercy (10.36-37). If there is a germ of secularization in Romans 13 that has contributed to drawing Christianity and society in Feuerbach's direction, this can perhaps be attributed to Jesus just as much as to Paul.

The question is whether this Pauline "reduction" actually benefits love of neighbour. Does love of neighbour become stronger if it is allowed to lead its own life – without a God? Is there more love of neighbour if the human being "does not have to" love God? Or is it not rather the case that the love

---

[175] Taubes, *The Political Theology of Paul*, 52-3.
[176] ". . . ein Feuerbach wird daraus": see the German-language transcription of Taubes' lecture. *Die Politische Theologie Des Paulus* (Munich: Wilhelm Fink, 1993), 74.
[177] This is pointed out by Gideon Baker, "Paul's Reduction of the Dual Commandment: The Significance of Worldliness to Messianic Life", *Political Theology* 21, no. 7 (2020): 609.

of neighbour is so exceptionally demanding that it requires an extraordinary faith, for example a faith in God, if it is to be followed and complied with?[178]

Conclusion: Philosophical perspectives on the Letter to the Romans

While biblical scholars have largely listened to Krister Stendahl's warning against reading Paul as an introspective thinker, philosophers have discovered even more aspects in the Pauline introspection in Romans. And where Stendahl held that later generations had misunderstood Paul by reading the apostle through Augustine, modern philosophers have had a tendency to see Paul through Augustine, who usually has a place in the canon of the history of philosophy. Stendahl's explanation of why Romans 7 had been read as a prime example of introspection and the expression of an unavoidable struggle in the universal human psyche was that Paul simply wrote too well. He thereby also acknowledged implicitly that the status of the Letter to the Romans as a classic in Western intellectual history was its utterly extraordinary potential of meaning.

The Letter to the Romans has been a special source of inspiration for thinkers with a psychoanalytic orientation to philosophize with the help of Paul. Romans has proved to be an attractive text for reflection on what the philosophers see as perennially valid aspects of human life, particularly in relation to the law, which in psychoanalysis is an unavoidable dimension of human existence. A strikingly large number agree with Nietzsche's interpretation of Paul as an apostle who wanted to abolish the law and replace it with faith. This means that this central premise in Nietzsche's polemic against the apostle is not in fact challenged, and the aspect of Paul – as an apologist both for the law and for a new type of piety vis-à-vis the law – that makes things complicated emerges only to a small extent in philosophical readings of Romans. That Paul would defend the law as holy and good is so unthinkable that the philosophers tend to overlook this standpoint in Romans. This means that they fail to grasp a

---

[178] When Sigmund Freud rejects the commandment to love one's neighbour as an ideal demand that is unrealistic for a humankind that has exposed itself as a flock of wild animals, he quotes the biblical commandment in its Pauline form or "reduction", with no reference to a god. Freud, "Civilization and Its Discontents".

more sophisticated and complex thinking about law and justice, where there is no simple antithesis between these two realities. Although justice takes precedence, the law remains a necessity for justice, while justice continually destabilizes the law and puts fundamental questions to it. This is not a definitive synthesis of law and justice, but a continuous back-and-forth between them.

While the philosophers choose "anti-philosophy", "universalism" or "introspection" as the principal categories to describe the centre of Paul's thinking, "justice" may be a more appropriate thematic entry point, if one wishes to read the Pauline Letters philosophically. Justice is not an idea imposed on the Letter to the Romans from the outside, but a concept that emerges from inside the Letter along with its principal thesis (1.16-17), namely, that God's justice has been revealed, first for Jews and then for Greeks. Justice is a concept linked to the law and is a fundamental motif in political philosophy. With an overarching concept of justice, inspired by Derrida and Levinas, it is possible to give a new orientation to the discussion of the philosophical relevance of Romans. While Badiou and Žižek have made Paul's universalism a crowbar against every form of communitarianism and multiculturalism, a comprehensive concept of justice can be linked to philosophical reflections that take their starting point in demands for a more just economic redistribution, as well as to demands by identity politics for justice in the form of the recognition of sexual, ethnic and gender differences.[179] The vulnerability and poverty of the Other can be caused by injustice connected to the class system, but also by cultural oppression. Justice, as a horizon outside the law and independent of the logic of the law, can inspire new forms of politics with regard to differences and to redistribution. Socioeconomic and cultural realities can provide motivation for new struggles for justice that take seriously the existence of various forms of injustice and confront them with political strategies that are both affirmative and transformative – depending on the situation and context. For Paul too is one who thinks about differences.[180]

---

[179] Nancy Fraser, "Sosial rettferdighet i identitetspolitikkens tidsalder", *Agora* 27, no. 4 (2009): 213-35.
[180] Løland, *Reception of Paul the Apostle in the Works of Slavoj Žižek*, 175-92.

4

Conclusion

Paul: A philosopher for atheists

The history of the interpretation of any text consists of layers of various readings. In this book, the history of the reception of Paul's Letters in modern philosophy has been both presented and developed further. When the history of reception is analysed, this history itself is necessarily also expanded, since we are located within its horizon. We have presented and discussed the picture of Paul in older and more recent voices in modern philosophy. We have included the readings of Paul in Spinoza, Sigmund Freud, Martin Heidegger and Max Weber, and we have built upon them. But it is above all various layers of readings of Paul in Nietzsche's writings that have been in focus here. These readings have been presented and compared with more recent philosophical readings in combination with my own readings, which can never completely be separated from those of the philosophers. But Nietzsche's picture of Paul as a fraud who was impelled by a boundless lust for power to tyrannize the masses has been rejected by recent philosophers such as Badiou, Agamben, Critchley, Derrida, Kristeva and Žižek. All these philosophers see Paul as a thinker who seeks truths, a thinker who has a philosophical value independently of a belief in God or in supernatural forces. As we have seen, this is not an atheism or secularity that is simply imposed on the Pauline Letters from the outside. There is a germ of various forms of secularization or even profanation in these Letters. There is a potential of secularizing meaning in Paul that is sometimes actualized in the quest for a radical philosophy. A religious figure like the apostle Paul thereby becomes the object of secular thinking in ways that destabilize and challenge accustomed distinctions between what we often take for granted are secular ideas and praxis, on the one hand, and religious ideas and praxis, on the other. The French philosopher Jean-Luc Nancy claims that "Christianity has desacralized, demythologized, and secularized itself in such a constant and irreversible way".[1] Interestingly, he traces this secularization back to the New Testament writers, and especially to Paul.[2]

Among all the biblical authors, it is Paul most of all who has attracted the interest of these philosophers. They thus implicitly confirm the image of Paul that Spinoza established in the early modern period as the one who philosophized more than any other apostle, and also Spinoza's perception of the Letter to the Romans as based on something more rational than a divine revelation. This does not mean that these atheistic philosophers do not encounter religious elements in Paul's thinking that they are obliged to doubt or reject; but it means that all of them share Alain Badiou's premise that a philosopher can draw out completely secularized ideas from the Letters of an apostle who is regarded as the second founder of Christianity. The philosophers' demythologization or secular refining can make Paul's thinking almost chemically free of religion. Paul can become an apostle for atheists. In the aftermath of Spinoza's praise of Paul's philosophical abilities, there is a way of reading Paul in the modern period and approaching the apostle as a thinker with profound philosophical insights. As Jacob Taubes points out, not even Friedrich Nietzsche always succeeds in hiding his admiration of the depth in the Pauline thinking.

This essay is not an invitation to reach a conclusion definitively about the meaning of Paul's Letters. It is an attempt to open up the intellectual and existential conversation about them. The interpretations in this book must also stand the test and be more or less meaningful for its readers. In addition to giving an overview of various philosophical readings of Paul, the intention here has been to indicate some possible strengths and weaknesses in these readings, from philosophical, historical and political perspectives. This essay has not been based on a supposition that a reading is either correct or false, but that it can be good or less good. Many interpretations are possible, but not all interpretations are good. All interpretations can be discussed, and their strengths and weaknesses can come to light through critical investigations

---

[1] Jean-Luc Nancy, "In the Midst of the World or, Why Deconstruct Christianity?", in *Re-Treating Religion. Deconstructing Christianity with Jean-Luc Nancy*, ed. Alena Alexandrova, et al. (New York: Fordham University Press, 2012), 4.
[2] Ibid., 13.

and dialogues about them. Nor need differing interpretations be mutually exclusive. For example, it is not necessary to choose between psychoanalytic readings of law in the Letter to the Romans and readings inspired by Derrida. Both perspectives can enrich our understanding of this text.

Similarly, this is not an argument for choosing between a premodern religious Paul and a modern secularized understanding of the apostle. The Uruguayan Jesuit and liberation theologian Juan Luis Segundo once wrote that Christians cannot assume that they do not need Freud, just because they already have Paul.[3] On the contrary, modern psychoanalysis could supply a deeper understanding of faith, which, according to Segundo, must be liberated from oppressive ideologies in order to become a liberating force for Latin America's poor. The faith that was intact after the criticism of religion had a right to live. Indeed, it was necessary, in order to create a better world. Faith had to be cleansed from alienating superstition. It had to be demythologized.

One reason why Paul Ricoeur called Karl Marx, Friedrich Nietzsche and Sigmund Freud the founders of "the school of suspicion" was their shared opposition to religion.[4] All three claim in various ways that religion alienates the human being from the truth about oneself, either about one's real role in the class struggle, one's fundamental will to power, or one's psychological self-deception. While Paul is absent from Marx's writings, the apostle played something of a role for Freud and occupied considerable space in Nietzsche's philosophy. In other words, Paul is an inseparable part of the genealogy of the modern criticism of religion.

One basic reason why recent philosophers appreciate Paul as a thinker is that, like Freud, they emphasize the credibility in the tragic descriptions of human life in the apostle's Letters. The Pauline original sin and its catastrophic consequences are much more credible for these modern philosophers than the Pauline salvation. They can buy Paul's diagnosis, but they are more doubtful about the medicine that the apostle wants to prescribe for his patients. There are nevertheless rare moments in modern philosophy where one or other form of Pauline salvation is acknowledged, as when Sigmund Freud acknowledges

---

[3] Juan Luis Segundo, *The Humanist Christology of Paul*, vol. 3, Jesus of Nazareth Yesterday and Today (Maryknoll: Orbis Books, 1986), 167.
[4] Paul Ricoeur, *Freud and Philosophy: An Essay on Interpretation* (New Haven: Yale University Press, 1970), 32.

in *Moses and Monotheism* that Paul's call to admit guilt is a "breakthrough".[5] This is interesting precisely because psychoanalytic therapy links the patient's admission of one's own guilt and that of others to a potential deliverance in the treatment.

There is something about the radically evil human nature or sinful inclination that creates a resonance in a modern philosophy that finds it difficult to dispense with psychoanalytical concepts such as aggressiveness, illusions, projections and denials. Psychoanalysis can be said to uncover some of the worst symptoms of original sin. Nor is this all: – its insights into the long-lasting effects of traumas, or into difficult emotional states in parents that are transformed into psychological pain for their children, can lead psychoanalysis to nod approvingly to the idea that sin is in some sense hereditary in an almost physical manner.

For modern philosophers who are interested in Paul, the absence of God is more obvious than most other things: the scepticism about God's existence weighs much more heavily than openness to the idea of a divine intervention in the world. This, however, does not mean that the philosophers' atheism consists in a consistent rejection of the words "God" or "religion" as meaningful for a modern human being. This book brings another self-declared atheist into the discussion of Paul, namely, Jacques Derrida. All the parallels make it clear that Derrida remains a kind of Pauline atheist who opens the door onto new readings of the apostle.

While Agamben, Badiou and Žižek all see Paul as an antinomian thinker with a revolutionary potential, the apostle can be understood against the background of Derrida's philosophy as a reform-oriented interpreter of the law. Both Paul and Derrida aim to formulate a philosophy about justice that contains the necessary conservation of the law, on the one hand, and its destruction, on the other hand. In the light of the justice that has become visible independently of the law, the one who wants to be just will rediscover the law again and again in love towards the Other.[6] It is difficult to reduce this

---

[5] Freud, *Moses and Monotheism*, 65.
[6] "In short, for a decision to be just and responsible, it must, in its proper moment if there is one, be both regulated and without regulation: it must conserve the law and also destroy or suspend it enough to have to reinvent it in each case, rejustify it." Derrida, "Force of Law: The 'Mystical Foundation of Authority'", in *Deconstruction and the Possibility of Justice*, ed. Drucilla Cornell, Michel Rosenfeld, and David Gray Carlson (New York and London: Routledge, 1992), 23.

to a political program. It constitutes a summons to a continuous re-evaluation of the regulation, the calculation, and the law while awaiting the incalculable justice that we must reckon with – if we are to be open to hear the Other. This receptivity – following in the footsteps of the crucified one – will inspire a constant revaluing, questioning and rediscovering of the law as the law of love. This love can lead to conservatism, to reform, or to revolution. Nothing is decided in advance. In the encounter with the Other, everything stands open – face to face.

Bibliography

Agamben, Giorgio. *The Church and the Kingdom*. London: Seagull Books, 2012.

Agamben, Giorgio. *The Coming Community*. Minneapolis: University of Minnesota Press, 1993.

Agamben, Giorgio. *The Kingdom and the Glory: For a Theological Genealogy of Economy and Government (Homo Sacer Ii, 2)*. Stanford: Stanford University Press, 2011.

Agamben, Giorgio. *Means without End: Notes on Politics*. Minneapolis: University of Minnesota Press, 2000.

Agamben, Giorgio. *The Time That Remains: A Commentary on the Letter to the Romans*. Stanford: Stanford University Press, 2005.

Allison, Dale C. *Constructing Jesus: Memory, Imagination, and History*. London: SPCK, 2010.

Anders, Martinsen. "Oversettelsesproblematikk og slaveri." *Teologisk tidsskrift* 7, no. 2 (2018): 114–31.

Babich, Babette. "Ad Jacob Taubes." *New Nietzsche Studies* 7, no. 3 (2007): 5–10.

Badiou, Alain. *Ethics: An Essay on the Understanding of Evil*. London: Verso, 2001.

Badiou, Alain. *Saint Paul: The Foundation of Universalism*. Stanford: Stanford University Press, 2003.

Barclay, John M. G. "Paul and the Philosophers: Alain Badiou and the Event." *New Blackfriars* 91, no. 1032 (2010): 171–84.

Barthes, Roland. *Image, Music, Text*. Translated by Stephen Heath. New York: Hill and Wang, 1977.

Benjamin, Walter. *Illuminations*. New York: Schocken books, 2007.

Blanton, Ward. *Displacing Christian Origins: Philosophy, Secularity, and the New Testament*. Chicago: University of Chicago Press, 2007.

Blanton, Ward. "Dispossessed Life." In *A Radical Philosophy of Saint Paul*, edited by Stanislas Breton. New York: Columbia University Press, 2011.

Blanton, Ward. *A Materialism for the Masses: Saint Paul and the Philosophy of Undying Life*. New York: Columbia University Press, 2014.

Blanton, Ward. "Paul and Contemporary Philosophy". In *The Oxford Handbook of Pauline Studies*, edited by Matthew V. Novenson and R. Barry Matlock, 668–87. Oxford: Oxford University Press, 2022.

Blanton, Ward and Hent de Vries. *Paul and the Philosophers*. New York: Fordham University Press, 2013.

Boer, Roland. *Criticism of Religion: On Marxism and Theology, Ii*. Leiden: Brill, 2009.

Boer, Roland. "Julia Kristeva, Marx and the Singularity of Paul." In *Marxist Feminist Criticism of the Bible*, edited by Jorunn Økland and Roland Boer, 204–28. Sheffield: Sheffield Phoenix Press, 2008.

Boer, Roland. "Paul of the Gaps. Agamben, Benjamin and the Puppet Player." In *Paul in the Grip of the Philosophers*, edited by Peter Frick, 57–68. Minneapolis: Fortress Press, 2013.

Bornkamm, Günther. *Paulus*. Translated by Tom Rønnow. Oslo: Land og Kirke, 1977.

Boyarin, Daniel. "Paul among the Antiphilosophers; or, Saul among the Sophists." In *St. Paul among the Philosophers*, edited by John D. Caputo and Linda Martín Alcoff, 109–41. Bloomington: Indiana University Press, 2009.

Bradley, Arthur and Andrew Tate. *The New Atheist Novel: Fiction, Philosophy and Polemic after 9/11*. London: Continuum, 2010.

Breed, Brennan W. *Nomadic Text: A Theory of Biblical Reception History*. Bloomington: Indiana University Press, 2014.

Britt, Brian. "The Schmittian Messiah in Agamben's the Time That Remains." *Critical Inquiry* 36, no. 2 (2010): 262–87.

Buch-Hansen, Gitte. "Beyond the New Perspective: Reclaiming Paul's Anthropology." *Studia Theologica* 71, no. 1 (2017): 4–28.

Bultmann, Rudolf. *Jesus Christ and Mythology*. New York: Scribner, 1958.

Bultmann, Rudolf. "New Testament and Mythology." In *The Historical Jesus: Vol. 1: The History of the Quest: Classical Studies and Critical Questions*, edited by Craig A. Evans, 323–58. London: Routledge, 2004.

Calarco, Matthew and Steven DeCaroli. *Giorgio Agamben: Sovereignty and Life*. Stanford: Stanford University Press, 2007.

Cicero, Marcus Tullius. "Pro Rabirio Perduellionis." In *The Loeb Classical Library. Cicero Ix*, 452–92. Cambridge, MA: Harvard University Press, 1927.

Conzelmann, Hans. "The Address of Paul on the Areopagus." In *Studies in Luke-Acts: Essays Presented in Honor of Paul Schubert*, edited by Paul Schubert, J. Louis Martyn, and Leander E. Keck, 217–30. Nashville: Abingdon Press, 1966.

Critchley, Simon. *Continental Philosophy: A Very Short Introduction*. Oxford: Oxford University Press, 2001.

Critchley, Simon. *The Faith of the Faithless: Experiments in Political Theology*. London: Verso, 2012.

Crossan, John Dominic and Jonathan L. Reed. *In Search of Paul: How Jesus's Apostle Opposed Rome's Empire with God's Kingdom*. New York: HarperSanFrancisco, 2004.

Crowe, Benjamin D. *Heidegger's Phenomenology of Religion: Realism and Cultural Criticism*. Bloomington: Indiana University Press, 2008.

Dawkins, Richard. *The God Delusion*. 2016 ed. London: Black Swan, 2006.

Derrida, Jacques. *Adieu to Emmanuel Levinas*. Translated by Pascale-Anne Brault and Michael Naas. Stanford: Stanford University Press, 1999.

Derrida, Jacques. *Archive Fever: A Freudian Impression*. Translated by Eric Prenowitz. Chicago: University of Chicago Press, 1996.

Derrida, Jacques. "Force of Law: The 'Mystical Foundation of Authority'. (Deconstruction and the Possibility of Justice)." *Cardozo Law Review* 11, nos. 5–6 (1990): 920–1045.

Derrida, Jacques. *The Gift of Death*. Chicago: University of Chicago Press, 1995.

Derrida, Jacques. "A Silkworm of One's Own." In *Acts of Religion*, edited by Gil Anidjar, 311–55. London and New York: Routledge, 2002.

Derrida, Jacques. *Specters of Marx: The State of the Debt, the Work of Mourning and the New International*. Translated by Peggy Kamuf. 2012 ed. New York: Routledge, 1994.

Dunn, James D. G. "The Justice of God: A Renewed Perspective on Justification." *Journal of Theological Studies* 43, no. 1 (1992): 1–22.

Eagleton, Terry. *Reason, Faith, and Revolution: Reflections on the God Debate*. New Haven: Yale University Press, 2009.

Elliott, Neil. *Liberating Paul: The Justice of God and the Politics of the Apostle*. 2006 ed. Minneapolis: Fortress Press, 1994.

Engberg-Pedersen, Troels. "Innledning." In *Paulus Og Jødedommen*, edited by Troels Engberg-Pedersen, 10–37. København: Akademisk Forlag, 2019.

Engberg-Pedersen, Troels. "Paul the Philosopher." In *The Oxford Handbook of Pauline Studies*, redigert av Matthew V. Novenson and R. Barry Matlock, 198–216. New York: Oxford University Press, 2022.

Fink, Bruce. *The Lacanian Subject: Between Language and Jouissance*. Princeton: Princeton University Press, 1995.

Forrás, Peter. "Kronos, kairos og arché." *Agora*, no. 4 (2011): 19–45.

Foucault, Michel. *The History of Sexuality: 3: The Care of the Self*. Vol. 3. Harmondsworth: Penguin, 1988.

Fredriksen, Paula. "Historical Integrity, Interpretative Freedom: The Philosopher's Paul and the Problem of Anachronism." In *St. Paul among the Philosophers*, edited by John D. Caputo and Linda Martín Alcoff. Bloomington: Indiana University Press, 2009.

Fredriksen, Paula. *Paul: The Pagans' Apostle*. New Haven: Yale University Press, 2017.

Fredriksen, Paula. "The Question of Worship." In *Paul within Judaism: Restoring the First-Century Context to the Apostle*, edited by Magnus Zetterholm and Mark D. Nanos, 175–202. Minneapolis: Fortress Press, 2015.

Freud, Sigmund. *Beyond the Pleasure Principle*. Translated by C. J. M. Hubback. DigiReads, 2009.

Freud, Sigmund. *The Future of an Illusion; Civilization and Its Discontents, and Other Works: (1927–1931)*. The Standard Edition of the Complete Psychological Works of Sigmund Freud. Edited by James Strachey and Anna Freud. Vol. 21. London: Hogarth Press and The Institute of Psycho-Analysis, 1961.

Freud, Sigmund. *Moses and Monotheism*. Buckinghamshire: Chrysoma, 2007.

Freud, Sigmund. *Totem and Taboo, and Other Works: (1913–1914)*. The Standard Edition of the Complete Psychological Works of Sigmund Freud. Edited by James Strachey and Anna Freud. Vol. 13. London: Hogarth Press and The Institute of Psycho-Analysis, 1958.

Gadamer, Hans-Georg. *Truth and Method*. London: Continuum, 2004.

Gignac, Alain. "Agamben's Paul. Thinker of the Messianic." In *Paul in the Grip of the Philosophers: The Apostle and Contemporary Continental Philosophy*. Paul in Critical Contexts, edited by Peter Frick, 165–91. Minneapolis: Fortress Press, 2014.

Gourgouris, Stathis. *The Perils of the One*. New York: Columbia University Press, 2019.

Granberg, Anne. "Verken Athen Eller Jerusalem – Heideggers Augenblick Som 'Kairologisk Tid'." *Norsk filosofisk tidsskrift* 40, no. 4 (2005): 214–34.

Gullestad, Siri Erika. "Arven fra Freud." *Nytt norsk tidsskrift* 23, no. 4 (2006): 317–30.

Haugsgjerd, Svein. *Lidelsens karakter i ny psykiatri*. Oslo: Pax, 1990.

Haugsgjerd, Svein. *Å møte psykisk smerte*. Oslo: Gyldendal, 2018.

Heidegger, Martin. *Being and Time*. Translated by John Macquarrie and Edward Robinson. Oxford: Basil Blackwell, 1962.

Heidegger, Martin. "Introduction to 'What Is Metaphysics?'." Translated by Walter Kaufmann. In *Pathmarks*, edited by William Hardy McNeill, 27–290. Cambridge: Cambridge University Press, 1998.

Heidegger, Martin. *The Phenomenology of Religious Life*. Translated by Matthias Fritsch and Jennifer Anna Gosetti-Ferencei. Bloomington: Indiana University Press, 2010.

Hume, David. "The Natural History of Religion." In *Hume on Religion*, edited by Julian Baggini, 77–124. London: Philosophy Press, 2010.

Israel, Jonathan. "Introduction." Translated by Michael Silverthorne and Jonathan Israel. In *Theological-Political Treatise*, viii–xxiv. Cambridge: Cambridge University Press, 2007.

Jennings, Theodore W. *Outlaw Justice: The Messianic Politics of Paul*. Stanford: Stanford University Press, 2013.

Jennings, Theodore W. *Reading Derrida / Thinking Paul*. Stanford: Stanford University Press, 2006.

Jervell, Jacob. *Gud og hans fiender: Forsøk på å tolke Romerbrevet*. Oslo: Universitetsforlaget, 1973.
Jewett, Robert. *Romans: A Commentary*. Minneapolis: Fortress Press, 2007.
Kant, Immanuel. *Religion Within the Limits of Reason Alone*. Translated by Theodore M. Greene and Hoyt H. Hudson. New York: Harper Torchbooks, 1960.
Kar, Prafulla C. and Paul St-Pierre. *In Translation: Reflections, Refractions, Transformations*. Amsterdam: Benjamins, 2007.
Karlsen, Mads Peter. "Alain Badious Paulus-Læsning." *Dansk teologisk tidsskrift* 73, no. 1 (2010): 56–77.
Karlsen, Mads Peter. "'Episoden i Antiokia': En teologisk scene i Alain Badious filosofiske teater." In *Den store fortælling: Festskrift til Geert Hallbäck*, edited by Søren Holst and Christina Petterson, 361–378. København: Anis, 2012.
Kearney, Richard and Jens Zimmermann. *Reimagining the Sacred. Richard Kearney Debates God with James Wood, Catherine Keller, Charles Taylor, Julia Kristeva, Gianni Vattimo, Simon Critchley, Jean-Luc Marion, John Caputo, David Tracey, Jens Zimmermann, and Merold Westphal*. Insurrections: Critical Studies in Religion, Politics, and Culture. New York: Columbia University Press, 2015.
Kierkegaard, Sören. *Tvende Ethish-Religieuse Smaa-afhandlinger*. København: Søren Kierkegaard Forskningscenteret, 2014.
Kristeva, Julia. *Black Sun: Depression and Melancholia*. New York: Columbia University Press, 1989.
Kristeva, Julia. *Passions of Our Time*. New York: Columbia University Press, 2018.
Kristeva, Julia. *Strangers to Ourselves*. New York: Columbia University Press, 1991.
Kristeva, Julia. *Tales of Love*. New York: Columbia University Press, 1987.
Lacan, Jacques. *The Ethics of Psychoanalysis, 1959–1960: The Seminar of Jacques Lacan*. Vol. VII. London and New York: Routledge, 2008.
Lloyd, Genevieve. *The Man of Reason. "Male" and "Female" in Western Philosophy*. Minnesota: University of Minnesota Press, 1993.
Løland, Ole Jakob. "The Modern Philosophers' Paul: Reclaiming Pauline Introspection and Reviving Legacies of Anti-Judaism." *Journal for Cultural and Religious Theory* 18, no. 1 (2019): 71–84.
Løland, Ole Jakob. *Pauline Ugliness. Jacob Taubes and the Turn to Paul*. Perspectives in Continental Philosophy. New York: Fordham University Press, 2020.
Løland, Ole Jakob. *Reception of Paul the Apostle in the Works of Slavoj Žižek*. London: Palgrave Macmillan, 2018.
Luther, Martin. "Preface to the Epistle of St. Paul to the Romans (1522, Revised 1546)." In *Martin Luther's Basic Theological Writings*, edited by Timothy F. Lull and William R. Russell, 76–85. Minneapolis: Fortress Press, 2012.
Luther, Martin. "Preface to the New Testament." In *Martin Luther's Basic Theological Writings*, edited by Timothy F. Lull, 112–17. Minneapolis: Fortress Press, 1989.

Magazine, Impose. "Slavoj Žižek Speaks at Occupy Wall Street: Transcript." https://imposemagazine.com/bytes/slavoj-zizek-at-occupy-wall-street-transcript.

Malabou, Catherine. "Before and Above: Spinoza and Symbolic Necessity." *Critical inquiry* 43, no. 1 (2016): 84–109.

Martin, Dale B. *The Corinthian Body*. New Haven: Yale University Press, 1995.

Martin, Dale B. "Heterosexism and the Interpretation of Romans 1:18–32." *Biblical Interpretation* 3, no. 3 (1995): 332–55.

Martin, Dale B. "The Promise of Teleology, the Constraints of Epistemology, and Universal Vision in Paul." In *St. Paul among the Philosophers*, edited by John D. Caputo and Linda Martín Alcoff, 91–108. Bloomington: Indiana University Press, 2009.

Meeks, Wayne A. *The First Urban Christians: The Social World of the Apostle Paul*. New Haven: Yale University Press, 1983.

Miller, Anna C. "Not with Eloquent Wisdom: Democratic Ekklesia Discourse in 1 Corinthians 1–4." *Journal for the Study of the New Testament* 35, no. 4 (2013): 323–54.

Mitchell, Margaret M. "Paul's Letters to Corinth: The Interpretative Intertwining of Literary and Historical Reconstruction." In *Urban Religion in Roman Corinth: Interdisciplinary Approaches*, edited by Daniel N. Schowalter and Steven J. Friesen, 307–38. Cambridge: Harvard Divinity School, 2005.

Moltmann, Jürgen. *The Coming of God: Christian Eschatology*. London: SCM Press, 1996.

Moriarty, Michael. *Pascal: Reasoning and Belief*. Oxford: Oxford University Press, 2020.

Moxnes, Halvor. "Asceticism and Christian Identity in Antiquity: A Dialogue with Foucault and Paul." *Journal for the Study of the New Testament* 26, no. 1 (2003): 3–29.

Nasrallah, Laura Salah. *Archaeology and the Letters of Paul*. Oxford: Oxford University Press, 2019.

Nasrallah, Laura Salah. "Grief in Corinth. The Roman City and Paul's Corinthian Correspondence." In *Contested Spaces: Houses and Temples in Roman Antiquity and the New Testament*, edited by David L. Balch and Annette Weissenrieder, 109–39. Tübingen: Mohr Siebeck, 2012.

Nietzsche, Friedrich. *The Anti-Christ, Ecce Homo, Twilight of the Idols, and Other Writings*. Translated by Judith Norman. New York: Cambridge University Press, 2005.

Nietzsche, Friedrich. *Daybreak: Thoughts on the Prejudices of Morality*. Translated by R. J. Hollingdale. Cambridge: Cambridge University Press, 1997.

Nietzsche, Friedrich. *The Essential Nietzsche: Beyond Good and Evil: The Genealogy of Morals*. New York: Chartwell Books, 2017.

Nietzsche, Friedrich. *The Gay Science: With a Prelude in German Rhymes and an Appendix of Songs*. Translated by Josefine Nauckhoff. Cambridge: Cambridge University Press, 2001.

Nietzsche, Friedrich. *Human, All Too Human: A Book for Free Spirits*. 1993 ed. Cambridge: Cambridge University Press, 1986.

Økland, Jorunn. "Innledende Essay." In *Paulus' Brev*. Verdens Hellige Skrifter, vii–lxxii. Oslo: Bokklubben, 2010.

Økland, Jorunn. "Sjelløs Lesning." In *Den levende kroppen: Mot en ny forståelse av menneske og natur*, edited by Drude von der Fehr, 261–84. Oslo: Vidarforlaget, 2016.

Onfray, Michel. *The Atheist Manifesto: The Case against Christianity, Judaism and Islam*. Translated by Jeremy Leggatt. New York: Arcade Publishing, 2007.

Parsons, William B. *Freud and Religion: Advancing the Dialogue*. Cambridge: Cambridge University Press, 2021.

Pascal, Blaise. *Pascal's Pensées*. New York: E.P. Dutton, 1958.

Penner, Todd. "Madness in the Method? The Acts of the Apostles in Current Study." *Currents in Biblical Research* 2, no. 2 (2004): 223–93.

Plato. *Gorgias*. Loeb Classical Library. London: Heinemann, 1925.

Plato. *Phaedrus*. Loeb Classical Library. London: Heinemann, 1914.

Polybius. *The Histories* 1.4. Loeb Classical Library. Cambridge, MA: Harvard University Press, 2010.

Reinhard, Kenneth. "Introduction." In *The Incident at Antioch/L'incident D'antioche: A Tragedy in Three Acts/Tragedie En Trois Actes*, edited by Susan Spitzer and Kenneth Reinhard, xxi–li. New York: Columbia University Press, 2013.

Reinhard, Kenneth. "Paul and the Political Love of the Neighbour." In *Paul and the Philosophers*, edited by Ward Blanton and Hent de Vries, 449–65. New York: Fordham University Press, 2013.

Renan, Ernest. *Life of Jesus*. New York: Random House, 1927. https://www.gutenberg.org/cache/epub/16581/pg16581.html.

Riches, John Kenneth. *Galatians through the Centuries*. Blackwell Bible Commentaries. Edited by John Sawyer, Christopher Rowland, Judith Kovacs, and David M. Gunn. Malden: Wiley-Blackwell, 2008.

Ricoeur, Paul. "What Is a Text? Explanation and Understanding." Translated by John B. Thompson. In *Hermeneutics and the Human Sciences: Essays on Language, Action, and Interpretation*, edited by John B. Thompson, 145–60. Cambridge: Cambridge University Press, 1981.

Ruin, Hans. "Faith, Grace, and the Destruction of Tradition: A Hermeneutic-Genealogical Reading of the Pauline Letters." *Journal for Cultural and Religious Theory* 11, no. 1 (2010): 16–34.

Sanders, E. P. *Paul and Palestinian Judaism: A Comparison of Patterns of Religion.* Philadelphia: Fortress Press, 1977.

Santner, Eric L. "Freud's Moses." In *Sexuation*, edited by Renata Salecl, 57–105. Durham: Duke University Press, 2000.

Santner, Eric L. *On the Psychotheology of Everyday Life: Reflections on Freud and Rosenzweig.* Chicago: University of Chicago Press, 2001.

Schweitzer, Albert. *The Mysticism of Paul the Apostle.* Translated by William Montgomery. 1998 ed. Baltimore: Johns Hopkins University Press, 1931.

Schweitzer, Albert. *The Quest of the Historical Jesus: A Critical Study of Its Progress from Reimarus to Wrede.* Baltimore: Johns Hopkins University Press, 1998.

Sloterdijk, Peter. *You Must Change Your Life: On Anthropotechnics.* Translated by Wieland Hoban. Cambridge: Polity Press, 2013.

Songe-Møller, Vigdis. "Metamorphosis and the Concept of Change." In *Metamorphoses: Resurrection, Body and Transformative Practices in Early Christianity*, edited by Turid Karlsen Seim and Jorunn Økland, 108–22. Berlin: Walter de Gruyter, 2009.

Spinoza, Benedictus de. *Theological-Political Treatise.* Translated by Jonathan I. Israel and Michael Silverthorne. Cambridge: Cambridge University Press, 2007.

Stendahl, Krister. *Paul among Jews and Gentiles and Other Essays.* Philadelphia: Fortress Press, 1976.

Stevenson, Leslie. "Kant versus Christianity." In *Kant and the Question of Theology*, edited by Chris L. Firestone and James H. Joiner, 119–37. Cambridge: Cambridge University Press, 2017.

Stowers, Stanley K. *A Rereading of Romans: Justice, Jews, and Gentiles.* New Haven: Yale University Press, 1994.

Svenungsson, Jayne. *Divining History: Prophetism, Messianism, and the Development of the Spirit.* New York: Berghahn, 2016.

Svenungsson, Jayne. "Nykter Motbild Till Filosofernas Paulus-Hajp." Svenska Dagbladet. https://www.svd.se/nykter-motbild-till-filosofernas-paulus-hajp.

Taubes, Jacob. *From Cult to Culture: Fragments towards a Critique of Historical Reason.* Stanford: Stanford University Press, 2010.

Taubes, Jacob. *Occidental Eschatology.* Stanford: Stanford University Press, 2009.

Taubes, Jacob. *The Political Theology of Paul.* Stanford: Stanford University Press, 2004.

Thucydides. *Peloponnesian War* 1.22. Loeb Classical Library. Cambridge, MA: Harvard University Press, 1928.

Tillich, Paul. *The Shaking of the Foundations*. London: SCM Press, 1949.
Tillich, Paul. *Theology of Culture*. Oxford and London: Oxford University Press, 1959.
Vries, Hent de. *Philosophy and the Turn to Religion*. Baltimore: Johns Hopkins University Press, 1999.
Weaver, Taylor M. *The Scandal of Community: Pauline Factions and the Circulation of Grace*. redigert av Taylor M. Weaver. Lanham: Lexington, 2021.
Weber, Max. *The Protestant Ethic and the Spirit of Capitalism*. London: Harper Collins, 1991.
Weigel, Sigrid. "In Paul's Mask: Jacob Taubes Reads Walter Benjamin." In *Genealogies of the Secular: The Making of Modern German Thought*, edited by Willem Styfhals and Stéphane Symons, 193–216. Albany: State University of New York Press, 2019.
Welborn, Larry L. *Paul, the Fool of Christ: A Study of 1 Corinthians 1–4 in the Comic-Philosophic Tradition*. London and New York: T&T Clark International, 2005.
Zetterholm, Magnus and Mark D. Nanos. *Paul within Judaism: Restoring the First-Century Context to the Apostle*. Minneapolis: Fortress Press, 2015.
Žižek, Slavoj. *Did Somebody Say Totalitarianism?: Five Interventions in the (Mis)Use of a Notion*. London: Verso, 2001.
Žižek, Slavoj. *The Fragile Absolute, or, Why Is the Christian Legacy Worth Fighting For?* 2008 ed. London; New York: Verso, 2000.
Žižek, Slavoj. *In Defense of Lost Causes*. 2nd ed. London: Verso, 2008.
Žižek, Slavoj. "The Jew Is within You, but You, You Are in the Jew." In *What Does a Jew Want? On Binationalism and Other Specters*, edited by Udi Aloni, 159–72. New York: Columbia University Press, 2011.
Žižek, Slavoj. *Less Than Nothing: Hegel and the Shadow of Dialectical Materialism*. London and New York: Verso, 2012.
Žižek, Slavoj. *Living in the End Times*. London: Verso, 2010.
Žižek, Slavoj. *On Belief*. London: Routledge, 2001.
Žižek, Slavoj. *The Puppet and the Dwarf: The Perverse Core of Christianity*. Cambridge, MA: MIT Press, 2003.
Žižek, Slavoj. *The Ticklish Subject: The Absent Centre of Political Ontology*. 2008 ed. London: Verso, 1999.

Name Index

Adorno, Theodor 48, 50
Agamben, Giorgio 5–7, 42, 47–9, 82–94, 97–8, 101, 109, 154, 181, 184
Althusser, Louis 61
Arendt, Hannah 50
Aristotle 15
Augustine 15, 37, 39, 45, 112, 120, 179

Badiou, Alain 5–7, 16, 22, 26–7, 43, 45–7, 61–9, 71–7, 79, 91–2, 98–9, 104–7, 109, 128, 132, 134–6, 139–45, 148–9, 154, 168, 180–2, 184
Barclay, John 16, 24
Barth, Karl 160
Barthes, Roland 22, 125
Benjamin, Walter 48–50, 83, 90, 92–3, 109, 163, 170
Blanton, Ward 30
Bloch, Ernst 93
Bornkamm, Günther 43, 73, 75
Boyarin, Daniel 22, 107
Breed, Brennan W. 22
Buber, Martin 31
Bultmann, Rudolf 43, 74–5, 92, 128

Calvin, John 45, 101
Cicero 58
Conzelmann, Hans 40–1
Critchley, Simon 39, 76, 109, 149–50, 181

Dawkins, Richard 4–8, 32
Derrida, Jacques 3–4, 15, 26, 50, 61, 78–9, 134, 149–63, 165–7, 169–73, 176, 180–1, 183–4

Eagleton, Terry 73, 79
Einstein, Albert 73, 79
Esler, Philip 166

Feuerbach, Ludwig 177–8

Foucault, Michel 61, 89, 96–7
Fredriksen, Paula 22–3, 148
Freud, Sigmund 3, 7, 25–6, 37–8, 116–28, 131, 141, 173, 181, 183

Gadamer, Hans-Georg 9

Hegel, Georg Wilhelm Friedrich 141–2
Heidegger, Martin 9, 13–15, 25, 61, 83, 163, 181
Holbein, Hans 129
Hume, David 102–3

Jennings Jr, Theodor W. 45, 154
Jesus of Nazareth 2–3, 5, 18–20, 26, 30–4, 39, 42, 53–5, 62–4, 91, 94–5, 99, 109, 111, 130–1, 177–8

Kafka, Franz 90, 150–4
Kierkegaard, Søren 46
Kristeva, Julia 26, 129–34, 140, 181

Lacan, Jacques 8, 26, 123–9, 133–4, 137, 143, 149–50
Lenin, Vladimir 1, 32, 79
Levinas, Emmanuel 26, 170–3, 176–7, 180
Luke, the Evangelist 40
Luther, Martin 16–18, 24, 38–9, 45, 80–1, 83, 112–13, 165

Martin, Dale 22, 85, 96, 99
Marx, Karl 3, 7, 32, 47–8, 68, 78, 146, 183
Moxnes, Halvor 97, 165

Nancy, Jean-Luc 182
Nietzsche, Friedrich 3–4, 7, 13, 19, 25–6, 29–36, 38–9, 42–5, 50, 53–61, 63–4, 80, 88, 91, 95, 97–9, 101–4, 108–12, 116–17, 136, 139–41, 154, 163, 168, 179, 181–3

Økland, Jorunn 39, 98–100
Onfray, Michel 5–6, 32, 139

Pascal 10, 39
Plato 30, 46–7, 69, 96, 106–7
Polybius 41

Reinhard, Kenneth 122
Renan, Ernest 18–19, 31
Riches, John 21
Ricoeur, Paul 135–6, 183
Rousseau, Jean-Jacques 76

Sanders, E. P. 22
Santner, Eric 122
Sartre, Jean-Paul 61
Schweitzer, Albert 20
Segundo, Juan Luis 183
Sloterdijk, Peter 16
Socrates 107
Spinoza 10–13, 21–3, 25, 27, 75, 178, 181–2
Stendahl, Krister 38, 112–16, 134, 179

Stowers, Stanley K. 37
Strauss, David Friedrich 19, 31
Svenungsson, Jayne 24

Taubes, Jacob 3–4, 13, 37, 44, 47–8, 56–61, 83, 89, 94, 105, 109, 112, 119–23, 140, 153–4, 177–8, 182
Taylor, Charles 69
Thomas Aquinas 45, 98
Thucydides 41
Tillich, Paul 123–4

Vattimo, Gianni 35

Weber, Max 70, 80–4, 88, 181
Welborn, Larry L. 107, 175
Wittgenstein, Ludvig 47

Žižek, Slavoj 1–2, 5–8, 22, 26, 31–3, 40, 42, 47, 62–3, 68–72, 76–80, 92, 109, 134, 136–9, 141–9, 154–5, 168, 180–1, 184

Subject Index

alienation 90–3, 124
anarchism 90
anthropology 37, 99, 115, 121, 134
antiquity 38, 42, 57–8, 69, 85, 90, 96, 106, 156
Antisemitism 119
atheism 1, 4–9, 25, 39, 71–2, 117, 128–9, 147, 149, 154, 170, 173, 181–4
autonomy 117, 129, 149

biopolitics 89, 93

canon, the Christian 13, 42, 51
canon, the philosophical 15, 26, 47, 129, 180
capitalism 2, 68–70, 77, 80–1, 83, 170
Christianity 3–5, 8–15, 19, 24, 29–33, 37–50, 53–64, 70–2, 80, 87, 95–8, 108, 112–16, 120, 129–34, 142, 155, 161, 178, 182–3
communitarianism 64, 69, 180
compassion 30, 171
criticism of ideology 2, 32, 70, 77–8, 129, 136, 143, 145–7
criticism of religion 4, 26, 102–3, 108, 131, 139–41, 149, 183

deconstruction 78, 156–66
democracy 45, 77–8, 94
demythologization 72–6, 128, 182
desire 97, 123–8, 135, 137, 143–4, 147, 149–50, 168
divine election 59–60, 66, 103, 105

Empire, the Roman 33, 39, 41, 43, 46, 59, 84, 94, 116
Enlightenment, the 16, 20, 22, 76, 129, 134
Eschatology 48, 80–1, 87, 169–74

fantasy 26, 37, 118, 130, 132, 149
feminism 47, 133

freedom from the law 26, 112, 117, 129, 136, 140–1, 144, 149, 154
freedom of expression 10, 94, 147–8
fundamentalism 1–2, 32–3, 145–7

gender 79, 133, 175–6, 180

Holocaust 114
Hysteria 6, 138, 147

instinct, human 54–5, 112, 117, 121, 127, 139

Judaism 31, 34, 36, 44, 46, 48, 50, 57, 114, 119
justice 45, 48, 69, 104, 114, 149, 154–67, 169–73, 175–7, 180, 184

law 2, 8, 25–6, 34, 36–8, 65–8, 90, 94, 111–17, 122–9, 133–69, 174–7, 179–80, 183–5
left, the political 2, 6, 32–3, 68, 76–80, 91, 109, 145–6, 148, 178
liberalism 1–2, 145–8
liberation 93, 117, 121–2, 147
life beyond death 101–5, 130
love, of neighbour 2, 30, 48, 51, 105, 131–2, 139–41, 149, 173–85

Marxism 32, 48, 69–70, 78, 90–1
masochism 5–6, 131–2, 139–41
messianism 7, 47–50, 59–60, 78, 84, 90–1, 93, 109
metaphysics 13, 172
militant, the 63, 68–72, 92, 132
miracles 11, 34, 73–5
modern biblical scholarship 11–14, 18–24, 39–44, 57, 113–14
moral responsibility 160–3, 170–2, 176

neurosis 117, 119, 136
nihilism 53, 93–4, 140

ontology   13, 72, 172
Original Sin   26, 37, 116, 118,
    120–1, 183–4
Other, the (Levinas)   150, 171–6, 178,
    180, 184–5
Other, the big (Lacan)   8, 143

perversity   103, 137–8, 141, 146
phenomenology   13–16
Platonism   29–30, 45, 95–7, 100–
    1, 105, 109
populism   106
Protestantism   11, 17, 25–6, 38, 70, 80–3,
    112–14, 129, 141, 153, 155, 165
psychoanalysis   8, 26, 37, 116–34,
    136–45, 149, 155, 179, 183–4

reception history, of the Bible   3, 20–5,
    115, 161, 181
resurrection, of Jesus   34, 40, 62–5, 71,
    73–4, 99, 114, 130, 133
revelation   12, 60, 157, 177, 182
revolution, of ideas   17, 57, 59, 105,
    121, 131, 177
rhetoric   3, 33, 37, 52, 58, 65–6, 69,
    105–7, 109, 115, 126, 148

rights   55, 68, 167

salvation   26, 37, 48–9, 58, 87, 105,
    113, 118, 130, 135–6, 140–1,
    183
Scandinavia   77, 166–7
science, modern   31, 49, 60–4, 72–4, 79,
    108, 120, 128
secularization   15, 27, 48, 72–6, 80,
    91, 120, 128, 130, 147, 162,
    178, 181–3
superego   117, 123, 137–9, 144, 149–50

Thing (Lacan)   124–8
translation, of Paul   44–5, 84, 87–
    9, 155, 175
truth event   5, 61–5, 67–8, 71–5, 77–9,
    91, 136, 140, 142, 144

universalism   1–3, 32, 62, 64, 67–9, 72,
    136, 149, 154, 174, 180

vocation   49, 80, 84, 86, 92

wisdom   9, 51–2, 55, 58, 60–1, 65–6, 71,
    77, 82, 105–9

www.ingramcontent.com/pod-product-compliance
Lightning Source LLC
Chambersburg PA
CBHW052117300426
44116CB00010B/1705